Network Security Technologies

Second Edition

Network Security Technologies

Second Edition

Kwok T. Fung

A CRC Press Company
Boca Raton   London   New York   Washington, D.C.

All terms mentioned in this book that are known to be trademarks or service marks have been appropriately capitalized. Use of a term in this book should not be regarded as affecting the validity of any trademark or service mark.

Library of Congress Cataloging-in-Publication Data

Fung, K. T. (Kwok T.)
    Network security technologies / Kwok T. Fung.--2nd ed.
      p. cm.
    Includes bibliographical references and index.
    ISBN 0-8493-3027-0 (alk. paper)
     1. Computer networks--Security measures. I. Title.

    TK5105.59.F86 2004
    005.8--dc22

                                             2004046417

Visit the Auerbach Web site at www.auerbach-publications.com

DEDICATION

To my wife, children, and Bigglesworth and Fox
and all others who have helped shape my values and priorities.

CONTENTS

ABOUT THE AUTHOR

Kwok T. Fung worked for AT&T Bell Laboratories/AT&T Laboratories in data networking and telecommunications for more than 20 years. He also taught computer science for a number of years at the University of Windsor, Ontario, Canada. He coauthored the book *Computer Design and Implementation* by Computer Science Press and has several papers published in technical journals and conference proceedings. He has also coauthored several patent applications. He received his M.S. and Ph.D. degrees in computer engineering from Cornell University and his B.S. in electrical engineering from the University of Manitoba, Canada.

PREFACE

With the advent of telecommunication and IT technologies and the increasingly dominant roles played by E-commerce in every major industry, development and implementation efforts in the many areas of network security draw technologies from more and more seemingly unrelated technical fields that did not previously have to cross paths or intimately interwork. These major fields include cryptography, network protocols, switch and router technology, and information technology, each with fully developed theories and standards, as well as well-established practices. Trying to develop expertise in all of these technical fields is a challenging task. This book presents the key network security-relevant technologies in these diverse fields, using an organized, hierarchical framework that greatly facilitates understanding of not only the technologies themselves but also their interrelationships and how they interwork.

This framework has been formulated in a systematic classification and categorization of network security technologies. First, fundamental network security functional elements are identified: confidentiality, authentication, authorization, message integrity, and non-repudiation. Technologies that implement these functional elements are then classified and categorized based on these functional elements. The result is a unique presentation of major legacy, state-of-the-art, and emerging network security technologies from all the relevant fields, which serves as an extremely useful and easy-to-follow guide.

The descriptions for most of the relevant technologies include enough technical depth to enable the reader to have a full understanding of the roles played by, and responsibilities required of, each technology. However, they are not intended to replace the corresponding detailed descriptions in such documents as standard specifications, RFCs, interface and implementation agreements, etc. Every effort is made to render the mathematical derivations used in the algorithms as self-contained as possible.

In several places where this proves to be too difficult without sacrificing the overall readability of the material, certain details that are not deemed absolutely necessary to understanding the operations of the associated algorithms are omitted, and references are always provided for readers to supplement the missing details. Regardless, for readers who desire intensive understanding of the in-depth theory and nitty-gritty details of each technology, references are provided at the end of each chapter.

The presentation of the materials in this book is unique in the following ways:

◼ Network security technologies are classified as basic, enhanced, integrated, and architectural as a means to associate their relative functional (not necessarily algorithmic, for example) complexities, providing a useful perspective on their interrelationships.
◼ Together with the introduction and description of security-related technologies, the interrelationship and interworking of these technologies are also discussed so that the readers can have an easier time grasping the relevance of each of these technologies within the network security landscape.

Thus, the book is intended to be used both as a textbook and study guide and also as a reference for network telecommunications students, all network and information technology staffs (e.g., network designers and architects, network and systems engineers and administrators, etc.) who have a need to better understand the basic theories, interrelationships and interworking of different security functionalities and technologies and how they relate to other network components. It is expected that vendor equipment users' manuals will provide the details and CLI command usage instructions needed for the actual configuration of security devices such as firewalls, router configurations, etc.

1

INTRODUCTION

As the role of enterprise networks keeps expanding in its support of both internal and external connectivity in the form of emerging Internet, intranet, and extranet applications, network components are being exposed more and more seriously to malicious as well as unintentional security breaches. Network security becomes an ever increasingly critical element of enterprise network designs and implementations. A typical network security exercise involves the planning and design of a company's networks and information technology (IT) security infrastructures so as to protect its valuable applications, sensitive data, and network resources from unauthorized access that results in either intentional or unintentional misuse and malicious alterations of the company's assets.

According to surveys of IT managers in major corporations done over the last few years, the following are the most consistently cited security concerns (in descending order of perceived severity according to most of those surveyed):

- Authorized access control
- Viruses
- Virtual private networks (VPNs)
- Confidentiality, privacy, and encryption
- Firewalls
- Access by remote users
- Education and staying up-to-date
- Usage monitoring and Internet usage abuse
- E-commerce
- Poorly designed software and systems
- E-mail and "spam"

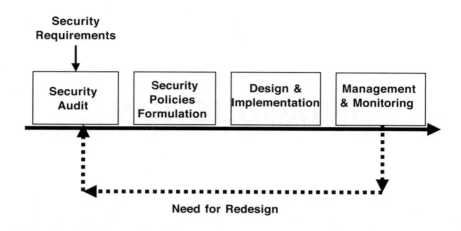

Figure 1.1   Network security methodology.

Of course, some of these security concerns have a wider impact on the worldwide IT community than others. For example, a bug in a router's widely deployed network operating system (NOS) is likely to result in much more extensive damage than a poorly designed piece of application software with limited local deployment in a company's remote or even central sites.

1.1   SECURITY IN NETWORK DESIGN AND IMPLEMENTATIONS

Network security in an enterprise environment refers to all the measures and software and hardware implementations, as well as to the associated personnel, documentation, and processes within the enterprise network infrastructure, that together protect the integrity and privacy of applications, data, and information flow. Figure 1.1 shows the major steps involved in a typical network security design process cycle.

The typical network security process for designing and implementing security capabilities in the enterprise network should be considered very much a mission-critical task that:

■ Evolves rapidly
■ Increases in complexity
■ Is critical for business success

In particular, the key characteristic is that the entire process is a constantly evolving one. Network security design and implementation efforts need to be upgraded or readjusted as new threats are identified or as new business needs dictate new security requirements.

When considering the design and implementation of network security, the following principles should always be kept in mind in order to ensure success:

- Network security needs should be initiated at the beginning of a network design and development process and adequately managed throughout the entire network's life cycle.
- The application of network security policies, procedures, and countermeasures should be corporatewide in scope and should be driven by well-defined and quantifiable needs.
- The responsible network security functional group must work closely with other engineering and technical function groups and all other relevant functional groups of the organization.
- High-level visibility and management support and commitment are essential for any network security program to be successful.
- The implementation of network security must not overburden the users (including the network and IT developers and maintenance personnel) or significantly impact network and system performance or mission objectives. It is always necessary to work toward a compromise.
- Cost-effective solutions must be sought as soon as possible to ensure that the network security program is as efficient and up-to-date as possible.
- Never assume that a solution previously used to solve a specific network security vulnerability problem will be sufficient for the same vulnerability the next time. Technology moves too fast not to reevaluate available options at the time the decision is made.

Network security starts with the formulation and adoption of a set of corporatewide security policies and processes. A network security policy is a set of rules or decisions that combine to determine an organization's stance with regard to network security. It determines the limits of acceptable behavior on the part of insiders and outsiders, and determines what the responses to deviations from acceptable behavior should be. The network security policy is used to guide the organization in determining the particular security steps to take. In particular, the policy must be defined before any network security technology is chosen.

Security policies and processes must be tailored to the specific needs of the company's business. For instance, many government agencies adopt e-authentication policies (e.g., assigning one of four electronic identity assurance levels to each e-government transaction) that have been defined for interagency communication and need to be followed. The definition of these policies is accomplished by determining the key business assets that are vulnerable because they are connected to the network. The next step is to determine what would be required, at a high level, to protect the endangered assets. The security policy will be the result of a compromise between expected or suspected dangers, business needs, the users' tolerance, and the cost of security technologies and their operational impact.

The security policy needs to consider both computer resources and network resources. Computer resources include, for example, applications, databases, and computer hardware. These are all business assets and are worth protecting at some level. Network resources include switches, routers, multiplexers, modems, and interconnecting links. They are usually not attacked purely for themselves (apart from a network provider's perspective) but rather, as a way to attack the computer resources that are connected to them. The final security policy will define what is to be protected and how it is to be protected.

All these point to the realization that network security should be considered an integral part of network design and implementations, and many of the classical security technologies, such as cryptography, should be well understood by traditional network designers and vice versa.

1.2 FRAMEWORK FOR NETWORK SECURITY TECHNOLOGIES

Development and implementation in many areas of network security draw together technologies from more and more seemingly unrelated technical fields that did not previously have to cross paths or intimately interwork. These major fields include, but are not limited to, cryptography, network protocols, switch and router technology, and information technology, each with fully developed theories and standards besides well-established industry practices. Trying to fully understand all this diverse knowledge is a necessary but challenging task for present-day network and IT architects and designers.

In the following text, we develop an organized, hierarchical framework to present many of the key network-security-relevant technologies in these diverse fields to facilitate a discussion of not only the technologies themselves but also their interrelationships and how they interwork.

1.2.1 Major Basic Network Security Functional Elements

The ultimate objective of network security is to ensure that protected applications and the information used as input and generated as output by these applications are not compromised by malicious or unintentional security breaches. As a result, it is possible to define the major basic network security functional elements that are needed to build a network security system, in terms of the following well-known security services needed for secure message exchanges: confidentiality authentication, authorization, message integrity, and non-repudiation.

Thus, the following are defined to be the five basic network security functional elements:

- Confidentiality: Confidentiality or privacy ensures that the content of the message is not visible to any persons other than the intended or authorized receivers. Encryption is typically used to achieve this. Confidentiality or the ability to hide the meaning of information from unauthorized persons is probably the most basic functional element that all other functional elements build on.
- Authentication: Authentication ensures the integrity of user identities through the identification of legitimate and illegitimate users. Legitimate users would be allowed to proceed with their business to some extent, even though they could still subsequently be limited in what they can do by other aspects of security controls, such as authorization.
- Authorization: Authorization is the control of access to network or systems resources so that only authenticated users who have specific authorization are allowed to access particular resources. This type of control would allow selective access to resources by the small population of users who have already been authenticated.
- Message Integrity: Message integrity refers to the condition that the received message is not altered unintentionally *en route* compared with the originally sent message.
- Non-repudiation: Non-repudiation guarantees that the sender is a legitimate sender of the received message and that the sender cannot later dispute the sending of the message. Sometimes, non-repudiation is extended to apply to the receiver also.

These five network security functional elements are implemented as hardware and software in network devices (e.g., routers and servers) that are found in places over the end-to-end path of a connection between two communicating endpoints (typically, a client computer and a server or host).

It is important to note that not all five functional elements are always included in any particular deployed network security system. Also, there are network security services that cannot easily be classified under any of the above functional elements but that work together with them to provide the desired network security capabilities.

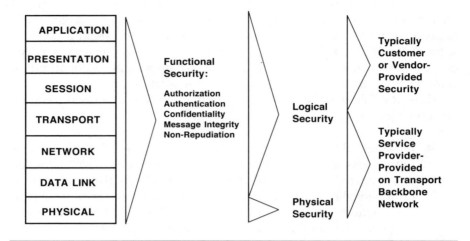

Figure 1.2 Network security and the OSI Network Model.

It should also be noted that in the above definitions, "authentication" refers to "user authentication" but "data authentication" is separately referred to as "message integrity." In network security literature, authentication often refers to both user and data authentication.

Most common security risks are the results of breakdowns or inadequacies in the protection provided by one or more of the functional elements. For example, denial-of-service (DoS) is most likely due to malicious attacks from outside hackers who have managed to gain unauthorized access to some network or systems resources. The hackers might, in turn, have managed to gain access because of unencrypted or easily compromised passwords. Also, the damage that viruses can potentially cause to system resources can be significantly reduced with stricter security policies and more carefully designed firewalls, for example.

1.2.2 Network Security and the OSI Model

It is useful to examine where the network security functional elements listed above fall under the Open Systems Interconnection (OSI) 7 Layer Reference Model. This is illustrated in Figure 1.2. This diagram can be useful as the different technologies that are available to implement these network security functional elements are studied in subsequent chapters.

The network security functional elements span all seven layers, although particular technologies will likely dictate which layer each will operate at. For example, SSL is a session-oriented technology and operates principally at the application layer.

If a customer uses service providers for backbone connectivity in their network, as is likely the case, many of the lower-layer security capabilities will be integrated into the backbone network infrastructure or offered as optional features.

1.2.3 Categorizing Network Security Technologies

Once the five network security functional elements have been identified, it is possible to examine the many different key legacy, state-of-the-art, and emerging technologies that have been defined and invented to implement these functional elements to meet specific security requirements under different operating environments. In order to formulate a structured view of the relationship between different, diverse network security technologies, we divide the technologies according to the way they implement the functional elements, into the following four categories (only technologies considered to be standards, *de facto* standards, or industry-accepted practices are described in this book):

- Basic Technologies: From each functional element's perspective, these are functionally simple technologies, each of which is typically designed to implement primarily only one specific functional element. Examples of these technologies are encryption technologies, Layer 2 VPNs such as Frame Relay (FR) permanent virtual circuits (PVCs) and switched virtual circuits (SVCs), and router access control lists (ACLs). Basic network security technologies can be considered to be the fundamental building blocks of all the other security technologies and are described in Chapters 2, 3, 4, 5, and 6 for the five different functional elements.
- Enhanced Technologies: These are network security technologies that are still designed to implement primarily one particular functional element, but we consider them to be more than basic technologies because they are relatively more complex and very often make heavy use of some of the basic technologies, and sometimes even include other functionally different basic technologies. One example is the digital signature for implementing source non-repudiation, as digital signatures are built on top of hashing algorithms, which are also considered to be basic technologies for implementing confidentiality. Enhanced technologies are described in Chapter 7.
- Integrated Technologies: These are network security technologies that are, in turn, defined using other more basic technologies and are designed or have evolved to support more than one functional element. Examples of these technologies are SSL and IP Security

(IPSec). (IPSec is normally considered a Layer 3 VPN.) Integrated technologies are described in Chapter 8.

■ Security Architectures: These are network security technology architectures that define standard or *de facto* security architectures based on basic, enhanced, and integrated technologies and are intended to provide guidelines for implementing security systems within the architecture's defined framework. The defined architecture typically implements a number of network security elements. The best example of this category is public key infrastructure (PKI). Security architectures are described in Chapter 9.

Note that this categorization is really intended primarily for ease of understanding and application. There are, of course, technologies that can readily be put into more than one category. For example, Encapsulation Security Payload (ESP) is considered to be a basic authentication technology but it also provides a confidentiality capability. Also, there are technologies implementing security functional services that might not fit in perfectly with any of the five network security functional elements defined in this book.

As will be evident from the rest of the book, the identification of the network security functional elements and the classification and categorization of these technologies together allow a much more structured way of learning about the many existing and developing — sometimes complementing and sometimes competing — network security technologies, as well as how they interrelate and interwork together.

1.2.4 The Framework

The classification into network security functional elements and the categorization of network security technologies as basic functional elements versus nonbasic elements, together provide a framework for a structured approach to studying the fast-evolving and sometimes increasingly confusing panorama of these technologies. Figure 1.3 shows a framework that provides such an organized, hierarchical view of security technologies.

This structured, hierarchical view is used in presenting all the legacy, state-of-the-art, and emerging network security technologies in the rest of the book. A summary of this view is given in Appendix A.

1.3 THE ORGANIZATION OF THE BOOK

The rest of the book discusses the industry's key network security technologies using this framework.

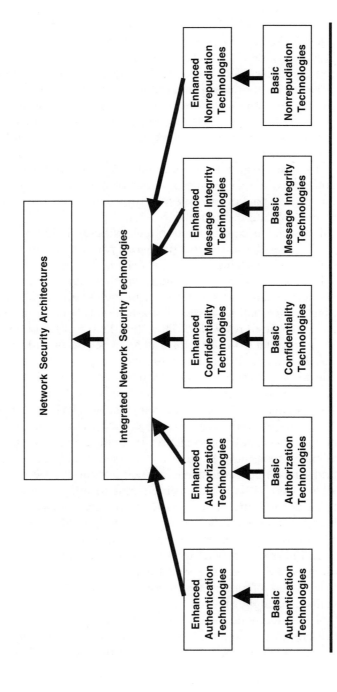

Figure 1.3   A framework for network security technologies.

Chapter 2 begins the presentation of network security technologies by discussing some of the key basic confidentiality technologies. There are two major types of confidentiality technologies: hashing functions such as Message Digest 5 (MD5) and SHA-1, and cryptographic algorithms such as Ron's (or Rivest's) Code (RC4), Data Encryption Standard (DES), Triple Data Encryption Standard (3DES), etc. As indicated earlier, confidentiality can be considered to be the most fundamental of all the network security functional elements and this will become evident in later chapters, as we find that the basic confidentiality technologies discussed in this chapter are used over and over again in other enhanced, integrated, and architectural technologies.

Chapter 3 discusses some basic authentication technologies. These include Authentication Header technologies such as AH and Encapsulating Security Payload (ESP), packet filtering techniques, and the use of userID and password authentication methods.

Chapter 4 discusses basic authorization technologies including physical access control, the use of userID and password for authorization, access control lists (ACLs), and demilitarized zones (DMZs).

Chapter 5 discusses basic message integrity technologies. These include Layer 2 VPNs such as FR and ATM VPNs, tunneling protocols such as Generic Routing Encapsulation (GRE), Point-to-Point Tunneling Protocol (PPTP), Layer 2 Tunneling Protocol (L2TP), Multi-Protocol Label Switching (MPLS), PPP over Ethernet (PPPoE), etc., and also the use of authentication headers such as AH and ESP for data integrity.

Chapter 6 discusses basic non-repudiation technologies, which include digital signatures, message authentication code (MAC) algorithms, network address translation (NAT), and port address translation (PAT) technologies.

Chapter 7 discusses enhanced technologies. These include the enhanced authentication and authorization technologies such as userID- and password-based technologies such as Password Authentication Protocol (PAP) and Challenge Handshake Authentication Protocol (CHAP), token cards, PPP-based VPNs of Extensible Authentication Protocol (EAP) and Microsoft Point-to-Point Encryption (MPPE), key-management technologies such as Internet Security Association and Key Management Protocol (ISAKMP), OAKLEY, Internet Key Exchange (IKE), and Simple Key Management for Internet Protocol (SKIP), digital signatures and digital certificates, wireless WEP, and IEEE 802.11i.

Chapter 8 discusses integrated technologies. Included in this category are SSO, firewalls, and higher-layer VPNs such as IP Security (IPSec), SSL, and Simple Key Management for Internet Protocol (TLS).

Chapter 9 discusses four security architectures — Remote Access, PKI, federal public key infrastructure (FPKI), and Secure Electronic Transaction (SET).

Chapter 10 discusses the Wireless LAN (WLAN) security architecture. A number of the key WLAN security technologies such as Wired Equivalent Privacy (WEP) and IEEE 802.11i are included in the discussion.

Chapter 11 looks at a number of topics that are related to the implementation of network security technologies. The topics can be generally categorized as vulnerability considerations and improvement considerations.

At the end of each chapter, a summary section is included to provide a useful perspective on certain important aspects of the technologies.

BIBLIOGRAPHY

1. IETF RFC 1825: Security Architecture for the Internet Protocol, R. Atkinson, August 1995.
2. Mike Horton and Clinton Mugge, *Network Security — Portable Reference*, McGraw-Hill/Osborne, 2003.
3. Saadat Malik, *Network Security Principles and Practices*, Cisco Press, 2003.
4. Authentication Policy for Federal Agencies, Draft E, Federal Register, Vol. 68, No. 133, July 11, 2003.
5. Layered Security: Re-Establishing the Trusted Network, NetScreen Technologies white paper, June 2003.

2

BASIC CONFIDENTIALITY TECHNOLOGIES

This chapter looks at some key basic confidentiality technologies. Confidentiality or privacy ensures that the content of a message is not visible to persons other than the intended or authorized recipients. During even a single session between two message exchanging parties, there might potentially be a number of different types of messages that require confidentiality. These include the original sensitive data, passwords, secret or private keys that are needed for encryption and decryption of the sensitive data and, maybe, a session that both sides agree on for cryptography purposes during bulk file transfer.

Two classes of technologies are commonly used to achieve confidentiality:

- Hashing algorithms
- Secret- and public-key cryptography

Both technologies have the ability to hide the meaning of the content of a message from an unauthorized person. This is the most important and fundamental capability in any network security system. This capability is routinely needed for sending such sensitive information as passwords, signed documents and, of course, important data itself. The more efforts the intruder needs to put in to understand the message, the more effective the technology.

Hashing algorithms such as Message Digest 5 (MD5) do not require special keys for encryption and decryption of messages. Rather, they rely on the natural randomness of messages to achieve a high probability of two separate messages not being "hashed" to the same resulting "hashed" messages. In each hashing technology the critical component is the hashing function used.

Key cryptographic algorithms such as Data Encryption Standard (DES), on the other hand, make use of keys for encryption and decryption of messages. Closely associated with cryptographic technologies are key-sharing and key-encryption technologies such as the Diffie–Hellman Algorithm, as well as key-management technologies such as Internet Key Exchange (IKE). Key-management technologies are considered as enhanced technologies and discussed in Chapter 7.

Software and packages that implement many of the hashing and cryptographic algorithms are commercially available, enabling the convenient use of these technologies in different network security applications.

2.1 HASHING ALGORITHMS

A hashing algorithm refers to a mathematical function that takes a variable-size string as input and transforms (hashes) it into a fixed-size string, which is called the hash value, as output. In network security applications, the mathematical function should have the essential properties that the transformation is one-way and that it is computationally infeasible for two different inputs to produce the same output.

One of the most common uses of hashing in network security is to produce condensed representations of messages or "fingerprints," often known as "message digests," by applying a hashing algorithm to an arbitrary amount of data — the message.

The two most commonly used hashing algorithms are MD5 and SHA-1 (part of the secure hash standard [SHS]), to be described in the following text.

2.1.1 The MD5 Algorithm

The MD5 message-digest algorithm defined in RFC 1321 takes as input a message of arbitrary length, applies some "independent and unbiased" bit-wise operations on the message blocks, and produces as output a 128-bit fingerprint or message digest of the input. With this hashing technique, the conjecture is that it is computationally infeasible to produce two messages having the same message digest, or to produce any message having a prespecified target message digest. MD5 is designed to be a fast and compact algorithm.

The MD5 algorithm is an extension of the MD4 message-digest algorithm by Ronald L. Rivest of MIT. It is slightly slower than MD4, but is more conservative in design, giving up a little in speed for a much greater likelihood of ultimate security.

Given a b-bit length message, the MD5 algorithm performs the following five steps to compute the message digest:

- *Step 1, append padding bits:* The message is padded (extended) so that its length (in bits) is congruent to 448, modulo 512. That is, the message is extended so that it is just 64 bits shy of being a multiple of 512 bits long. Padding is always performed, even if the length of the message is already congruent to 448, modulo 512.
- Step 2, append length: A 64-bit representation of b (the length of the message before the padding bits were added) is appended to the result of the previous step. In the unlikely event that b is greater than 2^{64}, then only the low-order 64 bits of b are used. (These bits are appended as two 32-bit words and appended low-order word first.) At this point, the resulting message (after padding with bits and with b) has a length that is an exact multiple of 512 bits. Equivalently, this message has a length that is an exact multiple of sixteen 32-bit words.
- Step 3, initialize the MD buffer: A four-word buffer (A, B, C, and D) is used to compute the message digest. Here, A, B, C, and D are 32-bit registers, which are initialized to the following values in hexadecimal, low-order bytes first:
  - Word A: 01 23 45 67
  - Word B: 89 ab cd ef
  - Word C: fe dc ba 98
  - Word D: 76 54 32 10
- Step 4, process message in 16-word blocks: This is the main part of the MD5 hashing algorithm and essentially consists of four rounds of independent and unbiased bit-wise operations on message blocks using the MD buffers A, B, C, and D (for details, see IETF RFC 1321).
- Step 5, output a 128-bit message digest.

The MD5 message-digest algorithm is simple to implement and provides a fingerprint or message digest of a message of arbitrary length. It is estimated that the difficulty of coming up with two messages having the same message digest is on the order of 2^{64} operations, and that the difficulty of coming up with any message having a given message digest is on the order of 2^{128} operations.

2.1.1.1 Common Use

The MD5 algorithm is intended to be used to generate message digests for digital signature applications (see Chapter 7), where a large file must be compressed in a secure manner before being encrypted with a private key under a public-key cryptography system such as RSA (see Section 2.4.2).

2.1.2 The SHS Standard

SHS is a Federal Information Processing Standards (FIPS) standard that specifies four secure hash algorithms: SHA-1, SHA-256, SHA-384, and SHA-512. SHA-1 generates a 160-bit message digest whereas SHA-256, SHA-384, and SHA-512 generate 256-bit, 384-bit, and 512-bit message digests, respectively.

All four algorithms utilize iterative, one-way hash functions that can process a message to produce a condensed representation called a message digest. These algorithms enable the determination of a message's integrity: any change to the message will, with a very high probability, result in a different message digest. This property is useful in the generation and verification of digital signatures and message authentication codes (MACs), and also in the generation of random numbers (bits).

Each algorithm can be described in two stages — preprocessing and hash computation:

- Preprocessing involves padding a message, parsing the padded message into m-bit blocks, and setting initialization values (IVs) to be used in the hash computation.
- Hash computation generates a message schedule from the padded message and uses that schedule, along with functions, constants, and word operations, to iteratively generate a series of hash values. The final hash value generated by the hash computation is used to determine the message digest.

The four algorithms differ most significantly in the number of bits of security provided for the data being hashed — this is directly related to the message digest length. When a secure hash algorithm is used in conjunction with another algorithm, there may be requirements specified elsewhere that require the use of a secure hash algorithm having a certain number of bits of security. For example, if a message is being signed with a digital signature algorithm that provides 128 bits of security, then that signature algorithm may require the use of a secure hash algorithm that also provides 128 bits of security (e.g., SHA-256).

Additionally, the four secure hash algorithms differ in terms of the size of the blocks and words of data that are used during hashing. Table 2.1 presents the basic properties of all four secure hash algorithms.

Table 2.1   SHS Algorithm Properties

Algorithm	Message Size (bits)	Block Size (bits)	Word Size (bits)	Message Digest Size (bits)	Security (bits)
SHA-1	$<2^{64}$	512	32	160	80
SHA-256	$<2^{64}$	512	32	256	128
SHA-384	$<2^{128}$	1024	64	384	192
SHA-512	$<2^{128}$	1024	64	512	256

Source: Adapted from FIPS PUB 180-2.

2.1.2.1   The SHA-1 Algorithm

SHA-1 is used to hash a message of length $<2^{64}$ in blocks of 512 bits. Its output is a 160-bit message digest. SHA-1 is, in particular, the most commonly used among the four SHS algorithms and is defined in a technical revision of SHA-FIPS 180-1. (SHA-1 is also defined in IETF RFC 3174.) In the revision, a circular left-shift operation has been added to the specifications. This revision improves the security provided by the SHA standard. SHA-1 is based on principles similar to those used by Ronald L. Rivest of MIT in the design of the MD4 message digest algorithm.

The following is an overview of the preprocessing and hash computation stages defined in the SHA-1 algorithm.

2.1.2.1.1   Preprocessing — Message Padding

The purpose of message padding is to make the total length of a padded message a multiple of 512. SHA-1 sequentially processes blocks of 512 bits when computing the message digest.

In summary, a "1" followed by m "0"s followed by a 64-bit integer are appended to the end of the message to produce a padded message of length $512 * n$ where m is the number of "0"s required for the padding and n is the number of 512-bit blocks in the padded message. The 64-bit integer appended at the very end is the length of the original message.

The padded message is then processed in the SHA-1 hash computation stage as n 512-bit blocks.

2.1.2.1.2   Hash Computation — Computing the Message Digest

The message digest is computed using the padded message. The computation is described using two buffers, each consisting of five 32-bit words and also a sequence of eighty 32-bit words. The words of the first five-word buffer are labeled A, B, C, D, and E. The words of the second five-word buffer are labeled H0, H1, H2, H3, and H4. The words of the 80-word sequence are labeled W(0), W(1), ..., W(79). A single-word buffer, TEMP, is also employed.

2.1.2.1.3 Predefined Functions and Constants

To describe the hash computation method, the following predefined set of functions and constants is required:

- A sequence of logical functions f(0), f(1), ..., f(79) is used. Each f(t), $0 <= t <= 79$, operates on three 32-bit words B, C, and D and produces a 32-bit word as output. f(t;B,C,D) is defined as follows: for words B, C, and D,
  - f(t;B,C,D) = (B AND C) OR ((NOT B) AND D)   ($0 <= t <= 19$)
  - f(t;B,C,D) = B XOR C XOR D   ($20 <= t <= 39$).
  (Exclusive OR [XOR] is the logical operation of comparing two binary bits. If the bits are different, the result is 1. If the bits are the same, the result is 0.)
  - f(t;B,C,D) = (B AND C) OR (B AND D)
    OR (C AND D)   ($40 <= t <= 59$)
  - f(t;B,C,D) = B XOR C XOR D   ($60 <= t <= 79$).
- A sequence of constant words K(0), K(1), ..., K(79) is used. In hexadecimal, these are given by
  - K(t) = 5A827999   ($0 <= t <= 19$)
  - K(t) = 6ED9EBA1   ($20 <= t <= 39$)
  - K(t) = 8F1BBCDC   ($40 <= t <= 59$)
  - K(t) = CA62C1D6   ($60 <= t <= 79$).
- A circular left-shift operation S^n(X) is defined by
  - S^n(X) = (X << n) OR (X >> 32 − n)

where X is a word and n is an integer such that $0 <= n < 32$.

2.1.2.1.4 Hash Computation Method

To generate the message digest, the 16-word (or 512-bit) message blocks M(1), M(2), ..., M(n) are processed in order. The processing of each M(i) involves 80 steps.

Before processing any blocks, the Hs are initialized as follows in hexadecimal:

- H0 = 67452301
- H1 = EFCDAB89

- H2 = 98BADCFE
- H3 = 10325476
- H4 = C3D2E1F0

Now M(1), M(2), ..., M(n) are processed. To process M(i), we proceed as follows:

a. Divide M(i) into 16 words W(0), W(1), ..., W(15), where W(0) is the leftmost word.
b. For t = 16 to 79 let:
    W(t) = S^1(W(t − 3) XOR W(t − 8) XOR W(t − 14) XOR W(t − 16)).
c. Let A = H0, B = H1, C = H2, D = H3, and E = H4.
d. For t = 0 to 79 do:
    TEMP = S^5(A) + f(t;B,C,D) + E + W(t) + K(t);
    E = D; D = C; C = S^30(B); B = A; A = TEMP;
e. Let H0 = H0 + A, H1 = H1 + B, H2 = H2 + C, H3 = H3 + D, and H4 = H4 + E.

After processing M(n), the message digest is the 160-bit string represented by the five words:

H0, H1, H2, H3, and H4.

The SHA-1 specification also defines a second hash computation method that saves sixty-four 32-bit words of storage, but this method is likely to lengthen the execution time due to the increased complexity of the address computations.

2.1.2.2 Message Digests and Digital Signatures

Figure 2.1 illustrates how SHA-1 can be used with a public-key cryptography technology such as the digital signature algorithm (DSA) in the generation and verification of digital signatures. The following briefly looks at the steps executed by the sender and the receiver of the message:

- The Sender:
    - Step 1: The message is hashed using SHA-1 to produce a message digest.
    - Step 2: The message digest is encrypted (signed) using DSA with the sender's private key.
    - Step 3: The resulting digital signature is appended to the message (which is likely also encrypted for confidentiality) and sent out over an unsecured network to the receiver.

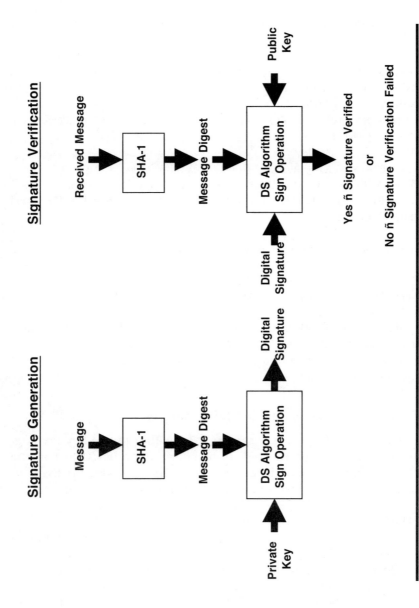

Figure 2.1 Generation and verification of digital signatures.

- The Receiver:
  - Step 1: The message (which needs to be first decrypted if the received message is encrypted) is hashed using SHA-1 to produce a message digest.
  - Step 2: The digital signature is decrypted (verified) with the sender's public key to produce a message digest.
  - Step 3: The two message digests are compared for a match.

If the two derived message digests match, the digital signature has been positively verified. If they do not match, the message most likely did not come from the intended sender or, to a lesser extent, the message has been altered *en route*.

Signing the message digest rather than the message typically improves the efficiency of the process because the message digest is usually much smaller in size than the message itself. The same hashing algorithm must be used by the verifier of a digital signature as was used by the creator of the signature.

2.1.2.3 Common Use

Just as the MD5 algorithm, the SHS hashing algorithms (in particular, SHA-1) are intended to be used for the generation of message digests in digital signature applications (e.g., DSA).

2.2 SECRET- AND PUBLIC-KEY CRYPTOGRAPHY

There are two classes of cryptography that are used in network security: secret key (or sometimes known as symmetric key) and public key (or sometimes known as asymmetric key). Secret-key cryptography is characterized by the fact that the same key that is used to encrypt the data is also used to decrypt the encrypted data.

Until the mid 1970s, secret-key cryptography was the only form of cryptography available, so the same secret key had to be known by all individuals participating in any application that provided a cryptographic security service. Although this form of cryptography was computationally efficient, it suffered from the shortcoming that only limited security services were offered, and it presented a difficult key-management problem because the secret keys had to be distributed securely to the communicating parties.

However, all this changed when Whitfield Diffie and Martin Hellman introduced the notion of public-key cryptography in 1976. This represented a significant breakthrough in cryptography because it enabled services that could not previously have been entertained, and it also significantly expedited the implementation of traditional security services.

Public-key cryptography is based on the use of key pairs. When using a key pair, only one of the two keys, which is referred to as the private key, must be kept secret and under the control of the owning party. The other key, referred to as the public key, can be disseminated freely for use by any party who wishes to participate in security services with the party holding the private key. This is possible because the keys in the pair are mathematically related, but it remains computationally infeasible to derive the private key from knowledge of the public key. In theory, any individual can send the holder of a private key a message encrypted using the corresponding public key, and only the holder of the private key can decrypt the secure message. Similarly, the holder of the private key can establish the integrity and origin of the data he sends to another party by digitally signing the data using his private key. Anyone who receives that data can use the associated public key to validate that the data came from the holder of the private key and to verify that the integrity of the data has been maintained.

Public-key cryptographic algorithms are much more CPU-intensive than secret-key cryptographic algorithms, but key management is easier to implement because only public keys need to be distributed. Because of the relative ease of key management due to advances in key-management technologies, public-key cryptographic technologies have become the major driving force behind E-commerce and many other applications over the Internet.

The following sections describe some of the major secret- and public-key cryptographic technologies used in the network security industry.

2.3 SECRET-KEY CRYPTOGRAPHY ALGORITHMS

These cryptography algorithms only make use of a secret key that is shared by the encryption and decryption operations. One special example of a shared secret key is a session key that has been agreed upon through exchanges of messages during the beginning of a Secure Socket Layer (SSL) session and prior to a typical secure file transfer in which the session key is used to encrypt and decrypt a large amount of data by the sender and the receiver, respectively.

2.3.1 Block Ciphers and Stream Ciphers

Each secret-key cryptography algorithm or cipher typically works in two phases: the key set-up phase and the ciphering or encrypt and decrypt phase. There are two major classes of these algorithms: block ciphers and

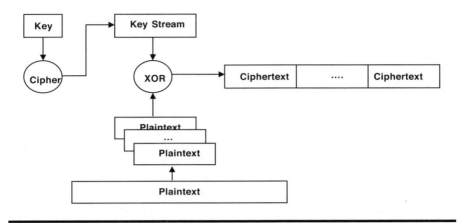

Figure 2.2   Block cipher operation.

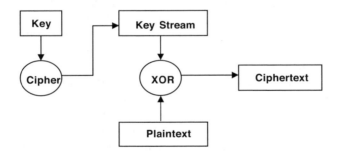

Figure 2.3   Stream cipher operation.

stream ciphers. Block ciphers encrypt plaintext in units of blocks and likewise decrypt ciphertext in units of blocks, whereas stream ciphers encrypt plaintext in one stream and decrypt ciphertext likewise.

Figure 2.2 depicts the operation of a block cipher. The block cipher fragments the frame into blocks of a predetermined size and performs the XOR function on each block with the key stream generated by the cipher algorithm. Each block must be of the predetermined size, and leftover frame fragments are padded to the appropriate block size. For example, if a block cipher fragments frames into 16-byte blocks, and a 38-byte frame is to be encrypted, the block cipher fragments the frame into two 16-byte blocks and one 6-byte block. The 6-byte block is padded with ten bytes of padding to meet the sixteen-byte block size.

Figure 2.3 depicts the operation of a stream cipher such as RC4. The stream cipher encrypts data by generating a key stream from the key and performing the XOR function on the key stream with the plaintext data. The key stream can be any size that matches the size of the plaintext frame to be encrypted.

2.3.2 DES and 3DES Encryption Standards

DES was originally developed by IBM as "Lucifer" in the early 1970s. The National Security Agency (NSA) and the National Institute of Standards and Technology (NIST) used a modified version of Lucifer and named it DES. DES was adopted as the federal standard in 1976 [specified in FIPS 46-3 and identical to the American National Standards Institute (ANSI) standard Data Encryption Algorithm (DEA) defined in ANSI X3.92]. However, DES became vulnerable as computers became more powerful, and simple DES has been cracked and is no longer secure. So NIST defined 3DES or Triple DES in 1999. 3DES uses three stages of DES and so is much more secure and suffices for most applications. In 2001, NIST replaced DES by the Advanced Encryption Standard (AES). AES is expected remain strong enough for the next ten to twenty years.

Data DES is a block cipher — i.e., it acts on a fixed-length block of plaintext and converts it into a block of ciphertext of the same size by using a secret key.

In DES, the block size for plaintext is 64 bits. The length of the key is also 64 bits but 8 bits are used for parity. Hence the effective key length is only 56 bits. In 3DES, three stages of DES are applied using a separate key for each stage. So the key length in 3DES is 168 bits.

Decryption in DES is done by applying the reverse transformation to the block of ciphertext using the same key. The DES method of operation is shown below.

2.3.2.1 The Basic DES Algorithm

DES encrypts a plaintext block by a process that has $r = 16$ rounds as shown in Figure 2.4 and is described below:

- The Encryption Process:
    - The block of plaintext is split into two halves (L_0, R_0), each of which is 32 bits long. Also, DES uses the original 56-bit key to generate 16 subkeys of 48 bits each (k_i). These subkeys are used in the 16 rounds.
    - In each round, the function F is applied to one half using a subkey k_i, and the result is XORed with the other half. The two halves are then swapped and the process is repeated. All

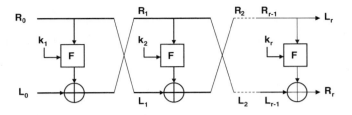

Figure 2.4 The DES algorithm.

the rounds follow the same pattern except the last one, where
there is no swap.
- The final result is the ciphertext (L_r, R_r). Hence, the plaintext
(L_0, R_0) is transformed to (L_r, R_r).
■ The Decryption Process:
- Decryption is structurally identical to encryption. So the same
mechanism as above is used. However, the input here is the
pair (R_r, L_r) instead of (L_0, R_0).
- Also, the input subkeys are applied in the reverse order. So the
ith subkey is k_{r-i+1} instead of k_i.
- The final result is the original text (L_0, R_0). So the ciphertext
(R_r, L_r) was decrypted to (L_0, R_0).

The function F is a key-dependent complex function known as the
cipher function, which takes the 48-bit subkey and a 32-bit plaintext half
as input and produces a 32-bit output for each round of the algorithm.
The reader is referred to the FIPS PUB 46-1 publication for a detailed
description of both the cipher function and the complete encryption and
decryption algorithms.

2.3.2.2 The 3DES Algorithm

3DES uses the same basic machinery of DES three times over, using three
keys k_1, k_2, and k_3. The plaintext (M) is encrypted using k_1. This result is
encrypted with k_2 and the result is then further encrypted with k_3 to get
the ciphertext (C). Thus $C = E_{k_3}(E_{k_2}(E_{k_1}(M)))$ where E_{k_i} stands for encryption using k_i. This mode of using 3DES is called the DES–EEE mode
because all three keys run in encryption mode. The other mode is called
DES–EDE, where the second stage is run in decryption mode, i.e.,
$C = E_{k_3}(E_{k_2}(E_{k_1}(M)))$; E_{k_2} stands for encryption using k_2.
   The three keys may or may not be independent. For the DES–EDE
mode, three options are defined:

- The keys k_1, k_2, and k_3 are independent.
- k_1 and k_2 are independent but $k_1 = k_3$.
- $k_1 = k_2 = k_3$; in this case, 3DES becomes backward compatible with DES.

2.3.2.3 Common Use

Both DES and 3DES are used in all common security technologies that utilize encryption and decryption with secret keys.

2.3.3 The AES Standard

The AES standard was developed to replace DES and 3DES. AES uses the Rijndael algorithm, a symmetric block cipher algorithm that can process blocks of 128 bits using cipher keys with lengths of 128, 192, and 256 bits.

2.3.3.1 The Rijndael Algorithm

This is an iterative block cipher, which means that the initial input block and cipher key undergo multiple transformation cycles before producing the final output. The algorithm can operate over a variable-length block using variable-length keys. A 128-, 192-, or 256-bit key can be used to encrypt data blocks that are 128, 192, or 256 bits long, and all nine combinations of key and block length are possible. (The accepted AES implementation contains only some of the Rijndael algorithm's total capabilities.) The algorithm is written so that block length and key length can easily be extended in multiples of 32 bits, and the system is specifically designed for efficient implementation in hardware or software on a range of processors.

The Rijndael algorithm is a substitution–linear transformation network with ten, twelve, or fourteen rounds, depending on the key size. A data block to be encrypted by the algorithm is split into an array of bytes, and each encryption operation is byte-oriented. The Rijndael algorithm's round function consists of four layers. In the first layer, an 8×8 substitution table also known as an S-box is applied to each byte. The second and third layers are linear mixing layers, in which the rows of the array are shifted and the columns are mixed. In the fourth layer, subkey bytes are XORed into each byte of the array. In the last round, column mixing is omitted.

NIST selected the Rijndael algorithm for AES because it offers a combination of security, performance, efficiency, ease of implementation, and flexibility. Specifically, it has the following advantages:

Table 2.2   AES versus 3DES

	AES	3DES
Type of Algorithm	Symmetric, block cipher	Symmetric, Feistel cipher
Key Size (in bits)	128, 192, 256	112 or 168
Speed	High	Low
Time to Crack (assume a machine could try 255 keys per second — NIST)	149 trillion years	4.6 billion years
Resource Consumption	Low	Medium

■ The Rijndael algorithm appears to be consistently a very good performer when implemented in both hardware and software across a wide range of computing environments, regardless of whether it is used in the feedback mode or in the nonfeedback mode.

■ Its key set-up time is excellent, and its key agility is good.

■ The very low memory requirements of the Rijndael algorithm make it very well suited for restricted-space environments while still demonstrating excellent performance.

■ The Rijndael algorithm operations are among the easiest to defend against power and timing attacks.

■ Additionally, it appears that a measure of defense can be provided against such attacks without significantly impacting the algorithm's performance.

■ Finally, the algorithm's internal round structure appears to have good potential for benefiting from instruction-level parallelism.

2.3.3.2   AES versus 3DES

Table 2.2 is not intended to provide absolute comparative merits but rather, some additional relevant information.

2.3.3.3   Common Use

Just as DES and 3DES, AES is used in all common security technologies that require cryptography utilizing secret keys.

AES, already a standard for new implementations in the U.S. government, is gradually being rolled out in many different encryption protocols including IEEE 802.11, IPSec, S/MIME, and TLS.

2.3.4 The RC4 Cipher

RC4 is a stream cipher designed by R. Rivest in 1987. It is a variable key-size stream cipher with byte-oriented operations. The algorithm is based on the use of random permutation operations. Analysis shows that the period of the cipher is overwhelmingly likely to be greater than 10^{100}. Eight to sixteen machine operations are required per output byte, and the cipher can be expected to run very quickly in software. RC4 is considered to be a secure algorithm.

RC4 uses a variable-length key from 1 to 256 bytes to initialize a 256-byte state table. The state table is used for the subsequent generation of pseudorandom bytes and then to generate a pseudorandom stream, which is XORed with plaintext to give ciphertext. Each element in the state table is swapped at least once.

The RC4 key is often limited to 40 bits because of U.S. export restrictions, but it is sometimes used as a 128-bit key for strong encryption. The algorithm has the capability of using keys between 1 and 2048 bits.

RC4 is used in many commercial software packages, such as Lotus Notes and Oracle Secure SQL. It is also defined in the Cellular Specifications.

2.3.4.1 The RC4 Algorithm

The RC4 algorithm works in two phases: key setup and ciphering.

Key setup is the first and more difficult phase of this algorithm. During an N-bit key setup (where N is the key length), the encryption key is used to generate an encrypting variable by utilizing two arrays, state and key, and N-number of mixing operations. These mixing operations consist of swapping bytes, modulo operations, and other formulas. A modulo operation is the process of obtaining the remainder from a division. For example, 11 ÷ 4 is 2 remainder 3; therefore, 11 mod 4 would be equal to 3.

Once the encrypting variable is produced from the key setup, it enters the ciphering phase, where it is XORed with the plaintext message to create an encrypted message. Once the receiver gets the encrypted message, he or she decrypts it by XORing it with the same encrypting variable.

2.3.4.2 Common Use

RC4 is widely used in commercial applications including Oracle SQL, Microsoft Windows, PERL, and the SSL technology (Chapter 8) for both file encryption and secure communication over the network, including Wireless LANs (WLANs).

2.4 PUBLIC-KEY CRYPTOGRAPHY

Public-key cryptography is based on the use of private and public key pairs. The private key must be kept secret and under the control of the owner, and the public key can be disseminated freely to the public.

2.4.1 Public Key Cryptography Standards

It is worth noting that Public Key Cryptography Standards (PKCS) are specifications produced by RSA Laboratories in cooperation with secure systems developers worldwide for the purpose of accelerating the deployment of public-key cryptographic technologies. First published in 1991 as a result of meetings with a small group of early adopters of public-key cryptographic technologies, the PKCS documents have become widely referenced and implemented. The PKCS standards cover RSA encryption, Diffie–Hellman key agreement, password-based encryption, extended-certificate syntax, private-key information syntax, and certification request syntax, as well as selected attributes.

The following table lists the standards defined by PKCS:

- PKCS #1: RSA Cryptography Standard
- PKCS #2: Has been incorporated into PKCS #1
- PKCS #3: Diffie–Hellman Key Agreement Standard
- PKCS #4: Has been incorporated into PKCS #1
- PKCS #5: Password-Based Cryptography Standard
- PKCS #6: Extended-Certificate Syntax Standard
- PKCS #7: Cryptographic Message Syntax Standard
- PKCS #8: Private-Key Information Syntax Standard
- PKCS #9: Selected Attribute Types
- PKCS #10: Certification Request Syntax Standard
- PKCS #11: Cryptographic Token Interface Standard
- PKCS #12: Personal Information Exchange Syntax Standard
- PKCS #13: Elliptic Curve Cryptography Standard
- PKCS #15: Cryptographic Token Information Format Standard

Contributions from the PKCS standards series have become part of many formal and *de facto* standards, including PKIX, SET, S/MIME, and SSL.

ANSI and Rivest–Shamir–Adleman (RSA) PKCS both define digital signature mechanisms with very similar underlying principles. RSA PKCS #1 v2.0 describes the RSA algorithm and ways to use that algorithm for both encryption and decryption and for digital signature generation and verification. ANSI X9.31 similarly defines a digital signature mechanism that is based on the same RSA algorithm and, overall, the two digital signature mechanisms have only small variations.

It should be noted that whereas the RSA algorithm is considered in our network security framework to be a basic cryptographic technology in this book, the overall digital signature mechanisms defined in the ANSI X9.31 and PKCS specifications are enhanced, non-repudiation technologies and will be discussed further in Chapter 7.

The RSA algorithm is summarized in the following text.

2.4.2   The RSA Algorithm

The RSA public- and private-key cryptographic algorithm is defined in ANSI X9.31 as part of the RSA PKCS. RSA PKCS are specifications produced by RSA Laboratories in cooperation with secure systems developers worldwide for the purpose of accelerating the deployment of public-key cryptography. First published in 1991 as a result of meetings with a small group of early adopters of public-key technology, the PKCS documents have become widely referenced and implemented. The RSA algorithm depends on a public and private key pair.

2.4.2.1   The Key-Generation Algorithm

The following steps are used to generate the public and private key pair:

- Step 1: Generate two large random primes, p and q, of approximately equal size such that their product $n = pq$ is of the required bit length, e.g., 1024 bits.
- Step 2: Compute $n = pq$ and $\phi = (p - 1)(q - 1)$.
- Step 3: Choose an integer e, $1 < e < \phi$, such that gcd $(e, \phi) = 1$.
- Step 4: Compute the secret exponent d, $1 < d < \phi$, such that ed 1 (mod ϕ).
- Step 5: The public key is (n, e) and the private key is (n, d). The values of p, q, and ϕ should also be kept secret.

2.4.2.2   Encryption by Sender A

Sender A does the following:

- Step 1: Obtains the recipient B's public key (n, e).
- Step 2: Represents the plaintext message as a positive integer $m < n$.
- Step 3: Computes the ciphertext $c = m^e$ mod n.
- Step 4: Sends the ciphertext c to B.

2.4.2.3   Decryption by Recipient B

Recipient B does the following:

- Step 1: Uses the private key (n, d) to compute $m = c^d \bmod n$.
- Step 2: Extracts the plaintext from the integer representative m.

2.4.2.4   Common Use

Contributions from the PKCS standards series have become parts of many formal and *de facto* standards, including the ANSI X9 documents and the RSA algorithms (including improved RSA algorithms such as RSA-PSS), and have found their way into many other network security technologies such as PKIX, SET, S/MIME, and SSL.

2.4.3   Digital Signature Cryptography Algorithms

The DSA algorithm and the Elliptic Curve Digital Signature Algorithm (ECDSA; defined in ANSI X9.62) are FIPS-approved digital cryptographic algorithms that are used in digital signature generation and verification within the digital signature standards (DSS) specifications. Digital signatures themselves are considered to be an enhanced technology and will be described in more detail in Chapter 7.

DSA and ECDSA allow a signatory to generate a digital signature on a piece of data and a verifier to verify the authenticity of the signature. Each signatory has a public and private key. The private key is used in the signature generation process and the public key is used in the signature verification process. The signature generation and verification processes involve the use of either algorithm (DSA or ECDSA) to encrypt and decrypt a message using the private and public keys, respectively. An adversary, who does not know the private key of the signatory, cannot generate the correct signature of the signatory. However, by using the signatory's public key, anyone can verify a correctly signed message. A means of associating public and private key pairs to the corresponding users (i.e., key management) is required (see Chapter 7 and Chapter 9 on key-management technologies).

It is important to note that the DSA and ECDSA encryption and decryption algorithms, just like the RSA algorithm, are considered to be basic cryptographic technologies even though they are defined in the specifications of the DSS, which is considered to be an enhanced, non-repudiation technology.

2.4.3.1   The DSA Algorithm

The following text summarizes the encryption (signature generation) and decryption (signature verification) operations in the DSA algorithm.

The DSA algorithm makes use of the following parameters:

- p = a prime modulus, where $2^{L-1} < p < 2^L$ for $512 = < L = <1024$, and L is a multiple of 64.
- q = a prime divisor of $p - 1$, where $2^{159} < q < 2^{160}$.
- $g = h^{(p-1)/q} \bmod p$, where h is any integer with $1 < h < p$ 1 such that $h^{(p-1)/q} \bmod p > 1$ (g has order $q \bmod p$).
- x = a randomly or pseudorandomly generated integer with $0 < x < q$.
- $y = g^x \bmod p$.
- k = a randomly or pseudorandomly generated integer with $0 < k < q$.

The integers p, q, and g can be public and can be common to a group of users. A user's private and public keys are x and y, respectively. They are normally fixed for a period of time. Parameters x and k are used for signature generation only, and must be kept secret. Parameter k must be regenerated for each signature.

2.4.3.1.1   DSA Signature Generation

The signature of a message M is the pair of numbers r and s computed according to the equations below:

$$r = (g^k \bmod p) \bmod q \text{ and } s = (k^{-1} (\text{SHA-1(M)} + xr)) \bmod q.$$

In the above, k^1 is the multiplicative inverse of k, mod q, i.e., $(k^1\ k)$ mod $q = 1$ and $0 < k^1 < q$. The value of SHA-1(M) is a 160-bit string output by the secure hash algorithm (SHA-1) specified in FIPS 180-1 (see Section 2.1.2.1).

As an option, one may wish to check if $r = 0$ or $s = 0$. If either $r = 0$ or $s = 0$, a new value of k should be generated and the signature should be recalculated (it is extremely unlikely that $r = 0$ or $s = 0$ if signatures are generated properly).

The signature is transmitted along with the message to the verifier.

2.4.3.1.2   DSA Signature Verification

Prior to verifying the signature in a signed message, p, q, and g plus the sender's public key and identity are made available to the verifier in an authenticated manner.

Let M', r', and s' be the received versions of M, r, and s, respectively, and let y be the public key of the signatory. To verify the signature, the verifier first checks to see that $0 < r' < q$ and $0 < s' < q$; if either condition is violated, the signature is rejected. If these two conditions are satisfied, the verifier computes

$$w = (s')^{-1} \bmod q$$
$$u1 = ((\text{SHA-1}(M'))w) \bmod q$$
$$u2 = ((r')w) \bmod q$$
$$v = (((g)^{u1} \text{ and } (y)^{u2}) \bmod p) \bmod q$$

If $v = r^1$, then the signature is verified and the verifier can have high confidence that the received message was sent by the party holding the secret key x corresponding to the public key y.

If v does not equal r^1, then the message may have been modified, the message may have been incorrectly signed by the signatory, or the message may have been signed by an impostor. The message should be considered invalid.

2.4.3.2 The ECDSA Algorithm

The ECDSA digital signature algorithm is a FIPS-approved cryptographic algorithm for digital signature generation and verification. ECDSA is the elliptic curve analog of the DSA. ECDSA is described in ANSI X9.62.

2.4.3.3 Common Use

Just as RSA, DSA and ECDSA are used in digital signature generation and verification. In fact, all three algorithms are FIPS approved for the generation and verification of digital signatures.

2.5 THE DIFFIE–HELLMAN KEY-EXCHANGE ALGORITHM

The Diffie–Hellman Key-Agreement Protocol (also called Exponential Key Agreement) was developed by Diffie and Hellman in 1976 and published in the groundbreaking paper "New Directions in Cryptography" in the *IEEE Transactions on Information Theory*. The protocol allows two users to securely exchange a shared key over an insecure medium without actually transmitting this key. The algorithm is utilized in the OAKLEY key-management protocol to allow two communicating entities to negotiate methods for encryption, key derivation, and authentication (described in Chapter 7).

Note that this key-exchange algorithm works with any key, whether it is a secret key, a private key, or a session key.

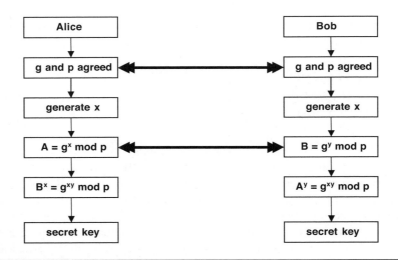

Figure 2.5   The Diffie–Hellman key-exchange algorithm.

2.5.1   An Overview of the Algorithm

The protocol has two system parameters p and g. They are both public and may be used by all the users in a system. Parameter p is a prime number and parameter g is the primitive root (usually called a generator) and is an integer less than p, which is capable of generating every element from one to $p - 1$ when multiplied by itself a certain number of times, modulo the prime p.

The diagram in Figure 2.5 illustrates the algorithm, which is explained in the following text. Alice and Bob agree upon a prime number p and a primitive root g. Alice generates a random number x, calculates $A = g^x$ mod p, and sends this to Bob. Bob also generates a random number y, calculates $B = g^y$ mod p, and sends this to Alice. Now Alice calculates g^{xy} mod p and Bob does the same.

The shared key is g^{xy} mod p. An attacker only gets to know the numbers g, p, A, and B but not x and y. The attacker needs x and y to compute the key. The Diffie–Hellman problem is based on the difficulty of calculating discrete logarithms, so it is not possible to calculate x from A, p, and g, or y from B, p, and g.

Thus, a shared key has been successfully exchanged without actually sending the key over the network. This is obviously a secure way to exchange keys.

2.5.2   Common Use

As indicated earlier, the Diffie–Hellman algorithm has been used in the definition of the OAKLEY key-management protocol which, in turn, has been partially used in defining the IPSec Internet Key Exchange Protocol (IKE). Both OAKLEY and IKE are described further in Chapter 7.

2.6 SUMMARY

Confidentiality functional elements play a central role in secure communications and, as a result, hashing algorithms and key-based (secret key, and public and private key pairs) cryptographic algorithms are the basic technologies that are employed over and over again in most other network security technologies and in various applications. In addition, programmed packages and software are readily available commercially and academically for different operating environments. For example, the hashing algorithm MD5 is used to produce message digests and, in turn, RSA is then used to generate digital signatures. Similarly, SHA-1 is used with public-key DSA in digital signature applications also.

The secret-key cryptographic algorithm AES, which is considered to be more secure than the earlier DES or 3DES algorithm, is used in many popular network security technologies including IPSec VPNs, Secure MIME (S/MIME), TLS (a follow-up to SSL), and WLAN.

RC4 is a secret-key stream cipher and is used in WLAN security as well as many other applications.

A number of public-key cryptographic algorithms have been defined for use in areas where public cryptography is applied: the RSA algorithm used in both PKCS #1 v.2 and ANSI 9.31 (both digital signature specifications), DSA, and ECDSA.

The Diffie–Hellman is a very heavily used secret-key-exchange algorithm because it accomplishes secure key exchange without actually sending the key over the network. For example, it is used in key-management technologies such as OAKLEY and IKE, and IKE forms a central part of the public-key architecture PKI, as is described in Chapter 9.

Bibliography

1. IETF RFC 1321: The MD5 Message-Digest Algorithm. April 1992.
2. FIPS PUB 46-2: Data Encryption Standard (DES), October 25, 1999.
3. 3DES and Encryption, tutorial by K. Castelino.
4. FIPS PUB 197: Specification for the Advanced Encryption Standard (AES), November 26, 2001.
5. IETF RFC 3565: Use of the Advanced Encryption Standard (AES) Encryption Algorithm in Cryptographic Message Syntax (CMS), July 2003.
6. PKCS #1 v2.1: RSA Cryptography Standard, RSA Laboratories, June 14, 2002.
7. Wireless LAN Security, Cisco White Paper, 2002.
8. FIPS PUB 186-2: Digital Signature Standard (DSS), National Institute of Standards and Technology, January 27, 2000.
9. FIPS PUB 180-2: Secure Hash Standard (SHS), National Institute of Standards and Technology, August 1, 2002.

10. W. Diffie and M.E. Hellman, New directions in cryptography, *IEEE Transactions on Information Theory,* IT 22: 644–654, 1976.

11. Robert Neumann, Security Association and Key Management, ISAKMP and OAKLEY protocols seminar work, January 28, 2003.

12. R. Rivest, RC4 Encryption Algorithm, History and Description of the Algorithm.

13. IETF RFC 2104: HMAC: Keyed-Hashing for Message Authentication, H. Krawczyk, M. Bellare, and R. Canetti, February 1997.

14. IETF RFC 3174: US Secure Hash Algorithm 1 (SHA1), D. Eastlake, 3rd, and P. Jones, September 2001.

15. Burt Kaliski, Raising the Standard for RSA Signatures: RSA-PSS, RSA Laboratories, February 26, 2003.

3

BASIC AUTHENTICATION TECHNOLOGIES

Authentication ensures the integrity of user identities through the identification of legitimate users and the rejection of others. Legitimate users would be allowed to proceed with their business to some extent, even though they can still subsequently be limited in what they can actually do or rejected by other aspects of security controls, such as authorization. In this chapter, we look at some basic authentication technologies, i.e., technologies that are intended primarily for the identification of legitimate users and the rejection of all others.

Authentication needs to be done during the setup of a connection to authenticate the identity of one or both of the two communicating parties. Authentication might also be needed for each subsequent exchange of data or messages.

Authentication Header (AH) and Encapsulating Security Payload (ESP) are key authentication mechanisms in IP network environments and are particularly useful in the authentication of individual data packets. Included in the authentication technologies to be described in this chapter are packet filtering and simple userID and password authentication methods including Password Authentication Protocol (PAP) and Shiva Password Authentication Protocol (SPAP).

3.1 IP-LAYER AUTHENTICATION MECHANISMS

Because IP is by definition a connectionless transport technology utilizing datagram exchanges over the network, special facilities are needed to ensure user authentication for each of the IP packets transmitted and received. There are two commonly used authentication mechanisms defined for IP. The first is AH, which provides integrity and authentication without confidentiality. The second is ESP, which always provides confidentiality and optionally also provides integrity and authentication. The two mechanisms may be used together or separately. In addition, there are also techniques available in the industry and not discussed here that can be used to provide protection against IP traffic analysis.

Both AH and ESP use an authentication algorithm to generate authentication information known as the Integrity Check Value (ICV), which is placed in the authentication data field in the corresponding header.

3.1.1 AH

AH defines an Authentication Header that contains the authentication information for the particular IP datagram and is used to provide connectionless data integrity and source identity authentication for IP datagrams (hereafter referred to as just "authentication") and protection against replays. This latter, optional service may be selected by the receiver when a Security Association is established. (Although the default calls for the sender to increment the Sequence Number used for anti-replay, the service is effective only if the receiver checks the Sequence Number.) AH provides authentication for as much of the IP header as possible, as well as for upper-level protocol data. However, some IP header fields may change in transit, and the value of these fields, when the packet arrives at the receiver, may not be predictable by the sender. The values of such fields cannot be protected by AH. Thus, the protection provided to the IP header by AH is somewhat piecemeal.

AH may be applied alone, in combination with ESP, or in a nested fashion through the use of a tunnel mode (see also Chapter 7). Security services can be provided between a pair of communicating hosts, between a pair of communicating security gateways, or between a security gateway and a host.

ESP may be used to provide similar security services as AH, and it also provides an added confidentiality (encryption) service. The primary difference between the authentication capabilities provided by ESP and AH is the extent of the coverage offered by each. Specifically, ESP does not protect any IP header fields unless those fields are encapsulated by ESP (i.e., in the tunnel mode).

In some cases, the AH technology might be combined with the ESP technology to obtain the desired security properties. AH always provides integrity and authentication and can provide non-repudiation if it is used with certain authentication algorithms (e.g., RSA). ESP always provides integrity and confidentiality and can also provide authentication if used

Next Header	Payload Len	RESERVED
Security Parameters Index (SPI)		
Sequence Number Field		
Authentication Data (variable)		

Figure 3.1   AH header format.

with certain authenticating encryption algorithms. Adding the AH header to an IP datagram prior to encapsulating the datagram using ESP might be desirable for users wishing to have strong integrity, authentication, and confidentiality, and perhaps also for users who require strong non-repudiation. When the two mechanisms are combined, the placement of the IP AH makes clear which part of the data is being authenticated. For more details on how to use AH and ESP in various network environments, see IP Security (IPSec), the Security Architecture for the Internet Protocol in RFC 240. An illustration of the use of an AH and ESP combination can be found in Chapter 9, Section 9.1.

3.1.1.1   AH Header Format

The AH header format is shown in Figure 3.1. The IP protocol header (IPv4, IPv6, or Extension) immediately preceding AH will contain the value 51 in its Protocol (IPv4) or Next Header (IPv6, Extension) field, where

- *Next Header* is an 8-bit field that identifies the type of the next payload after AH. The value of this field is chosen from the set of IP Protocol Numbers defined in the most recent "Assigned Numbers" RFC from the Internet Assigned Number Authority (IANA).
- *Payload Length* is an 8-bit field that specifies the length of AH in 32-bit words (4-byte units), minus "2."
- *Reserved* is a 16-bit field reserved for future use.
- *Security Parameters Index (SPI)* is an arbitrary 32-bit value that, in combination with the destination IP address and security protocol (i.e., AH), uniquely identifies the Security Association for this datagram.
- *Sequence Number* is an unsigned 32-bit field that contains a monotonically increasing counter value (sequence number).
- *Authentication Data* is a variable-length field that contains the ICV for this packet. The field must be an integral multiple of 32 bits in length.

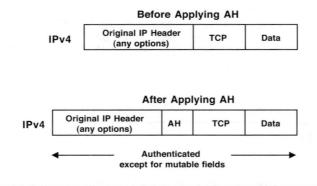

Figure 3.2   IPv4 packet with and without AH.

3.1.1.2   AH Authentication Operation

AH may be employed in one of two ways or modes: transport mode or tunnel mode. The transport mode is applicable only to host implementations and provides protection for upper-layer protocols, in addition to selected IP header fields. In this mode, inbound and outbound IP fragments may require an IPSec implementation to perform extra IP reassembly or fragmentation in order to both conform to this specification and provide transparent IPSec support.

In transport mode, AH is inserted after the IP header and before an upper-layer protocol, e.g., TCP, UDP, ICMP, etc., or before any other IPSec headers that have already been inserted. In the context of IPv4, this calls for placing AH after the IP header (and any options that it contains), but before the upper-layer protocol. (Note that the term "transport" mode should not be misconstrued as restricting its use to TCP and UDP. For example, an ICMP message *may* be sent using either "transport" mode or "tunnel" mode.) Figure 3.2 illustrates AH transport mode positioning for a typical IPv4 packet, on a "before and after" basis.

In the IPv6 context, AH is viewed as an end-to-end payload and thus should appear after hop-by-hop, routing, and fragmentation extension headers. The destination options extension headers could appear either before or after AH, depending on the semantics desired. Figure 3.3 illustrates AH transport mode positioning for a typical IPv6 packet.

ESP and AH headers can be combined in a variety of modes. The IPSec Architecture document (RFC 2401) describes the combinations of security associations that must be supported.

Tunnel-mode AH may be employed in either hosts or security gateways. When AH is implemented in a security gateway (to protect transit traffic), tunnel mode must be used. In tunnel mode, the "inner" IP header carries

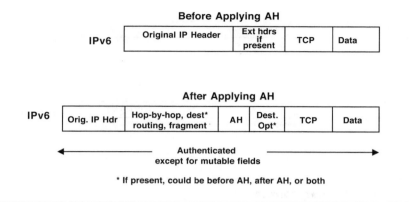

Figure 3.3   IPv6 packet with and without AH.

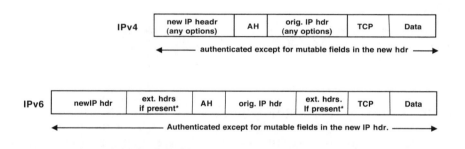

Figure 3.4   Tunnel-mode AH.

the ultimate source and destination addresses, whereas the "outer" IP header may contain distinct IP addresses, e.g., addresses of security gateways. In tunnel mode, AH protects the entire inner IP packet, including the entire inner IP header. The position of AH in the tunnel mode, relative to the outer IP header, is the same as for AH in the transport mode.

Figure 3.4 illustrates the AH tunnel-mode positioning for typical IPv4 and IPv6 packets.

3.1.1.3   Authentication Algorithm

The authentication algorithm employed for the ICV computation is specified by the Security Association (SA) that has been established for communication between users. For point-to-point communication, suitable authentication algorithms include keyed Message Authentication Codes (MACs) based on symmetric encryption algorithms (e.g., DES) or on one-way hash functions (e.g., MD5 or SHA-1).

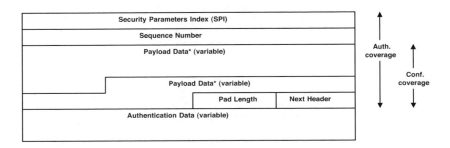

Figure 3.5   ESP packet format.

3.1.2   ESP

As indicated earlier, ESP may be used to provide the same security services as AH, but ESP also provides a confidentiality (encryption) service.

3.1.2.1   ESP Packet Format

The ESP packet format is shown in Figure 3.5. The protocol header (IPv4, IPv6, or Extension) immediately preceding the ESP header will contain the value 50 in its Protocol (IPv4) or Next Header (IPv6, Extension) field, where

- *Security Parameters Index (SPI)* is an arbitrary 32-bit value that, in combination with the destination IP address and security protocol (ESP), uniquely identifies the Security Association for this datagram.
- *Sequence Number* is an unsigned 32-bit field that contains a monotonically increasing counter value (sequence number).
- *Payload Data* is a variable-length field containing data described by the Next Header field.
- *Padding* is for Encryption.
- *Pad Length* indicates the number of pad bytes immediately preceding it.
- *Next Header* is an 8-bit field that identifies the type of data contained in the Payload Data field, e.g., an extension header in IPv6 or an upper-layer protocol identifier.
- *Authentication Data* is a variable-length field containing an Integrity Check Value (ICV) computed over the ESP packet minus the Authentication Data.

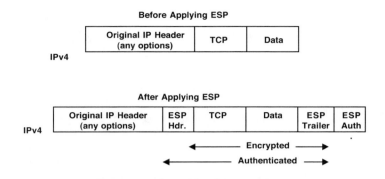

Figure 3.6   IPv4 packet with and without ESP.

3.1.2.2   ESP Authentication Operation

As in the case of AH, ESP may be employed in two ways: transport mode or tunnel mode. The former mode is applicable only to host implementations and provides protection for upper-layer protocols, but not the IP header. In this mode, inbound and outbound IP fragments may require an IPSec implementation to perform extra IP reassembly or fragmentation in order to both conform to this specification and provide transparent IPSec support.

In transport mode, ESP is inserted after the IP header and before an upper-layer protocol, e.g., TCP, UDP, ICMP, etc., or before any other IPSec headers that have already been inserted. In the context of IPv4, this translates to placing ESP after the IP header (and any options that it contains), but before the upper-layer protocol. (Note that the term "transport" mode should not be misconstrued as restricting its use to TCP and UDP. For example, an ICMP message *may* be sent using either transport mode or tunnel mode.)

Figure 3.6 illustrates ESP transport-mode positioning for a typical IPv4 packet, on a before and after basis. (The "ESP trailer" encompasses any Padding, as well as the Pad Length, and Next Header fields.)

In the IPv6 context, ESP is viewed as an end-to-end payload and thus should appear after hop-by-hop, routing, and fragmentation extension headers. The destination options extension headers could appear either before or after the ESP header, depending on the semantics desired. However, because ESP protects only fields following the ESP header, it generally may be desirable to place the destination options headers after the ESP header.

Figure 3.7 illustrates ESP transport-mode positioning for a typical IPv6 packet.

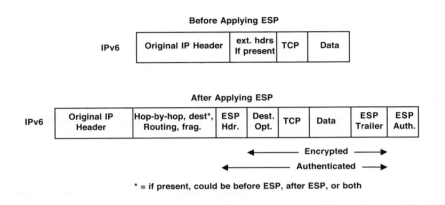

Figure 3.7 IPv6 packet with and without ESP.

As previously indicated, ESP and AH headers can be combined in a variety of modes. The IPSec Architecture document describes the combinations of security associations that must be supported.

Tunnel-mode ESP may be employed in either hosts or security gateways. When ESP is implemented in a security gateway (e.g., to protect subscriber transit traffic), tunnel mode must be used. In tunnel mode, the inner IP header carries the ultimate source and destination addresses, whereas an outer IP header may contain distinct IP addresses, e.g., addresses of security gateways. In tunnel mode, ESP protects the entire inner IP packet, including the entire inner IP header. The position of ESP in the tunnel mode, relative to the outer IP header, is the same as for ESP in the transport mode.

Figure 3.8 illustrates ESP tunnel mode positioning for typical IPv4 and IPv6 packets.

3.1.2.3 Encryption Algorithm

The encryption algorithm employed in ESP is specified by SA. ESP is designed for use with symmetric encryption algorithms.

Key management is an important part of the IPSec Architecture that uses symmetric encryption algorithms. ESP does not specify any key-management protocol to decouple the key-management mechanisms from the security-protocol mechanisms. The only coupling between the key-management protocol and the security protocol is the SPI. This decoupling permits different key-management mechanisms to be used. More importantly, it permits the key-management protocol to be changed or corrected without unduly impacting the security protocol implementations.

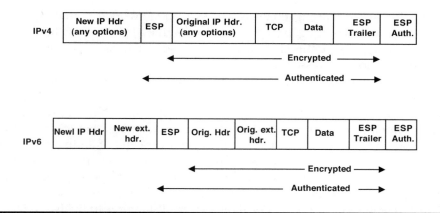

Figure 3.8   Tunnel-mode ESP.

3.1.2.4   *Common Use*

ESP and AH headers can be combined in a variety of modes and are used in such security technologies as IPSec.

3.2   PACKET FILTERING

Packet filtering or screening are typically described as a function in network interfaces or firewalls (see Chapter 8, Section 8.3 for a discussion of firewalls). Packet filtering, which can be performed at different protocol layers (defined according to the OSI Reference Model), basically specifies what type of traffic is allowed into and out of an interface (e.g., an IP interface in a router). The packet filtering feature is normally specified based on exceptions by setting packet filters per interface and configuring them to do one of the following:

- Pass through all traffic except packets prohibited (denied) by filters.
- Discard all traffic except packets allowed (permitted) by filters.

Packet filtering is considered to be a basic authentication technology because in its most basic form, individual packets are screened for violation against a set of predefined security rules.

3.2.1   Packet Filter Types

It is generally possible to classify packet filtering into two types: static and dynamic.

Static packet filtering controls access to a network by analyzing the incoming and outgoing packets and letting them pass or halting them based on some predefined static security rules such as allowable source and destination addresses.

Dynamic packet filtering, more commonly known as "stateful" inspection, examines a packet based on the information in its header. Packets are handled on a circuit or connection basis. In a circuit-level firewall, all connections are monitored and only those connections that are found to be valid are allowed to pass through. Because of this, filtering decisions are based not only on predefined security rules (as in static packet filtering) but also on the context that has been established by prior packets that have passed through. For example, the CBAC (Context-Based Access Control) feature in Cisco routers allows access list entries to be dynamically added as packets are being inspected through the firewall.

Stateful inspection can also be extended to higher layers in the OSI Reference Model giving rise to application layer gateways (ALGs). When packets arrive at the gateway, they are examined and evaluated to determine whether the security policy allows the packet to enter into the internal network. Not only does the server evaluate IP and even higher-layer addresses, it can also look at the data in the packets for corruption and alteration.

Packet filtering and ALGs will be discussed further when firewalls are discussed in Chapter 8.

3.2.1.1 Common Use

Packet filtering technologies are crucial in the implementation of firewalls and router configurations.

3.3 USERID AND PASSWORD AUTHENTICATION METHODS

The most basic technologies for authentication based on userIDs and passwords are PAP and SPAP.

3.3.1 PAP

PAP is a simple proprietary userID and password authentication protocol. With PAP, the password is sent across the network to be compared against an encrypted password file on the access server. If the password matches the associated userID, the connection is established (see Figure 3.9). Because the password can potentially be intercepted by a hacker, PAP is not considered to be secure.

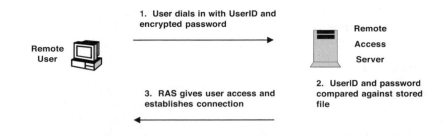

Figure 3.9   PAP authentication.

A number of other userID and password authentication technologies with improved security have also been designed, primarily to be employed during a user log-in process. A good example is Password Challenge Handshake Authentication Protocol (CHAP). In a network environment, because the log-in process first authenticates the user and then establishes a session (a logical connection) for the user if the user is indeed authorized, these special authentication protocols will be described in Chapter 7 as enhanced authentication and authorization technologies.

3.3.2   SPAP

SPAP is a proprietary authentication mechanism for PPP connection nego-tiation available in some commercial systems. SPAP uses a reversible encryption algorithm for password encryption, resulting in better security than PAP.

3.3.2.1   Common Use

UserID and password authentication is an integral part of most authenti-cation and authorization technologies such as Remote Access.

3.4   SUMMARY

Authentication refers to user authentication, and AH and ESP are authen-tication technologies that append special headers with authentication information to every IP packet. Authentication is achieved through the computation of MACs by applying algorithms such as SHA-1 or MD5 and DES. Both are used in many other network security technologies where authentication (and possibly data integrity as well) is needed.

Packet filtering is considered to be a primitive authentication technol-ogy because the most basic function that packet filtering can do is to filter out packets with bad addresses.

PAP and SPAP are simple userID and password authentication and authorization technologies.

BIBLIOGRAPHY

1. W. E. Burr, Public Key Infrastructure (PKI) Technical Specifications: Part A — Technical Concept of Operations, Working Draft, September 4, 1998.
2. Symeon Xenitellis, The Open-source PKI Book: A Guide to PKIs and Open-source Implementations, 2000.
3. Federal PKI Directory Concept of Operations, Cygnacom Solutions, April 20, 1999.
4. IETF RFC 2402 (Obsoletes RFC 1826): IP Authentication Header, S. Kent, and R. Atkinson, November 1998.
5. IETF RFC 2401: Security Architecture for the Internet Protocol, S. Kent, and R. Atkinson, November 1998.
6. IETF RFC 2406: IP Encapsulating Security Payload (ESP), S. Kent, and R. Atkinson, November 1998.

4

BASIC AUTHORIZATION TECHNOLOGIES

In this chapter, we look at some key basic authorization technologies, i.e., technologies that are used to control access to the network or systems so that only authorized users are allowed to gain access to specific network and system resources such as particular applications (e.g., e-mail server, host applications, etc.).

Authorization of a user is typically performed after the user's identity has been authenticated. If the user is then authorized to access the requested resources, then some network services, some data or applications, or connections or sessions to those resources are established. Thus, authorization typically takes place as a follow-up to user authentication at the beginning of a connection request. There are a number of technologies that conveniently handle both authentication and authorization functionalities as a tightly coupled sequence of access control operations.

The technologies presented in this chapter, which deal with handling authorization, can be classified into two types:

- Access control
- Demilitarized zone (DMZ)

Access control technologies validate access requests for authorization, whereas the DMZ serves as a buffer and go-between for the protected resources and all outside (external) users, some of whom are potential authorized users.

4.1 ACCESS CONTROL

Different access arrangements call for different access control mechanisms. As an example, suppose that a remote user is trying to gain access to an enterprise network. The user, being remote, does not have direct physical access to the network and systems equipment. The first line of defense in this case is network access control to prevent unauthorized users from even gaining access to the remote access network. This form of control can be provided in a number of ways: with add-on security hardware, restricted node addresses, caller identification, and dial-back. The add-on, hardware-based security device (e.g., a token card or a smart card) relies on the use of either a serial number or a pass-code that is to be verified by the remote access server before network access is granted. Restricted addressing, caller ID, and dial-back ensure that a remote user can only call in from certain predetermined locations.

Note that if the access network is through a service provider, only very limited security can be offered at this first line of defense because the network is normally shared by, and needs to be made accessible to, many different users and companies. Other additional, more sophisticated security measures (e.g., using virtual private networks [VPNs]) are needed.

The following subsections describe a number of access control mechanisms.

4.1.1 Physical Access Control

Physical protection requires key network equipment such as servers, switches, and routers to be placed in very secure places where access is controlled and absolutely limited to only authorized personnel. In addition, many other important concerns that affect network security should be regularly addressed, particularly those related to everyday methods and procedures of operations. The following are some key components needed in the physical protection of equipment:

- Physical safety: This includes the need for secured locations to be used for the placement of equipment and redundant power supplies, as well as for highly reliable equipment modules and components.
- Constant review and maintenance of software, including operating systems (OSs) and network operating systems (NOSs): Vendors' bug fixes and anti-virus patches should be installed as quickly as possible. Old software versions should be upgraded to proven newer versions. However, the need for upgrades should still be primarily driven by new feature requirements and should be weighted against any potential software instability in new code.

- Well-documented and streamlined operational procedures and processes (e.g., router configuration updates, etc.): Stringent configuration and reconfiguration requirements and well-established procedures are key to all aspects of network management and operations.
- Well-protected network management (NM) connections: Out-of-band NM circuits are desirable, in-band NM connections should be secure, and other NM components including operations support systems (OSSs) should be robust and reliable.

4.1.1.1 Common Use

Physical access control is obviously needed for all customer premises and service-provider environments.

4.1.2 UserID and Password

The use of some form of userID and password verification access to network and system resources is a well-established authorization technology.

Chapter 7 discusses a number of enhanced technologies that accomplish both authorization and authentication as a sequence of message exchanges with an authentication and authorization server.

Also, Chapter 8 discusses single sign-on (SSO), which is a technology that helps to solve the need for juggling multiple userIDs, passwords, and log-on procedures for each user in a client/server (C/S) environment without compromising network security.

4.1.2.1 Levels of Access Privilege

One key requirement for using this access control technology is to divide users into different levels of access privilege, associating the privilege levels with the corresponding userIDs and passwords. For example, the general users in an enterprise should be grouped at a minimum into the following three privilege levels:

- Employees as users with general access privileges for free access around the network to default network and systems resources
- Partners as users with lower access privileges for access to some limited, predetermined network and systems resources
- Outside users with authority to access very limited systems resources (probably only some pieces of data or applications) through some proxy servers (see Chapter 9).

Additional special privilege levels are likely needed, e.g., for administrators as users with higher access privileges, which are required to gain access to and to administer network and systems components like servers, routers, etc.

An enterprisewide set of privilege-level rules should be formulated and carefully mapped into equipment-specific implementations.

4.1.2.2   Common Use

The use of userID and password for authorization is typically tightly coupled with the steps taken to authenticate the userID and password combination. See Chapter 7, Chapter 8, and Chapter 9 for further descriptions of these uses.

4.1.3   Access Control Lists

An access control list (ACL) in its generic definition refers to a list of security protections that applies to an object. Using Microsoft's terminology, an object can be a file, a process, or an event, and each object has a security attribute that identifies the object's access control list. The access control list has an entry for each system user with access privileges. The most common privileges include the ability to read a file (or all the files in a directory), to write to the file or files, and to execute the file (if it is an executable file or program). This generic definition has been significantly expanded when ACLs are used in network elements such as routers.

4.1.3.1   Systems ACLs

Microsoft's Windows NT and Windows 2000, Novell's NetWare, Digital's OpenVMS, and Unix-based systems are among the operating systems that use access control lists. The list is implemented differently by each operating system. Each ACL has one or more access control entries (ACEs) consisting of the name of a user or a group of users. The user can also be a role name, such as *programmer* or *tester*. For each of these users, groups, or roles, the access privileges are stated in a string of bits called an *access mask*. Generally, the system administrator or the object owner creates the ACL for an object when the object is first defined.

In such environments, an ACL is a table that tells a computer operating system which access rights each user has to a particular system object, such as a file directory or an individual file. Each object has a security attribute that identifies its access control list. The list has an entry for each system user with access privileges. The most common privileges include the ability to read a file (or all the files in a directory), to write to the file or files, and to execute the file (if it is an executable file or program).

4.1.3.2 Router ACLs

In a router-based network security setting, an ACL, on the other hand, typically refers to a set of router commands that prevents the unauthorized use of network as well as some systems resources. Many vendors, including Cisco, define two types of access lists: standard and extended.

Standard ACLs only allow authorization based on the source IP addresses, i.e., doing source IP address filtering. Extended ACLs, on the other hand, can permit or deny packets, based on additional entities such as their protocols, source or destination IP addresses, source or destination TCP/UDP ports, or ICMP or IGMP message types.

Extended access lists also support selective logging for improved administrative operations. Both standard and extended IP access lists can be applied to router interfaces, IPSec, routing protocols, and many router features. Only standard IP access lists can be applied to Simple Network Management Protocol (SNMP). It therefore follows that extended ACLs support packet filtering in the sense of authentication (see Chapter 3).

The fact that many vendors use ACLs to support not only authorization based on source IP addresses but also authentication through packet filtering suggests that router-based ACLs can also be categorized as an integrated technology, according to this book's framework.

It should further be pointed out that ACLs have, in practice, been used by many vendors to do much more than just authorization and authentication. They have also been used to perform prioritization of traffic, to support multiple customer queuing classes, and to control access to applications like Telnet, etc. The router examines each packet to determine whether to forward or to drop the packet, based on the criteria specified in the associated ACL. In addition, some routers have the capability (e.g., the context-based access control (CBAC) in Cisco routers) to dynamically inject ACLs. These criteria can include the source address, destination address, upper-layer protocols, and other packet header information.

4.1.3.2.1 ACL Syntax Example

For reference, the following gives the syntax for Cisco router's standard and extended IP ACLs.

The basic structure for an access list rule is shown below:

access-list *list-number* {**deny** | **permit**} *condition*

The access list number tells Cisco IOS which access list the rule should be a part of, and what kind of access list it is. The condition field, which is different for each kind of access list, specifies the packets that match the rule. Conditions typically involve protocol information and addresses but do not involve application-level information.

The following is the syntax for a statement (rule) in a standard IP access list:

> **access-list** *list-number* {**deny** | **permit**} *source* [*source-wildcard*] [**log**]
> where
>> *list-number* is the number of the access list and can be any decimal number from 1 to 99.
>> **deny** denies access if the condition is matched.
>> **permit** permits access if the condition is matched.
>> *source* is the IP address of the network or host from which the packet is being sent.
>> *source-wildcard* is the wildcard bits to be applied to the *source*.
>> The optional keyword **log** may be applied to log matches to the rule.

The following is the simplified syntax for a statement in an extended IP access list:

> **access-list** *list-number* {**deny** | **permit**} *protocol*
> source source-wildcard source-qualifiers
> destination destination-wildcard destination-qualifiers [**log** | **log-input**]
> where
>> *list-number* is the number of the access list and can be any decimal number from 100 to 199.
>> **deny** denies access if the condition is matched.
>> **permit** permits access if the condition is matched.
>> *protocol* is the name or number of an IP-related protocol. It can be one of the following keywords: eigrp, gre, icmp, igmp, igrp, ip, ipinip, nos, ospf, tcp, or udp, or it can be an integer in the range 0 to 255, representing an IP protocol number. (Some protocols allow further qualifiers; source or destination ports can be specified for tcp or udp, and message types can be specified for icmp or igmp.)
>> *source* is the IP address of the network or host from which the packet is being sent.
>> *source-wildcard* is the wildcard bits to be applied to the *source*. The keyword **any** can be used in place of *source* and *source wildcard*.
>> *source-qualifiers* are optional details on the packet source, including port numbers and other protocol-specific information.
>> *destination* is the IP address of the network or host to which the packet is being sent.

destination-wildcard is the IP address wildcard bits to be applied to the *destination*. The keyword **any** can be used in place of *destination* and *destination wildcard*.

destination-qualifiers are optional details on the packet destination, including port numbers and other protocol-specific information.

log, if present, causes a message about the packet that matches the statement to be logged, and **log-input** causes a message that includes the interface.

4.1.3.3   Common Use

ACLs are used in firewalls and also in interfaces that connect two or more networks together.

4.2   DMZ

One way of enhancing network security is to create a DMZ between a company's access network and its internal enterprise network. A DMZ acts as a buffer zone to minimize the effects of any such malicious acts of intrusion. Bastion (or proxy) servers are provided within the DMZ to act as go-betweens, and they serve to establish two-step connections between the remote access user and the enterprise servers and hosts that the outside users want to connect to. This two-step indirect connection process helps to protect servers and hosts from outside attacks.

Figure 4.1 shows an example of a DMZ that has only an SMTP bastion server. Note that in this particular configuration, the router that runs the Cisco PIX firewall has three physical ports: one used to connect to the outside network, one used to connect to the inside (internal) private network, and a third one used as the DMZ (firewalls are considered as integrated security technologies, and are described in Section 8.3). A

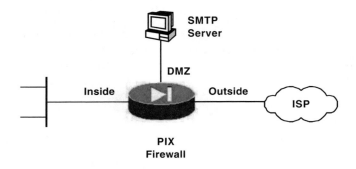

Figure 4.1   A DMZ example.

different approach would be to have the outside and inside connections reside on two separate routers, and to consider the connection between the two routers as the DMZ.

There are several possible slight variations to the topology of a DMZ. In a router-based network, the DMZ typically extends from the on-premises access network router to a router that is connected to the enterprise network. The DMZ is usually separated from the protected enterprise network by a security firewall that provides additional user authentication (e.g., non-repudiation), and packet or frame screening.

4.2.1 Common Use

DMZs are commonly deployed as an important component in the Remote Access Architecture described in Chapter 8.

4.3 SUMMARY

Controlling a user's access to network and system resources can be accomplished at different levels, ranging from controlling physical access to those resources, to the use of assigning different levels of user privileges and, further, to the use of ACLs to limit the extent to which unauthorized users can do damage to protected resources.

DMZ is a very critical network architectural innovation in keeping the protected part of a network out of the direct reach of unauthorized users.

All these are basic authorization technologies that are employed in other integrated technologies such as firewalls and Remote Access architectures, which will be described further in later chapters.

BIBLIOGRAPHY

1. Router Security Configuration Guide by System and Network Attack Center (SNAC), National Security Agency, Updated: March 25, 2002, Version: 1.0k, Report Number: C4-054R-00.
2. Managing ACLs Using ACL Manager v1.3, Cisco Tutorial, April 2001.
3. Configuring IP Access Lists, Cisco Document, 2003.
4. Bastien, G. and Abera Degu, C. *Cisco Secure PIX Firewall Advanced,* Cisco Press, 2003.

5

BASIC MESSAGE INTEGRITY TECHNOLOGIES

In this chapter, we look at some basic message integrity technologies, i.e., technologies that are used to ensure that the received message has not been unintentionally altered *en route* compared with the originally sent message. Ensuring message integrity is also called *message authentication* as opposed to *user authentication* described in Chapter 3.

One way to attain a high degree of confidence that each message is sent and received with integrity in any network infrastructure, including a shared one like the Internet, is to make the communication link behave like a private line circuit. In this regard, the most basic approach is to use Layer 2 virtual private network (VPN) technologies to ensure the separation of traffic in the network. Layer 2 VPNs are based on the use of hop-to-hop identifications such as data-link control identifiers (DLCIs) in Frame Relay (FR) permanent virtual circuits (PVCs) and virtual path identifiers or virtual circuit identifiers (VPI or VCIs) in Asynchronous Transfer Mode (ATM) to achieve separation of traffic over the entire virtual connection.

The basic message integrity technologies described in the following sections can be divided into three main classes:

- Layer 2 VPNs that include FR, ATM, Multi-Protocol Label Switching (MPLS), and Ethernet VLANs
- Tunneling protocols that include Point-to-Point Protocol (PPP)-based protocols
- Authentication protocols

All these technologies provide only basic separation of traffic and, unless supplemented by enhancements, do not support additional security capabilities.

A VPN is sometimes defined loosely as a network infrastructure in which the connectivity among multiple sites of a company is deployed on a shared infrastructure but that is provided with the same access and security policies equivalent to those of a private network. A VPN thus serves as a cost-effective alternative to expensive leased lines or circuit-switched infrastructures. If this loose definition of VPN is used, all the basic technologies described in this chapter can actually be considered as VPNs. We distinguish between Layer 2 VPNs, such as FR PVCs and SVCs (switched virtual circuits), and tunneling protocols, simply to highlight the different technical approaches utilized in the two classes of message integrity technologies.

A number of the technologies that are used for the authentication of users (described in Chapter 3) also support message authentication and are briefly discussed later in this chapter.

As an introduction, we first provide in the next section an overview of VPN technologies. Many of the VPN technologies that include more advanced security capabilities in their definitions are presented in Chapter 8 as integrated technologies.

5.1 OVERVIEW OF VPN TECHNOLOGIES

A VPN technology transports the payload traffic over tunnels established between the two ends over the transport network. There are two basic techniques of establishing such tunnels, giving two classes of VPNs:

- Encapsulation: With the encapsulation technique, a VPN uses an encapsulation protocol to encapsulate the payload. The tunnel is identified and secured by the encapsulation protocol's header information.
- Cryptography: With the encryption technique, a VPN uses cryptographic technologies to establish a secure connection. One example of a VPN technology that uses cryptography is IPSec.

VPNs that are based on the encapsulation technique are typically built over transport networks that are classified as Layer 2 and below, according to the OSI Reference Model. On the other hand, VPNs that are based on cryptography generally operate over higher layers, and they are described in Chapter 8.

Note that the two techniques can be used together. In this section, we continue to focus on VPNs that are based on the encapsulation technique.

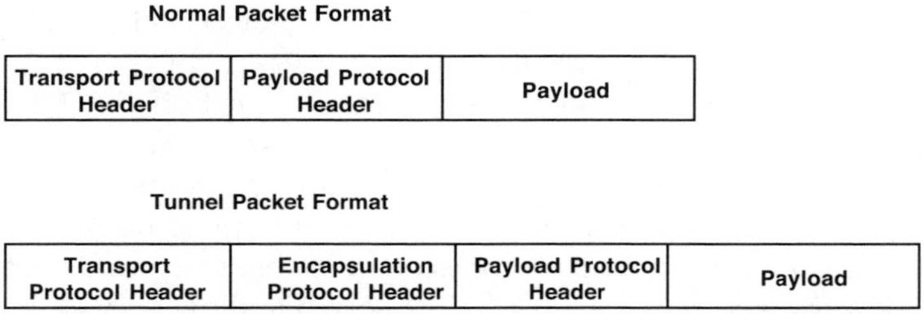

Normal Packet Format

Transport Protocol Header	Payload Protocol Header	Payload

Tunnel Packet Format

Transport Protocol Header	Encapsulation Protocol Header	Payload Protocol Header	Payload

Figure 5.1   Packet format with tunnel.

5.1.1   Encapsulation Techniques

The tunnel is achieved through encapsulation of the payload traffic by an encapsulation protocol. There are many such VPN technologies available, and each is defined in terms of the encapsulation protocol used. Thus, a VPN is characterized by the following three protocols:

■ Payload protocol
■ Encapsulation protocol
■ Transport protocol

The transport protocol is the protocol on which the VPN rides. The encapsulation protocol is dependent on the tunneling technology that is used. Figure 5.1 illustrates the relationship between the three protocols.

We now look at the most commonly used VPNs that are based on the encapsulation technique.

5.2   LAYER 2 VPNS

It is useful to consider a distinction between a "Layer 2 VPN service" and a "VPN service that supports L2 traffic."

A Layer 2 VPN service (or simply, a Layer 2 VPN) refers to a VPN that is built on top of an L2 network. Some of these VPNs can either support Layer 2 traffic only, or Layer 3 traffic only, or both Layers 2 and 3 traffic. For example, Any Transport over MPLS (AToM) supports the transport of both Layer 2 and Layer 3 traffic, using encapsulation. Higher-layer VPNs are discussed in Chapter 8.

When considering the underlying transport network, it is also helpful to consider a distinction between an IP network and an IP-based network: an IP network provides an IP layer, possibly built over some other end-to-end transport network, whereas an IP-based network is built to transport only IP traffic (e.g., IP router-based, IP over SONET, etc.). Other traffic types can be supported using encapsulation.

Currently most of these VPN infrastructures are built on FR or ATM Layer 2 networks, connecting each company's sites via either PVCs or SVCs. Because PVCs and SVCs are more suitable for supporting hub and spoke topologies, the current move of many enterprise networks toward an any-to-any mesh topology increases the complexity and number of VCs needed. Newer generations of VPN services allow service providers to offer a more economical way of supporting either partially or fully meshed connectivity.

5.2.1 FR

FR is a high-performance WAN protocol that operates at the physical and data-link layers of the OSI Reference Model. FR originally was designed for use across Integrated Services Digital Network (ISDN) interfaces. Today it is used over a variety of other network interfaces as well. This chapter focuses on FR's specifications and applications in the context of WAN services.

FR is an example of a packet-switched technology. Packet-switched networks enable end stations to dynamically share the network medium and the available bandwidth. The following two techniques are used in packet-switching technology:

- Variable-length packets
- Statistical multiplexing

Variable-length packets are used for more efficient and flexible data transfers. These packets are switched between the various segments in the network until the destination is reached.

Statistical multiplexing techniques control network access in a packet-switched network. The advantage of this technique is that it accommodates more flexibility and more efficient use of bandwidth. Most of today's popular LANs, such as Ethernet and Token Ring, are packet-switched networks.

FR often is described as a streamlined version of X.25, offering fewer of the robust capabilities such as windowing and retransmission of last data that are offered in X.25. This is because FR typically operates over WAN facilities that offer more reliable connection services and a higher degree of reliability than the facilities available during the late 1970s and early 1980s that served as the common platforms for X.25 WANs. As mentioned earlier, FR is strictly a Layer 2 protocol suite, whereas X.25 provides services at Layer 3 (the network layer) as well. This enables FR to offer higher performance and greater transmission efficiency than X.25 and makes FR suitable for current WAN applications such as LAN interconnection.

FR is specified in CCITT recommendations I.122 and Q.922, which add relay and routing functions to the data-link layer (Layer 2 of the OSI Reference Model).

5.2.1.1 FR Virtual Circuits

FR provides connection-oriented data-link layer communications. This means that a defined communication path exists between each pair of devices and that these connections are associated with a connection identifier. This service is implemented by using a FR virtual circuit, which is a logical connection created between two data terminal equipment (DTE) devices across an FR packet-switched network.

Virtual circuits provide a bidirectional communication path from one DTE device to another and are uniquely identified by a DLCI. A number of virtual circuits can be multiplexed into a single physical circuit for transmission across the network. This capability often can reduce the equipment and network complexity required to connect multiple DTE devices.

A virtual circuit can pass through any number of intermediate data communication equipment DCE devices (switches) located within the FR network.

FR virtual circuits fall into two categories: SVCs and PVCs.

5.2.1.1.1 SVCs

SVCs are temporary connections used in situations requiring only sporadic data transfer between DTE devices across an FR network. A communication session across an SVC consists of the following four operational states:

- Call setup — The virtual circuit between two FR DTE devices is established.
- Data transfer — Data is transmitted between the DTE devices over the virtual circuit.
- Idle — The connection between DTE devices is still active, but no data is transferred. If an SVC remains in an idle state for a defined period of time, the call can be terminated.
- Call termination — The virtual circuit between DTE devices is terminated.

After the virtual circuit is terminated, the DTE devices must establish a new SVC if there is additional data to be exchanged. It is expected that

SVCs will be established, maintained, and terminated using the same signaling protocols that are used in ISDN.

Few manufacturers of FR DCE equipment support SVC connections. Therefore, their actual deployment is minimal in today's FR networks.

Although previously not widely supported by FR equipment, SVCs are now the norm. Companies have found that SVCs save money ultimately because the circuit is not open all the time.

5.2.1.1.2 PVCs

PVCs are permanently established connections that are used for frequent and consistent data transfers between DTE devices across an FR network. Communication across a PVC does not require the call setup and termination states that are used with SVCs. PVCs always operate in one of the following two operational states:

- Data transfer — Data is transmitted between the DTE devices over the virtual circuit.
- Idle — The connection between DTE devices is active, but no data is transferred. Unlike SVCs, PVCs will not be terminated under any circumstances when in an idle state.

DTE devices can begin transferring data whenever they are ready because the circuit is permanently established.

5.2.1.1.3 DLCI

FR virtual circuits are identified by DLCIs. DLCI values typically are assigned by FR service providers.

FR DLCIs have local significance, which means that their values are unique in the LAN, but not necessarily in the FR WAN.

5.2.1.2 FR Frame Format

To understand much of the functionality of FR, it is helpful to understand the structure of the FR frame. Figure 5.2 depicts the standard format of the FR frame.

Flags indicate the beginning and end of the frame. Three primary components make up the FR frame: the header and address area, the user-data portion, and the frame check sequence (FCS). The address area, which is 2 bytes in length, is comprised of 10 bits representing the actual circuit identifier and 6 bits of fields related to congestion management. This identifier commonly is referred to as the DLCI.

Field Length in bytes

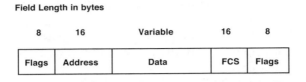

Figure 5.2 FR frame format.

The following descriptions summarize the basic FR frame fields:

- Flags — delimit the beginning and end of the frame. The value of this field is always the same and is represented either as the hexadecimal number 7E or as the binary number 01111110.
- Address — contains the following information:
  - DLCI — The 10-bit DLCI is the essence of the FR header. This value represents the virtual connection between the DTE device and the switch. Each virtual connection that is multiplexed onto the physical channel is represented by a unique DLCI. The DLCI values have local significance only, which means that they are unique only to the physical channel on which they reside. Therefore, devices at opposite ends of a connection can use different DLCI values to refer to the same virtual connection.
  - Extended address (EA) — The EA is used to indicate whether the byte in which the EA value is 1 is the last addressing field. If the value is 1, then the current byte is determined to be the last DLCI octet. Although all the current FR implementations use a two-octet DLCI, this capability does allow longer DLCIs to be used in the future. The eighth bit of each byte of the Address field is used to indicate the EA.
  - C/R — The C/R is the bit that follows the most significant DLCI byte in the Address field. The C/R bit is not currently defined.
  - Congestion control — This consists of the last three bits in the Address field, which control the FR congestion-notification mechanisms: the FECN, BECN, and DE bits.
    - *Forward-explicit congestion notification (FECN)* is a single-bit field that can be set to a value of 1 by a switch to indicate to an end DTE device, such as a router, that congestion was experienced in the direction of frame transmission (i.e., from source to destination). The primary benefit of the use of the FECN and BECN fields is the capability of higher-layer protocols to react intelligently to these congestion indicators. Today, DECnet and OSI are the only higher-layer protocols that implement these capabilities.

> ■ *Backward-explicit congestion notification (BECN)* is a single-bit field that, when set to a value of 1 by a switch, indicates that congestion was experienced in the network in the direction opposite to frame transmission (i.e., from destination to source).
> ■ *Discard eligibility (DE)* is set by a DTE device, such as a router, to indicate that the marked frame is of lesser importance relative to other frames being transmitted. Frames that are marked as "discard eligible" should be discarded before other frames in a congested network. This allows for a basic prioritization mechanism in FR networks.

■ Data — contains encapsulated upper-layer data. Each frame in this variable-length field includes a user-data or payload field that varies in length up to 16,000 octets. This field serves to transport the higher-layer protocol packet data unit (PDU) through an FR network.

■ FCS — ensures the integrity of transmitted data. This value is computed by the source device and verified by the receiver to ensure integrity of transmission.

5.2.1.2.1 Common Use

FR is commonly used as a replacement of private line circuits. FR can also be used to support higher-layer VPNs.

5.2.2 ATM

ATM is a connection-oriented data transport technology. Before sending cells that carry user data, a virtual connection between the source and the destination has to be established. All packets on a connection follow the same path within the network. During the connection setup, each ATM switch generates an entry in the VPI or VCI translation table. This enables the switch to move an incoming packet from its VP or VC to the corresponding outgoing VP or VC. As an added advantage, this kind of routing requires a small header as only a locally valid address (i.e., VPI or VCI) has to be carried in the packet.

5.2.2.1 ATM Cell Header Format

ATM transmits, switches, and multiplexes information in fixed-length cells. The length of a cell is 53 bytes, consisting of a 5-byte cell header and 48 bytes of data (Figure 5.3).

Header (5 bytes)	Payload (48 bytes)

Figure 5.3 ATM cell.

Table 5.1 ATM Cell Header Format (UNI)

	8	7	6	5	4	3	2	1
Byte 1	GFC				VPI			
Byte 2	VPI				VCI			
Byte 3	VCI							
Byte 4	VCI				PTI			CLP
Byte 5	HEC							

5.2.2.1.1 Header Format

The ATM header contains information about the destination, type, and priority of the cell:

- The Generic Flow Control (GFC) field allows a multiplexer to control the rate of an ATM terminal. The GFC field is only available at the User-to-Network Interface (UNI). At the Network-to-Network Interface (NNI), these bits belong to the VPI.
- The VPI and the VCI hold the locally valid relative address of the destination. These fields may be changed within an ATM switch.
- The Payload Type (PT) marks whether the cell carries user data, signaling data, or maintenance information.
- The Cell Loss Priority (CLP) bit indicates which cells should be discarded first in case of congestion.
- The Header Error Control (HEC) field is to perform a CRC check on the header data. Only the header is error checked in the ATM layer. The error check for user data is left to higher-layer protocols and is performed on an end-to-end base.

This header format is shown in Table 5.1.

5.2.2.2 Quality of Service (QoS)

ATM networks are designed to transmit data with varying performance characteristics. Different types of applications (e.g., file transfer, inquiry–response, packetized voice, video on demand, etc.) need different QoS.

Table 5.2 QoS Parameters

	CBR	Rt-VBR	Nrt-VBR	UBR	ABR
Traffic parameters:					
PCR and CDVT	Specified				
SCR, MBS, CDVT	N/A	Specified		N/A	
MCR	N/A				Specified
QoS parameters:					
Peak-to-peak CDV	Specified			Unspecified	
MaxCTD	Specified			Unspecified	
CLR	Specified			Unspecified	Network specific
Other attributes:					
Feedback	Unspecified				Specified

Note: N/A = Not applicable.

Some applications like packetized voice may be very sensitive to delay, but rather insensitive to loss, whereas others like compressed video are quite sensitive to loss.

To support different types of applications, the ATM Forum defines several QoS categories or classes of service (CoS):

- CBR (constant bit rate)
- rt-VBR (real-time variable bit rate)
- nrt-VBR (non-real-time variable bit rate)
- ABR (available bit rate)
- UBR (unspecified bit rate)

In ATM implementations, these QoS categories are realized through the specification or negotiation of traffic parameters. Table 5.2 shows the negotiated parameters for each QoS category, where:

- CDV: cell delay variation
- CDVT: CDV tolerance
- CLR: cell loss ratio
- CTD: cell transfer delay
- MBS: maximum burst size
- MCR: minimum cell rate
- PCR: peak cell rate
- SCR: sustainable cell rate

5.2.2.3 Security Mechanisms in ATM

Although ATM is commonly offered by service providers purely as a transport network like FR services, the ATM Forum has defined mechanisms for authentication, confidentiality, data integrity, and access control for the user plane, and mechanisms for authentication and integrity for the control plane (UNI and NNI signaling), as well as the infrastructure needed to support the following security services: negotiation of security services and parameters, key exchange, key update, synchronization, and certification infrastructure.

5.2.2.3.1 Common Use

Just as FR, ATM is commonly used as a replacement for private line circuits and can also be used to support higher-layer VPNs.

5.3 MPLS VPNS

MPLS is an emerging connection-oriented networking technology that evolved from Epsilon's tag technology, in which tags are assigned to similar Layer 3 IP traffic data streams for faster Layer 2 switching. MPLS permits Layer 3 switching at faster Layer 2 speeds by looking at labels instead of network addresses as each frame or packet passes through the Layer 2 switches.

MPLS makes this possible by decoupling the frame or packet routing and forwarding, two functions that are normally done together in a Layer 3 router. Routing is done only at the edge of the MPLS network, where similar frames or packets are assigned labels. Inside the MPLS network, frames or packets are forwarded across the network through connections, using only the labels.

IETF RFC 3346 defines a mechanism for traffic engineering in MPLS and IETF RFC 2547 defines an MPLS and Border Gateway Protocol (BGP) extension that can be used to establish route separation.

5.3.1 The MPLS Protocol

MPLS provides a framework for the efficient designation, routing, forwarding, and switching of traffic flows through the network.

MPLS performs the following functions:

- Specifies mechanisms to manage traffic flows of various granularities, such as flows between different hardware, machines, or even applications
- Remains independent of the Layer 2 and Layer 3 protocols used

- Provides a means to map IP addresses to simple, fixed-length labels used by different packet-forwarding and packet-switching technologies
- Interfaces to existing routing protocols such as Resource Reservation Protocol (RSVP) and Open Shortest Path First (OSPF)
- Supports the IP, ATM, and FR Layer 2 protocols

In MPLS, data transmission occurs on label-switched paths (LSPs). LSPs are sequences of labels at each and every node along the path from source to destination. LSPs are established either prior to data transmission (control-driven) or upon detection of a certain flow of data (data-driven). The labels, which are underlying protocol-specific identifiers, are distributed using label distribution protocol (LDP) or RSVP, or piggybacked on routing protocols like BGP and OSPF. Each data packet encapsulates and carries the labels during their journey from the source to the destination. High-speed switching of data is possible because the fixed-length labels are inserted at the very beginning of the packet or cell and can be used by hardware to switch packets quickly between links.

5.3.1.1   LSRs and LERs

The devices that participate in the MPLS protocol mechanisms can be classified into label edge routers (LERs) and label switching routers (LSRs).

An LSR is a high-speed router device in the core of an MPLS network that participates in the establishment of LSPs, using the appropriate label signaling protocol and high-speed switching of data traffic based on established paths.

An LER is a device that operates at the edge of the access network and MPLS network. LERs support multiple ports connected to dissimilar networks (such as FR, ATM, and Ethernet) and forward this traffic on to the MPLS network after establishing LSPs, using the label signaling protocol at the ingress and distributing traffic back to the access networks at the egress. The LER plays a very important role in the assignment and removal of labels, as traffic enters or exits an MPLS network.

5.3.1.2   FEC

The forward equivalence class (FEC) is a representation of a group of packets that share the same requirements for their transport. All the packets in such a group are treated the same way *en route* to the destination. As opposed to conventional IP forwarding, in MPLS, the assignment of a particular packet to a particular FEC is done just once, as the packet enters the network. FECs are based on service requirements for a given set of packets or just for an address prefix. Each LSR builds a table to specify how a packet must be forwarded. This table, called a label information base (LIB), is composed of FEC-to-label bindings.

5.3.1.3 Labels and Label Bindings

A label, in its simplest form, identifies the path a packet should traverse. A label is carried or encapsulated in a Layer 2 header along with the packet. The receiving router examines the packet for its label content to determine the next hop. Once a packet has been labeled, the rest of the journey of the packet through the backbone is based on label switching. The label values are of local significance only; i.e., they pertain only to hops between LSRs.

Once a packet has been classified as a new or existing FEC, a label is assigned to the packet. The label values are derived from the underlying data-link layer. For data-link layers (such as FR or ATM), Layer 2 identifiers such as DLCIs in the case of FR networks, or VPIs or VCIs in the case of ATM networks can be used directly as labels. The packets are then forwarded based on their label value.

Labels are bound to an FEC as a result of some event or policy that indicates a need for such binding. These events can be either data-driven bindings or control-driven bindings. The latter is preferable because of its advanced scaling properties, which can be used in MPLS.

Label assignment decisions may be based on forwarding criteria such as the following:

- Destination unicast routing
- Traffic engineering
- Multicast
- VPN
- QoS

MPLS labels created at an LER are distributed using LDP.

The generic label format is illustrated in Figure 5.4; the MPLS shim header is "shimmed" between the network- and link-layer headers, where:

- Exp: Experimental (3 bits)
- S: Bottom of label stack (1 bit)
- TTL: Time-to-live (8 bits)

The MPLS protocol is defined to be independent of any underlying protocol and, as a result, can run on any Layer 2 or Layer 3 protocol. Because many service providers currently offer FR and ATM networks and

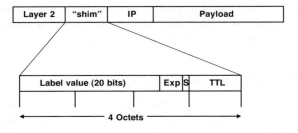

Figure 5.4 MPLS generic label format.

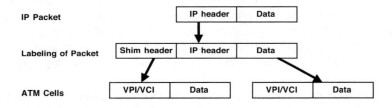

Figure 5.5 ATM as the data-link layer.

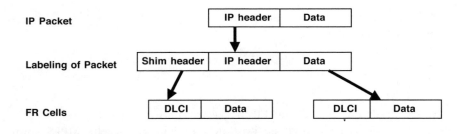

Figure 5.6 FR as the data-link layer.

ATM is the predominant transport technology used in these networks' core infrastructures, many MPLS deployments are over ATM. In this case, ATM switches are used as LSRs, and the label can be embedded in the header of the data-link layer (the ATM VCI or VPI) shown in Figure 5.5.

FR can also be used to support MPLS, in which case the MPLS label is contained in the DLCI field with possibly additional shim fields or headers, as shown in Figure 5.6.

Table 5.3 MPLS Value Propositions

	Customer's Perspective	Service Provider's Perspective
Cost savings	Operations: e.g., addition of new sites Access BW	Network convergence
QoS	Prioritization of applications Traffic engineering for improved performance	Prioritization of traffic types using EXP bits and management of congestion across varying BW rates Potential for end-to-end CoS offering with DSCP marking
Scalability	Any-to-any connectivity No routing required inside core Short cycle time for implementation of network requirements	Support of large numbers of VPNs of different sizes
Security	Approaching that of FR or ATM networks	VPN traffic kept separate using unique route identifiers
Reliability	Approaching that of FR or ATM networks	Robust QoS mechanisms
Manageability	SLAs with Web-based tools for performance monitoring and reporting	Web-based tools for performance monitoring and reporting

5.3.2 MPLS VPNs

An MPLS-based VPN delivers network-based VPN services, typically, over a shared IP network with any-to-any connectivity. It offers a CoS implementation based on DiffServ and MPLS traffic engineering for QoS.

MPLS VPNs can be used for forwarding packets over the backbone network, and BGP is used for distributing routes over the backbone network. The method is simple for the customer, and scalable and flexible for the service provider. It also allows the service provider the ability to provide Internet access to these customers as well.

MPLS VPN is a "true peer VPN" model that performs traffic separation at Layer 3 through the use of separate IP VPN forwarding tables. MPLS VPN enforces traffic separation between customers by assigning a unique VRF to each customer's VPN. This compares well with the security of a FR or ATM network because users in a specific VPN cannot see traffic outside their VPN. See Table 5.3 for a list of some of the key value propositions.

5.3.3 AToM

MPLS has been principally defined to switch packets of any network-layer protocol although these packets are commonly IP packets.

AToM allows service providers who offer Layer 2 connectivity to expand their service offerings by connecting Ethernet, ATM, FR, and Serial or PPP networks through an MPLS backbone. AToM is a scalable architecture based on label switching that allows multiplexing of connections. It is also a standards-based open architecture and can be extended to other yet to be defined transport types.

Deployment of AToM networks is of interest to customers who:

- Wish to protect their network investment by implementing AToM on existing MPLS networks
- Require scaling of FR and ATM implementations to OC-192 speed and performance
- Need "virtual leased line"-like services with QoS and MPLS Traffic Engineering
- Benefit from provisioning with point-to-point connections of several types in a simple network infrastructure

5.3.3.1 AToM-Supported Transport Protocols

The following is a list of transport mechanisms that are supported in equipment supplied by many AToM vendors (e.g., Cisco):

- Ethernet over MPLS
- ATM AAL5 over MPLS
- FR over MPLS
- ATM cell relay over MPLS
- PPP over MPLS
- HDLC over MPLS

5.3.3.1.1 Common Use

Service providers are commonly deploying MPLS over their existing infrastructures as a means of providing services with better scalability, improved performance, and more advanced features such as CoS in support of higher-layer customer VPNs.

5.4 ETHERNET VLAN

A virtual LAN (VLAN) acts like an ordinary LAN, but the connected devices do not have to be physically connected to the same LAN segment.

Although clients and servers may be located anywhere on a network, they are grouped together by VLAN technology, and broadcasts are only sent to devices within the VLAN. VLANs configured using Media Access Control (MAC) addresses can recognize when a station has been moved to another port on a switch, and VLAN management software can then automatically reconfigure that station into its appropriate VLAN without the need to change the station's MAC or IP address.

It is possible to classify VLAN into three types depending on how a packet gets assigned to a VLAN:

- Port-based VLANs, where the administrator assigns each port of a switch to a VLAN
- MAC address-based VLANs, where the VLAN membership of a packet is determined by its source or destination MAC address
- Layer 3 (or protocol)-based VLANs, where the VLAN membership of a packet is based on protocols (IP, IPX, NetBIOS, etc.) and Layer 3 addresses

There has been a lack of standards for vendors to implement VLANs that can interoperate. IEEE 802.1Q, which is part of the IEEE 802 series of LAN standards, has been defined to tackle this problem.

5.4.1 IEEE 802.1Q

The IEEE 802.1Q specification establishes a standard method for inserting VLAN membership information into Ethernet frames. The ability to move end stations to different broadcast domains by setting membership profiles for each port on centrally managed switches is one of the main advantages of IEEE 802.1Q VLANs.

The architectural framework of IEEE 802.1Q is based on a three-layer model, consisting of the following layers:

- Configuration — Specification of VLAN configurations and assignment of VLAN parameters
- Distribution of configuration information — Distribution of registration and topology information
- Relay — Execution of ingress, forwarding, and egress rules

Because of the rapidly increasing proliferation of Ethernet technology, extending from pure LAN environments to metropolitan area network (MAN) and beyond, technologies based on IEEE 802.1Q are becoming more and more significant in the networking landscape.

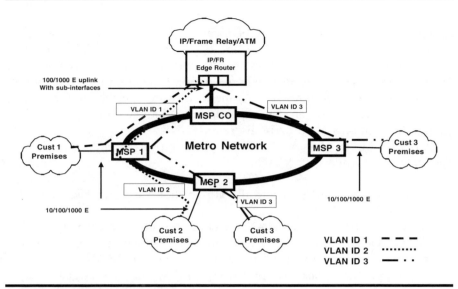

Figure 5.7   Sample Ethernet VLANs.

5.4.2   802.1Q Ethernet VPNs

With the advent of Ethernet technology and the increasingly widespread deployment of Gigabit Ethernet switches, VLAN has found a place in network infrastructures that allow multiple companies to share Ethernet connectivity, especially in access arrangements. An Ethernet VLAN can be considered to be a Layer 2 VPN that can interwork with other Layer 2 VPNs. The standard protocol used to support these types of Ethernet VPNs is IEEE 802.1Q.

Figure 5.7 shows a typical Ethernet VPN configuration. In this configuration, the metro network is likely a GigaEthernet network (with points of presence MSP CO, MSP 1, MSP 2, MSP 3, etc.) that interfaces through an Edge Router to an FR WAN or ATM WAN network, using an IP interface. 802.1Q VLAN ID tags are used to separate customers. These VLAN IDs allow multiple customers to share an IP or FR or ATM Ethernet interface similar to DLCI for FR or VPI or VCI for ATM.

5.4.3   PPPoE

PPP over Ethernet (PPPoE) is an emerging technology that is described in the next section as part of the PPP suite of tunneling protocols.

5.4.3.1   Common Use

Ethernet VPNs are used as high-speed access networks to corporate networks.

Protocol 8/16 bits	Information *	Padding *

Figure 5.8   PPP encapsulation.

5.5   TUNNELING PROTOCOLS

Both FR and ATM networks are connection oriented; i.e., messages are sent and received over point-to-point connections, either switched or permanent (provisioned). On non-connection-oriented networks such as an IP-based network, it is necessary to establish tunnels over the network to establish the equivalence of virtual circuits. Tunneling is typically done through the use of data encapsulation. There are many tunneling protocols defined for various application purposes. Some tunneling protocols such as IP Security (IPSec) define elaborate security mechanisms. They are categorized as integrated security technologies and discussed in Chapter 8. The tunneling protocols that are considered to be on par with FR and ATM Layer 2 VPNs are considered in the following subsections.

5.5.1   PPP

PPP is an industry-standard method of utilizing point-to-point links to transport multi-protocol datagrams based on IETF RFC 1661.

PPP encapsulation is used to disambiguate multi-protocol datagrams. This encapsulation requires the use of framing to indicate the beginning and end of the encapsulation.

A summary of PPP encapsulation is shown in Figure 5.8. The fields are transmitted from left to right.

The Protocol field is one or two octets in length, and its value identifies the datagram encapsulated in the Information field of the packet. The field is transmitted and received most significant octet first.

PPP is a simple tunneling protocol. It performs the following functions:

■ Provides multi-protocol data-link layer encapsulation — PPP creates frames that contain separate IP datagrams, IPX datagrams, or NetBEUI frames.
■ Establishes, maintains, and ends the logical link — The PPP protocol uses the Link Control Protocol (LCP) to establish and configure the parameters of the data-link connection. Part of the LCP negotiation is authenticating the credentials of the remote access client.

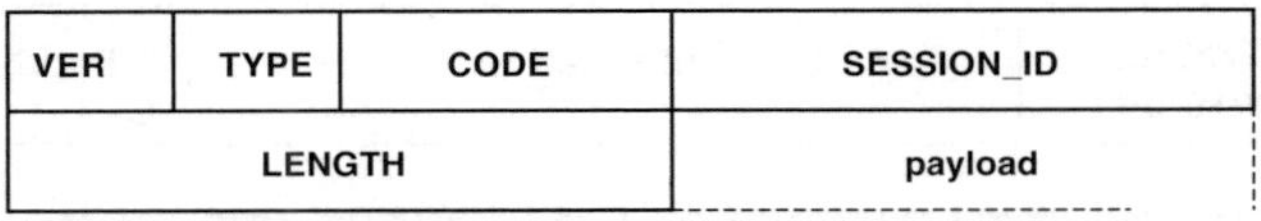

VER	TYPE	CODE	SESSION_ID
LENGTH			payload

Figure 5.9   PPPoE format.

- Provides protocol configuration — After the data-link connection has been negotiated, network-layer protocols such as IP, IPX, and AppleTalk are configured. For example, in TCP/IP, an IP address is allocated to the remote access client by the remote access server. Compression and encryption are also negotiated.

PPP is one of the earliest commonly used tunneling protocols.

5.5.2   PPPoE

As Ethernet technology becomes increasingly prevalent with the increasingly widespread deployment of Gigabit Ethernet switches, it becomes important for such point-to-point protocols as PPP to be securely supported over Ethernet. PPPoE was introduced to accomplish such support.

PPPoE operates in two distinct stages. There is a Discovery stage and a PPP Session stage. When a Host wishes to initiate a PPPoE session, it must first perform Discovery to identify the Ethernet MAC address of the peer and establish a PPPoE SESSION_ID. Although PPP defines a peer-to-peer relationship, Discovery is inherently a client/server (C/S) relationship. In the Discovery process, a Host (the client) discovers an Access Concentrator (the server). Based on the network topology, there may be more than one Access Concentrator that the Host can communicate with. The Discovery stage allows the Host to discover all Access Concentrators and then select one. When the Discovery stage completes successfully, both the Host and the selected Access Concentrator have the information they will use to build their point-to-point connection over Ethernet.

The Discovery stage remains stateless until a PPP session is established. Once a PPP session is established, both the Host and the Access Concentrator *must* allocate the resources for a PPP virtual interface.

The Ethernet payload for PPPoE is as shown in Figure 5.9, where:

- The VER field is four bits and *must* be set to 0x1 for this version of the PPPoE specification.
- The TYPE field is four bits and *must* be set to 0x1 for this version of the PPPoE specification.

- The CODE field is eight bits and is used to define the different Discovery and PPP Session stages.
- The SESSION_ID field is 16 bits. It is an unsigned value in network byte order. Its value is set to 0 for most Discovery Packets. The value is fixed for a given PPP session and, in fact, defines a PPP session along with the Ethernet SOURCE_ADDR and DESTINATION_ADDR. A value of 0xffff is reserved for future use and *must not* be used.
- The LENGTH field is 16 bits. The value, in network byte order, indicates the length of the PPPoE payload. It does not include the length of the Ethernet or PPPoE headers.

5.5.3 PPP over SONET or SDH

The use of PPP encapsulation over SONET or SDH links is defined in IETF RFC 2615. Because SONET or SDH is by definition a point-to-point circuit, PPP is well suited to use over these links.

The real differences between SONET and SDH (other than terminology) are minor; for the purposes of encapsulation of PPP over SONET or SDH, these differences are inconsequential or irrelevant.

PPP treats SONET or SDH transport as octet-oriented synchronous links. SONET or SDH links are full-duplex by definition.

5.5.3.1 The Interface Format

PPP in HDLC-like framing presents an octet interface to the physical layer. There is no provision for suboctets to be supplied or accepted.

The PPP octet stream is mapped into the SONET STS-SPE/SDH higher-order VC, with the octet boundaries aligned with the SONET STS-SPE/SDH Octet boundaries.

Scrambling is performed during insertion into the SONET STS-SPE/SDH higher-order VC to provide adequate transparency and protect against potential security threats. For backward compatibility with RFC 1619 (STS-3c-SPE or VC-4 only), the scrambler *may* have an on and off capability, where the scrambler is bypassed entirely when it is in the off mode. If this capability is provided, the default *must* be set to "scrambling enabled."

For PPP over SONET or SDH, the entire SONET or SDH payload (SONET STS-SPE/SDH higher-order VC minus the path overhead and any fixed stuffed bytes) is scrambled using a self-synchronous scrambler of polynomial $X^{43} + 1$.

The proper order of operation is:

When transmitting:
IP $\rightarrow$ PPP $\rightarrow$ FCS generation $\rightarrow$ Byte stuffing $\rightarrow$ Scrambling $\rightarrow$ SONET or SDH framing

Figure 5.10 GRE tunneling.

When receiving:
SONET or SDH framing → Descrambling → Byte destuffing → FCS
 detection → PPP → IP

The PPP frames are located by row within the SONET STS-SPE/SDH higher-order VC payload. Because the frames are variable in length, they are allowed to cross SONET STS-SPE/SDH higher-order VC boundaries.

5.5.3.2 Common Use

PPP is typically used on point-to-point links and remote access connectivity, and PPPoE is used to extend PPP sessions over Ethernet.

5.5.4 GRE

Generic Routing Encapsulation (GRE) tunnels provide a specific pathway across the shared WAN and encapsulate traffic with new packet headers to ensure delivery to specific destinations (see the example in Figure 5.10). The network is private because traffic can enter a tunnel only at an endpoint. Tunnels do not provide true confidentiality (encryption does) but can carry encrypted traffic.

GRE tunneling can also be used to encapsulate non-IP traffic into IP and send it over the Internet or an IP network. The Internet Package Exchange (IPX) and AppleTalk protocols are examples of non-IP traffic.

5.5.4.1 Common Use

GRE tunnels have been used to carry traffic, such as multicast and dynamic routing information, which cannot be carried over VPNs such as IPSec, MPLS, etc. In this type of applications, GRE traffic will, in turn, be encapsulated over the particular VPN's protocol.

5.5.5 PPTP

Point-to-Point Tunneling Protocol (PPTP) defined in RFC2637 provides a GRE-like tunneling function for PPP connections. PPTP specifies a protocol that allows PPP to be tunneled through an IP network.

PPTP does not specify any changes to the PPP protocol but rather describes a new vehicle for carrying PPP traffic in a C/S environment. A C/S architecture is defined to decouple the functions that exist in current network access servers (NAS) and to support VPNs. The PPTP Network Server (PNS) is envisioned to run on a general purpose operating system whereas the client, referred to as a PPTP Access Concentrator (PAC), operates on a dial access platform. PPTP specifies a call-control and management protocol that allows the server to control access from dial-in circuit switched calls originating from a PSTN or ISDN connection or to initiate outbound circuit-switched connections. PPTP makes use of an enhanced GRE mechanism to provide a flow- and congestion-controlled encapsulated datagram service for carrying PPP packets.

The GRE header used in PPTP is enhanced slightly from that specified in the current GRE protocol specification. The main difference involves the definition of a new Acknowledgment Number field, used to determine if a particular GRE packet or a set of packets has arrived at the remote end of the tunnel. This acknowledgment capability is not used in conjunction with any retransmission of user-data packets. It is used instead to determine the rate at which user-data packets are to be transmitted over the tunnel for a given user session.

The security of user data passed over the tunneled PPP connection is addressed by PPP, as is authentication of the PPP peers.

Because the PPTP control channel messages are neither authenticated nor integrity protected, it might be possible for an attacker to hijack the underlying TCP connection. It is also possible to manufacture false control channel messages and alter genuine messages in transit without detection.

The GRE packets forming the tunnel itself are not cryptographically protected. Because the PPP negotiations are carried out over the tunnel, it may be possible for an attacker to eavesdrop on and modify those negotiations.

Unless the PPP payload data is cryptographically protected, it can be captured and read or modified.

5.5.5.1 Common Use

PPTP is used to carry PPP traffic over an IP network and is intended to be used in remote access applications (see Chapter 7).

5.5.6 L2TP

Layer 2 Tunneling Protocol (L2TP) is defined in IETF RFC 2661 and incorporates the best attributes of PPTP and Cisco's Layer 2 Forwarding (L2F) protocol.

5.5.6.1 *Common Use*

L2TP tunnels are used primarily for dial-up remote access for both IP and non-IP traffic (see Chapter 9).

5.6 THE AUTHENTICATION PROTOCOLS AH AND ESP

A number of the technologies that are used for authentication of users (described in Chapter 3) also support message authentication.

In AH, the IP header, TCP header, and the data are all included in the authentication and generation of the AH authentication data. Thus, authentication of the IP and higher-layer addresses also authenticates message integrity.

In ESP, the TCP header, as well as the data, is included in the authentication and generation of the authentication data (the IP header is included only in the tunnel mode). Thus, authentication of the TCP and higher-layer addresses also authenticates message integrity.

5.6.1 Common Use

ESP and AH technologies can be combined in a variety of modes and are used in such security technologies as IPSec.

5.7 SUMMARY

The simplest type of message integrity technologies is Layer 2 VPNs (such as FR and ATM PVCs, and Ethernet VLANs) that ensure separation of traffic and provide security levels that are comparable to those in private lines. MPLS has become a very widely deployed technology of the type in service provider networks because of a number of key features, including its ability to provide connection-oriented characteristics for IP-based networks and its support of IP-layer CoS capabilities.

Another type of basic VPN is one that are based simply on tunneling, such as PPP, PPPoE, PPPoSONET or SDH, GRE, PPTP, and L2TP.

AH and ESP are basic data integrity technologies that rely on the use of authentication headers to ensure data integrity (in addition to user authentication). They use various algorithms to compute Integrity Check Values (ICVs); e.g., AH uses MD5, SHA-1, or DES to compute MACs.

BIBLIOGRAPHY

1. ATM Security Specification Version 1.1, af-sec-0100.002, ATM Forum, March 2001.
2. RFC 2637: Point-to-Point Tunneling Protocol, July 1999.

3. RFC 1701: Generic Routing Encapsulation (GRE), Hanks, S., Li, T., Farinacci, D. and P. Traina, October 1994.
4. IETF RFC 1702: Generic Routing Encapsulation (GRE) over IPv4 Networks, Hanks, S., Li, T., Farinacci, D. and P. Traina, October 1994.
5. IETF RFC 2661: Layer Two Tunneling Protocol (L2TP), August 1999.
6. IETF RFC 3031: Multiprotocol Label Switching Architecture, E. Rosen, Viswanathan, and R. Callon, January 2001.
7. Multiprotocol Label Switching (MPLS) Tutorial, International Engineering Consortium.
8. IETF RFC 2547: BGP/MPLS VPNs, E. Rosen and Y. Rekhter, March 1999.
9. Any Transport over MPLS (AToM), Cisco Documents.
10. IEEE Std 802.1Q: IEEE Standards for Local and Metropolitan Area Networks: Virtual Bridged Local Area Networks, 1998.
11. IETF RFC 1661 (obsoletes RFC 1548): The Point-to-Point Protocol (PPP), W. Simpson, Editor, July 1994.
12. IETF RFC 2516: A Method for Transmitting PPP Over Ethernet (PPPoE), L. Mamakos, K. Lidl, J. Evarts, D. Carrel, D. Simone, and R. Wheeler, February 1999.
13. IETF RFC 2615 (obsoletes RFC 1619): PPP over SONET/SDH, A. Malis and W. Simpson, June 1999.
14. Andrew G. Mason, *Cisco Secure Virtual Private Networks,* Cisco Press, 2002.

6

BASIC NON-REPUDIATION
TECHNOLOGIES

In this chapter, we look at some basic non-repudiation technologies. Non-repudiation in security systems typically is defined as the mechanism to guarantee that a message can be proved to have originated from a specific sender. This definition can also be called source non-repudiation. Non-repudiation can sometimes be more strictly defined as the assurance that the sender of a message is provided with proof of delivery and that the recipient is provided with proof of the sender's identity, so that neither can later deny having processed the message.

Non-repudiation technologies primarily support the authentication of source identities so as to guarantee that the sender is, indeed, a legitimate source of a received message:

- Digital signatures are the most common technologies used to ensure the authenticity of the sender.
- The use of message authentication codes (MACs) is another method for non-repudiation.

In addition, address-translation techniques such as network address translation (NAT) can also be classified as non-repudiation technologies because they help to ensure that IP packets are coming from and destined for authorized and predefined sources and destinations, respectively.

6.1 DIGITAL SIGNATURES

In Chapter 2, it was indicated that the holder of a private key in a network security application using public-key cryptography can establish the integrity and origin of the data that he or she sends to another party by digitally signing the data using his or her private key. Anyone who receives that data can use the associated public key to validate that it came from the holder of the private key, thus achieving source non-repudiation. This property is used in digital signature technology.

6.1.1 Types of Digital Signatures

Digital signature is the main technology used for source non-repudiation. A digital signature is used by the sender to sign off a message to accomplish source non-repudiation (and also message integrity in typical applications of digital signatures). The signing of a message can be done with the private key of a pair of public and private keys.

Because the message has been signed with a private key of a key pair, the recipient can use the public key to verify the digital signature. This situation is most desirable in application environments where a signatory (someone who is regarded as a signature authority) serves a large population — the area of public-key cryptography, which is described in more detail in Chapter 7 (digital signatures) and Chapter 9 (public key infrastructure [PKI] and federal public key infrastructure [FPKI]).

In practice, the entire message will not be used to generate the digital certificate. Rather, a digest of a message is first created by hashing the message, using a mutually agreed-upon hashing algorithm such as MD5 or SHA-1. Next, a digital signature for the message is generated by encrypting the message digest with a secret or private key that is known to the message sender only. This digital signature is appended to the message, and the entire signed message is sent over the network to the intended receiver.

Upon receiving a digitally signed message, a receiver can verify the identity of the sender by verifying the digital signature. Digital signature standard (DSS), defined for standardizing the overall combined mechanism of generation and verification of digital certificates, is considered to be an enhanced technology and is described in Chapter 7.

6.1.2 Common Use

Digital signatures are used in all integrated technologies that require or support source non-repudiation, such as higher-layer virtual private networks (VPNs) and Secure Sockets Layer (SSL). Digital signatures have also become an integral part of digital certificates (discussed in Chapter 7).

6.2 MAC

A MAC is an authentication tag (also called a checksum) that is derived by applying an authentication scheme, together with a secret key, to a message. Unlike digital signatures, MACs are computed and verified with the same key so that they can only be verified by the intended recipient.

If a message has been signed with a shared key, the same key has to be used to verify the digital signature. Because the shared key is likely a secret key or the entire authentication tag is some result of a hashing algorithm, only a small number of authorized recipients will be able to verify the digital signature.

There are different types of MAC technologies based on different authentication schemes, and they are further discussed in Chapter 7.

6.2.1 Common Use

Just as digital signatures, MACs are used in integrated technologies where source non-repudiation (as well as message integrity) is needed as part of their capabilities.

6.3 NAT AND PAT

Hosts or servers within enterprises that use IP networks can typically be divided into three categories:

1. Hosts that do not require access to hosts in other partnering enterprises or the Internet at large. Hosts within this category may use IP addresses that are unambiguous within an enterprise but may be ambiguous between enterprises.
2. Hosts that need access to a limited set of outside (external) services (e.g., e-mail, FTP, netnews, remote log-in) that can be handled by mediating gateways (e.g., application layer gateways [ALGs]). For many hosts in this category, unrestricted external access (provided via IP connectivity) may be unnecessary and even undesirable for privacy and security reasons. Such hosts, just like hosts within the first category, may use IP addresses that are unambiguous within an enterprise but may be ambiguous between enterprises.
3. Hosts that need network-layer access outside the enterprise (provided via IP connectivity). Hosts in the last category require IP addresses that are globally unambiguous.

We refer to the hosts in the first and second categories as "private," and these hosts can be assigned private IP addresses. The hosts in the third category, on the other hand, are referred to as "public" and require the use of public, globally unique addresses.

The Internet Assigned Numbers Authority (IANA) has reserved the following three blocks of the IP address space for private IP network usage (see RFC 1918):

- 10.0.0.0–10.255.255.255 (10/8 prefix)
- 172.16.0.0–172.31.255.255 (172.16/12 prefix)
- 192.168.0.0–192.168.255.255 (192.168/16 prefix)

Also, IP addresses in the range of 169.254.0.0 to 169.254.255.255 are reserved by some operating systems (namely, Microsoft Windows) for automatic private IP addressing. All these IP addresses should not be used on the Internet.

In the past, the common practice was to assign globally unique public addresses to all hosts that use TCP/IP. In order to extend the life of the IPv4 address space, address registries have been requiring more justification for getting public "registered" IP addresses than ever before, making it harder for organizations to acquire additional public registered address spaces. Organizations of any reasonable size have been forced to use private IP addresses in more and more places in their enterprise networks.

In addition, to contain the growth of routing overheads, a typical Internet service provider (ISP) normally obtains a block of address space from an address registry and then assigns to its customers addresses from within that block, based on each customer's requirements. The result of this process is that routes to many customers will be aggregated together and will appear to other service providers as a single route.

An environment has been created where the use of private and public IP address spaces makes non-repudiation (and other security concerns) a challenging task. NAT and port address translation (PAT) become critical technologies for ensuring that public and private IP address spaces are correctly separated and mapped.

6.3.1 NAT

NAT, defined in RFC 1631, is a function found typically in a router that performs one-to-one IP address mapping from a private address to a registered "real" IP address and vice versa. From the "inside" (internal) secured network and for each data packet that is bound for the unsecured "outside" world, the NAT function looks at the destination and source IP addresses. NAT then strips off any private addressing and replaces it with one of the "real" registered IP addresses from a preassigned address pool. NAT will keep track, through an internal mapping process, of the assigned registered IP addresses to private addresses. When the remote server replies, NAT will receive an inbound IP packet, which it readdresses to the original private address.

6.3.1.1 NAT Function Example

Figure 6.1 illustrates the operation of the NAT function when applied to a Cisco PIX firewall implementation.

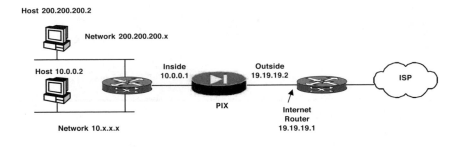

Figure 6.1   NAT function.

In this example, the ISP has provided the network manager with a range of addresses, e.g., from 199.199.199.1 to 199.199.199.63. The network manager has decided to assign 199.199.199.1 to the inside interface on the Internet router and 199.199.199.2 to the outside interface of the PIX.

The network administrator already had a Class C address assigned to his or her network, 200.200.200.0/24 (i.e., network mask 255.255.255.0) and has some workstations using these addresses to access the Internet. These workstations will not require any address translation as they already have valid addresses. However, new workstations are being assigned addresses in the 10.0.0.0/8 network, and they will need to be translated because 10.X.X.X is one of the unroutable (private) address spaces, as per RFC 1918.

To accommodate this network design, the network administrator must use two NAT statements and one global pool in the PIX configuration, as follows:

- global (outside) 1 199.199.199.3–199.199.199.62 netmask 255.255.255.192
- nat (inside) 0 200.200.200.0 255.255.255.0 0 0
- nat (inside) 1 10.0.0.0 255.0.0.0 0 0

This configuration will not translate the source address of any outbound traffic from the 200.200.200.0/24 network. It will translate a source address in the 10.0.0.0/8 network into an address from the range 199.199.199.3 to 199.199.199.62.

6.3.1.2   Common Use

As demonstrated in the PIX firewall example, NAT is typically incorporated into a firewall implementation. NAT is generally required when two or more networks interface with each other.

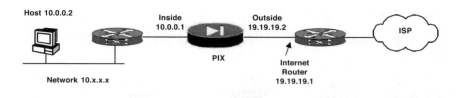

Figure 6.2 PAT function.

6.3.2 PAT

The PAT function works in a similar fashion to the NAT function; a registered IP address merely replaces the private address in an outgoing Internet session. PAT allows a number of users to share in the use of a pool of one or more public addresses.

6.3.2.1 PAT Function Example

Figure 6.2 illustrates the operation of the PAT function, again when applied in a Cisco PIX firewall implementation.

In this example, the ISP has again provided the network manager with a range of addresses from 199.199.199.1 to 199.199.199.63 for his or her company's use. The network manager has decided to use 199.199.199.1 for the inside interface on the Internet router and 199.199.199.2 for the outside interface on his or her PIX firewall. So, we are left with 199.199.199.3 to 199.199.199.62 to use for our NAT pool. However, the network manager knows that at any one time he may have more than 60 people trying to go out of the PIX firewall. He has decided to take 199.199.199.62 and make it a PAT address so that multiple users can share in the use of one address at the same time.

- global (outside) 1 199.199.199.3–199.199.199.61 netmask 255.255.255.192
- global (outside) 1 199.199.199.62 netmask 255.255.255.192
- nat (inside) 1 0.0.0.0 0.0.0.0 0 0

These commands instruct the PIX firewall to translate the source address to 199.199.199.3 to 199.199.199.61 for the first 59 internal users to pass across the PIX firewall. After these addresses have been exhausted, the PIX firewall will then translate all subsequent source addresses to 199.199.199.62 until one of the addresses in the NAT pool becomes free.

6.3.2.2 Common Use

Just as NAT, PAT is typically incorporated into a firewall implementation and on network interfaces.

6.4 SUMMARY

Digitally signing a message is the main technique for achieving non-repudiation. The overall digital signature technology, considered to be an enhanced technology, makes use of hashing algorithms such as MD5 and SHA-1, and secret-key and public-key cryptography technologies. Messages can also be signed with various MAC algorithms, using just hashing algorithms and secret-key cryptography.

NAT and PAT are address-translation technologies that are considered to be non-repudiation technologies because they help to ensure that IP packets are coming from and destined for authorized and predefined sources and destinations, respectively.

Bibliography

1. FIPS PUB 186-2: Digital Signature Standard (DSS), U.S. Department of Commerce/National Institute of Standards and Technology, January 27, 2000.
2. Using NAT and PAT Statements on the Cisco Secure PIX Firewall, Cisco Document, December 10, 2002.
3. IETF RFC 1918: Address Allocation for Private Internets, Y. Rekhter, B. Moskowitz, D. Karrenber, G. J. de Groot, E. Lear, February 1996.

7

ENHANCED TECHNOLOGIES

Basic network security technologies have been presented in the previous chapters. In this chapter, some of the key enhanced technologies are presented. Enhanced network security technologies are those that are designed to implement one particular primary functional element but are considered to be more than basic technologies because they are more complex and very often make heavy use of some of the basic technologies, and sometimes even include other functionally different basic technologies. Furthermore, these enhanced technologies might also implement to some degree some secondary functional elements in addition to the primary one (but in theory to a less degree than the integrated technologies to be presented in Chapter 8).

The enhanced technologies discussed in this chapter include the following:

- Authentication and authorization technologies (e.g., userID and password with PAP [Password Authentication Protocol] and CHAP [Challenge Handshake Authentication Protocol], Kerberos, etc.)
- Token cards
- PPP Extensible Authentication Protocol (EAP)
- Microsoft Point-to-Point Encryption (MPPE)
- Key-management protocols, e.g., Internet Security Association and Key Management Protocol (ISAKMP), Internet Key Exchange (IKE), etc.
- Digital certificates
- Digital signatures
- Message authentication codes (MACs)
- Wireless Encryption Technologies (e.g., WEP, 802.11i)

7.1 USERID AND PASSWORD AUTHENTICATION AND AUTHORIZATION

When a userID and a password pair are needed for the establishment of an access connection, two steps typically take place in a single successful access request session: the authentication of the userID and password pair and the ensuing authorization based on information stored in an authorization server (possibly the same server that performs the authentication).

There are two basic protocols most commonly used for the authentication of a Point-to-Point Protocol (PPP) connection: PAP (which has been described as a basic authentication technology in Chapter 3) and CHAP. Both protocols allow for the validation of a userID and password pair entered by the remote access server (RAS). PAP uses a cleartext password that is encrypted before it is transmitted over the network and is the less sophisticated authentication protocol. CHAP is the more secure protocol because it does not require the password to be transmitted over the network.

With PAP, which is a simple protocol, the encrypted password is sent across the network to be compared against an encrypted password file on the access server. If the password matches that associated with the particular userID, the connection is established. Because the password can potentially be intercepted by a hacker, PAP is not considered to be secure.

7.1.1 CHAP

CHAP is defined in IETF RFC 1994 and addresses the PAP deficiencies by having a server send a randomly generated "challenge" to the client along with the hostname. The hostname is used by the client to look up the appropriate password, which is then combined with the challenge and encrypted using a one-way hashing function to produce a result that is then sent to the server along with the client userID. The server performs the same computation using the password and compares the result with the result that has been sent back by the client. If there is a match, the connection will be established. Because the challenge is different in every session, a hacker cannot replay the sequence.

CHAP allows different types of encryption algorithms to be used. Most commercial RASs support Data Encryption Standard (DES) and Message Digest 5 (MD5). DES, the U.S. government standard, was designed to protect against password discovery and playback. MD5, the message digest algorithm defined in RFC 1321 (see Chapter 2), is a hashing scheme used by various PPP vendors for hashed password authentication. The specific method to be used can be negotiated by a client when connecting to an RAS.

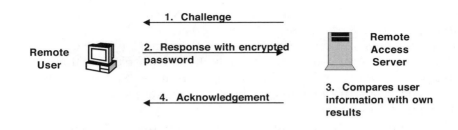

Figure 7.1   The CHAP handshake protocol.

Figure 7.1 and the following show the steps in the handshakes that occur after an initial PPP link has been established. The handshakes may be repeated anytime after the link has been established.

1. After the Link Establishment phase is complete, the authenticator (RAS) sends a challenge message to the peer.
2. The peer (client) responds with a value calculated using a one-way hash function.
3. The authenticator checks the response against its own calculation of the expected hash value. If the values match, the authentication is acknowledged; otherwise, the connection should be terminated.
4. At random intervals, the authenticator sends a new challenge to the peer and repeats steps 1 to 3.

7.1.1.1   Common Use

PAP and CHAP are used in remote access services (see Chapter 9 for Remote Access Architecture descriptions).

7.1.2   Kerberos

Kerberos is a system for authenticating users and services on a network and was originally introduced by MIT. It is built upon the a priori assumption that the network is unsafe. For example, data sent over the network can be eavesdropped on and altered, and addresses can also be faked or spoofed. Therefore, they cannot be used directly for authentication purposes.

The Kerberos protocol uses strong cryptography so that a client can prove its identity to a server (and vice versa) across an insecure network connection. After a client and server have used Kerberos to prove their identities, they can also encrypt all of their communications to assure privacy and data integrity as they go about their business.

Kerberos is a trusted third-party service, which means that there is a third party (the Kerberos server) that is trusted by all the entities on the network (users and services, usually called principals). All the principals share a secret password (or key) with the Kerberos server and this enables the principals to verify that the messages from the Kerberos server are authentic. Thus, trusting the Kerberos server, users and services can authenticate each other.

The following provides an overview of how Kerberos works.

7.1.2.1 Basic Mechanism

In Kerberos, the principals use "tickets" to prove that they are who they claim to be. The Kerberos server, which is also called the Key Distribution Center (KDC), serves as both an authentication server (AS) and a ticket-granting service (TGS).

The authentication process has three stages: the AS Exchange, the TGS Exchange, and the Client/Server (C/S) Exchange. In the following example, A is the initiator of the authentication exchange, usually a user, and B is the service that A wishes to use.

To obtain a ticket for a specific service, A sends a ticket request to the Kerberos server. The request basically contains A's and B's names. The Kerberos server checks that both A and B are valid principals.

Having verified the validity of the principals, the Kerberos server creates a packet containing A's and B's names, A's network address ($A@sub\{addr\}$), the current time ($@var\{t@sub\{issue\}\}$), the lifetime of the ticket ($life$), and a secret "session key" ($K@sub\{AB\}$). This packet is encrypted with B's secret key ($K@sub\{B\}$). The actual ticket ($@var\{T@sub\{AB\}\}$) looks like this:

$$(\{A,\ B,\ A@sub\{addr\},\ @var\{t@sub\{issue\}\},\ life,\\ K@sub\{AB\}\}@var\{K@sub\{B\}\}).$$

The reply to A consists of the ticket ($T@sub\{AB\}$), B's name, the current time, the lifetime of the ticket, and the session key, all encrypted in A's secret key ($\{B,\ t@sub\{issue\},\ life,\ K@sub\{AB\},\ @var\{T@sub\{AB\}\}@var\{K@sub\{A\}\}$). A decrypts the reply and retains it for later use.

Before sending a message to B, A creates an authenticator consisting of A's name, A's address, the current time, and a "checksum" chosen by A, all encrypted with the secret session key ($\{A,\ A@sub\{addr\},\ @var\{t@sub\{current\}\},\ checksum\}K@sub\{AB\}$). This is sent together with the ticket received from the Kerberos server to B. Upon reception, B decrypts the ticket using B's secret key. Because the ticket contains the session key that the authenticator was encrypted with, B can now also decrypt the authenticator. To verify that A really is A, B now has to compare the contents of the ticket with that of the authenticator. If everything matches, B now considers A as properly authenticated.

The KDC has a copy of every password associated with each Kerberos client. Hence, it is necessary that the KDC be as secure as possible.

7.1.2.2 Common Use

Kerberos is used as the authentication and authorization mechanism in GSS-API (see Chapter 8) and in many commercial products including a number of single sign-on (SSO) systems.

7.2 TOKEN CARDS

Token cards have been increasingly popular as a means to provide increased levels of security during the user authentication and authorization process. They have been used for remotely located company employees to gain access to their corporate networks, as smart cards are for E-commerce transactions.

A very typical application of token cards is E-banking. In E-banking, a customer is issued a credit-card-sized token card with a numeric keypad that is used to safely "unlock" the customer's account information. To access accounts, the customer must possess both the token card and a PIN to unlock the token card itself. The customer must then key in the string of numbers that represents a network access code generated by the card on a one-time basis and valid for a limited period of time. The token card's built-in security mechanism is always kept in sync with the bank's back-end server, with which the authorization code generated by the token card will be verified. Each token card has a unique serial number that forms part of the cryptographic key used for generating dynamic network access codes that change every time the customer needs to log on to the application. This provides a high level of security.

To prevent eavesdroppers from listening to or manipulating network traffic, the network path can be further protected by the implementation of a secure channel using, e.g., Secure Sockets Layer (SSL) technology (see Chapter 8). Additional security measures such as the use of a challenge-and-response mechanism as described earlier for the CHAP technology can be used for user authentication and authorization.

7.2.1 Token Card Authentication Methods

A token card uses a variety of available authentication methods, including the four standard methods defined in the key-management protocols ISAKMP and OAKLEY (discussed in Section 7.4.1.1 and Section 7.4.1.2):

digital signatures using either the digital signature standard (DSS) or the RSA algorithm, RSA public-key encryption, and preshared secret keys.

Token card vendors such as Security Dynamics/RSA (maker of SecurID cards) and AXENT Technologies, however, rely on some other methods, such as the use of time-variant passwords or challenge–response systems for the authentication of users. Both these methods use external servers for authentication. Neither scheme fits well within the four supported ISAKMP authentication methods because all four ISAKMP methods rely on cryptographic techniques in which some secret key (either the private half of a public–private key pair or a shared secret key) is always kept closely guarded and never transmitted across the network, even in encrypted form. The token card schemes also do not provide a key that can be used for the protection of the ISAKMP Phase 1 exchange.

The standard authentication mechanisms all provide some form of protection against what is known as a "man-in-the-middle" attack, where a malicious party located between the client and the server swaps in his or her own Diffie–Hellman public values in place of the client's and server's, thus allowing him or her to intercept and decrypt all traffic intended to be encrypted between the two parties. This attack can only be prevented by the use of either shared secret or public–private pair cryptographic mechanisms. One simple approach to prevent such attacks is the use of a preshared user or group key, which would not authenticate the user but which would stop any man-in-the-middle attacks from anyone who does not possess the user or group key.

7.2.1.1 Security Considerations

The security of this solution depends on the secrecy of the group password used to secure the security association (SA) creation during ISAKMP Phase 1 and on the strength of the underlying token mechanisms. Care should be taken to protect group password (preshared key), including regular changes, and use of passwords that will not fall to common dictionary attacks. In addition, PINs and other secrets must be protected to keep the underlying tokens secure.

7.2.1.2 Common Use

Token card technology is typically used as part of the authentication process (e.g., within ISAKMP) for security technologies such as IP Security (IPSec).

When combined with the Public Key Infrastructure (PKI) and micro-processor technologies, token cards can provide a high level of security serving as a tamper-resistant and secure data storage where the private key is created and stored. Furthermore, PKI-enabled token cards can be used for encrypted, digitally signed, and other confidential electronic transactions.

7.3 EAP AND MPPE

PPP provides a standard method for transporting multi-protocol datagrams over point-to-point links. PPP also defines an extensible Link Control Protocol (i.e., EAP), which allows for the negotiation of an Authentication Protocol for authenticating its peer before allowing network-layer protocols to transmit over the PPP link.

MPPE stands for Microsoft Point-to-Point Encryption and is a protocol designed for transfering encrypted datagrams over point-to-point links.

7.3.1 EAP

EAP typically runs directly over the link layer without requiring IP, and therefore includes its own support for in-order delivery and retransmission. Although EAP was originally developed for use with PPP, it is also now in use with IEEE 802.

To establish communications over a point-to-point link, each end of the PPP link must first send link configuration packets to configure the data link during the Link Establishment Phase. After the link has been established, PPP provides for an optional Authentication Phase before proceeding to the Network-Layer Protocol Phase.

By default, authentication is not mandatory. If authentication of the link is desired, an implementation *must* specify the Authentication-Protocol Configuration Option during the Link Establishment Phase.

These authentication protocols are intended for use primarily by hosts and routers that connect to a PPP network server via switched circuits or dial-up lines, but might be applied to dedicated links as well. The server can use the identification of the connecting host or router in the selection of options for network-layer negotiations.

EAP is a general protocol for PPP authentication that supports multiple authentication mechanisms. EAP does not select a specific authentication mechanism at Link Control Phase, but rather postpones this until the Authentication Phase. This allows the authenticator to request more information before determining the specific authentication mechanism. This also permits the use of a back-end server that actually implements the various mechanisms, whereas the PPP authenticator merely passes through the authentication exchange.

The following are the basic steps involved in the EAP authentication process:

Figure 7.2   PPP frame with EAP packet.

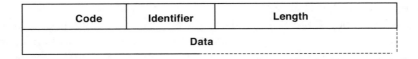

Figure 7.3   EAP packet format.

1. After the Link Establishment phase is complete, the authenticator sends one or more Requests to authenticate the peer. The Request has a type field to indicate what is being requested. Examples of Request types include Identity, MD5-challenge, One-Time Passwords, Generic Token Card, etc. The MD5-challenge type corresponds closely to the CHAP authentication protocol. Typically, the authenticator will send an initial Identity Request followed by one or more Requests for authentication information. However, an initial Identity Request is not required, and *may* be bypassed in cases where the identity is presumed (leased lines, dedicated dial-ups, etc.).
2. The peer sends a Response packet in reply to each Request. As with the Request packet, the Response packet contains a type field that corresponds to the type field of the Request.
3. The authenticator ends the authentication phase with a Success or Failure packet.

7.3.1.1   EAP Packet Formats

Exactly one PPP EAP packet is encapsulated in the Information field of a PPP data-link-layer frame where the protocol field indicates type hex C227 (PPP EAP). Figure 7.2 shows a PPP frame with an EAP packet.

A summary of the EAP packet format is provided in Figure 7.3. The fields are transmitted from left to right, where:

■ Code field is one octet and identifies the type of EAP packet. EAP codes are assigned as follows:
  1 for Request
  2 for Response
  3 for Success
  4 for Failure

Code	Identifier	Length
Type	Type-Data	

Figure 7.4   Request and response packet format.

- Identifier: The Identifier field is one octet and aids in matching responses with requests.
- Length: The Length field is two octets and indicates the length of the EAP packet including the Code, Identifier, Length, and Data fields. Octets outside the range of the Length field should be treated as data-link-layer padding and should be ignored on reception.
- Data: The Data field is zero or more octets. The format of the Data field is determined by the Code field.

A summary of the Request and Response packet format is shown in Figure 7.4. The fields are transmitted from left to right, where:

- Code:
  1 for Request
  2 for Response
- Identifier: The Identifier field is one octet. The Identifier field *must* be the same if a Request packet is retransmitted due to a timeout while waiting for a Response.
- Length: The Length field is two octets and indicates the length of the EAP packet including the Code, Identifier, Length, Type, and Type-Data fields.
- Type: The Type field is one octet. This field indicates the Type of Request or Response. Only one Type *must* be specified per EAP Request or Response.
- Type-Data: The Type-Data field varies with the Type of Request and the associated Response.

The Type field specifies the authentication method used. Most of the commonly available authentication methods are supported in EAP and they include basic technologies such as MD5, SHA-1, and enhanced and integrated technologies such as EAP-TLS, EAP-TTLS, PEAP, RSA SecurID, AXENT, etc.

Because EAP does not select a specific authentication mechanism at the Link Control Phase but rather postpones this until the Authentication Phase, this allows the authenticator to request more information before determining the specific authentication mechanism. It also permits the use of a back-end authentication server that actually implements the various mechanisms, whereas the PPP authenticator merely passes through the authentication exchange.

7.3.1.2 Common Use

EAP is used in the definition of advanced network security technologies TTLS (also called EAP-TTLS) and PEAP (see Chapter 8), both of which are developed to work within the 802.1x authentication framework in Wireless LANs (WLANs).

7.3.2 MPPE

One particular tunneling protocol that incorporates some basic data encryption capabilities is the MPPE scheme, which is a means of representing PPP packets in an encrypted form to enhance confidentiality of PPP-encapsulated packets. MPPE uses the RC4 algorithm to provide data confidentiality. The length of the session key to be used for initializing encryption tables can be negotiated as part of the PPP Compression Control Protocol. MPPE currently supports 40-bit and 128-bit session keys. MPPE is defined in RFC 3078.

7.3.2.1 Common Use

MPPE is used for transferring encrypted data over PPP links.

7.4 KEY-MANAGEMENT PROTOCOLS

Interestingly, one important area of usage or application of public-key cryptography is in the establishment of keys that generally require two critical functions: key transport and key generation. Key transport refers to an application that securely allows a secret key, possibly a session key, to be sent from one party to the receiving party. Key generation refers to the computation of a secret key using public information.

An example of key transport is the use of the RSA algorithm to encrypt a randomly generated session key (to be used for encryption during subsequent communications, e.g., to do bulk file transfers) with the recipient's public key. The encrypted random key is then sent to the recipient, who decrypts it using his or her private key. At this point, both sides have the same session key, even though it was created based on input from only one side of the communication. One benefit of the key-transport method is that it has less computational overhead than some other algorithms such as the Diffie–Hellman algorithm.

The Diffie–Hellman algorithm illustrates key generation using public-key cryptography. For a more detailed description of this algorithm, see Chapter 2. The Diffie–Hellman algorithm begins by two users exchanging public information. Each user then mathematically combines the other's public information along with his or her own secret information to compute a shared secret value. This secret value can be used as a session key or as a key-encryption key for encrypting a randomly generated session key. This method generates a session key based on public and secret information held by both users. The benefit of the Diffie–Hellman algorithm is that the key used for encrypting messages is based on information held by both users and the independence of keys from one key exchange to another provides perfect forward secrecy.

It should be noted that there are a number of variations on each of these two key-generation and key-transport schemes, i.e., the RSA algorithm and the Diffie–Hellman algorithm, and these variations do not necessarily interoperate.

Key exchanges may be authenticated during key-exchange protocol execution or after key-exchange protocol completion. Authentication of key exchanges during protocol execution is provided when each party provides proof that it has the secret session key before the end of the protocol. Such proof can be provided by encrypting some known data in the secret session key during the protocol exchange execution. Authentication after the key exchange protocol completion, on the other hand, must occur in subsequent communications. In general, authentication during the protocol is preferred so that subsequent communications are not initiated if the secret session key is not established with the desired party.

A key exchange provides symmetry if either party can initiate the exchange and exchanged messages can cross in transit without affecting the key that is generated. This is desirable so that computation of the keys does not require either party to know who initiated the exchange. Although key-exchange symmetry is desirable, symmetry in the entire key-management protocol may be a cause for vulnerability to reflection attacks.

An authenticated key-exchange protocol provides perfect forward secrecy if disclosure of long-term secret keying material does not compromise the secrecy of the exchanged keys from previous communications. The property of perfect forward secrecy does not apply to key exchange without authentication.

7.4.1 Key Management

Key management refers to key establishment and the rules and protocols for generating and establishing keys, and the subsequent handling of those keys. As the size of a key-management system or the number of entities using a system grows, the need for key establishment can lead to a key-management problem. A number of techniques have been defined in voluntary consensus industry standards. However, the proliferation of techniques, many with questionable security attributes, has led to concern that some techniques may not provide suitable security to meet the needs of many E-commerce applications, as well as federal government security needs, and may not promote interoperability. As a result, standard key-management protocols have been introduced.

The following subsections present a number of important key-management technologies. The Internet Security Association and Key Management Protocol (ISAKMP) is defined primarily as a very comprehensive framework for key management offering maximum flexibility, and OAKLEY is defined based on the Diffie–Hellman key-exchange algorithm. IKE, on the other hand, is defined primarily to be the key management for the IPSec Architecture and makes use of parts of the ISAKMP and OAKLEY definitions.

7.4.1.1 ISAKMP

Defined in IETF RFC 2408, ISAKMP has been developed to provide a framework for establishing SAs and keying material. ISAKMP only describes the procedures, i.e., how something is done. It is independent of the security protocols, cryptographic algorithms, and key-generation and key-exchange techniques that are actually used. This provides the flexibility needed in the future when new mechanisms and methods are developed.

The main design guidelines used during development of ISAKMP are flexibility, independence, and updatability. ISAKMP combines the concepts of SA, key management, and authentication. An SA is a set of information that describes how the communicating entities will utilize security. It is a relationship between these communicating entities and can be considered a contract that all participants must agree upon. Key management handles key generation and key exchange between the entities. The level of security in a communication is strongly dependent on these techniques. Another aspect of security is authentication, which enables an entity to trust the other participants. Different methods for authentication exist, based on public keys or certificates, for example.

7.4.1.1.1 Overview

ISAKMP defines procedures and packet formats to establish, negotiate, modify, and delete SAs. SAs contain all the information required for the

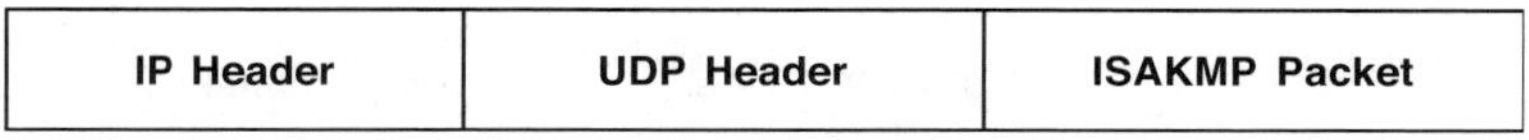

IP Header	UDP Header	ISAKMP Packet

Figure 7.5   IP packet with ISAKMP packet.

execution of various network security services, such as the IP-layer services including header authentication and payload encapsulation, transport or application-layer services, or self-protection of negotiation traffic. ISAKMP defines payload formats for exchanging authentication and key-generation data. These formats provide a consistent framework for transferring key and authentication data, which is independent of the key-generation techniques, encryption algorithms, and authentication mechanisms that are actually used.

ISAKMP is defined independently of key-exchange protocols in order to cleanly separate the details of security association management (and key management) from the details of key exchange. There may be many different key-exchange protocols, each with different security properties, but a common framework is required for agreeing to the formats of SA attributes, and for negotiating, modifying, and deleting SAs. ISAKMP serves as this common framework.

7.4.1.1.2   ISAKMP Phases

ISAKMP offers two phases of negotiation. In the first phase, the two entities (e.g., ISAKMP servers) agree on how to protect further negotiation traffic between themselves, establishing an ISAKMP SA. This ISAKMP SA is then used to protect the negotiations for the Protocol SA being requested. Two entities (e.g., ISAKMP servers) can negotiate (and have active) multiple ISAKMP SAs.

The second phase of negotiation is used to establish security associations for other security protocols. The security associations established by ISAKMP during this phase can be used by a security protocol to protect many message or data exchanges.

7.4.1.1.3   ISAKMP Packets

ISAKMP can be implemented over any transport protocol. However, all implementations must include send and receive capabilities for ISAKMP using UDP on port 500. The diagram in Figure 7.5 shows the format of an IP packet containing an ISAMKP-embedded payload.

Figure 7.6 is a high-level view of the placement of ISAKMP within a systems context in a network architecture. An important part of negotiating

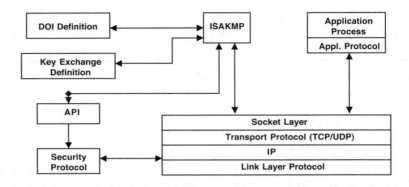

Figure 7.6 ISAKMP relationships.

Initiator Cookie				
Responder Cookie				
Next Payload	Mjr Ver.	Mnr Ver	Exchange Type	Flags
Message ID				
Length				

Figure 7.7 ISAKMP header format.

security services is to consider the entire stack of individual SAs as a unit. This is referred to as a protection suite.

7.4.1.1.4 ISAKMP Message Exchanges

ISAKMP operates through the exchange of ISAKMP messages. Each message is made up of one or more ISAKMP payloads.

Figure 7.7 shows the format of an ISAKMP message header, where:

■ Initiator Cookie (8 bytes): cookie of entity that initiated SA establishment, SA notification, or SA deletion.
■ Responder Cookie (8 bytes): cookie of entity responding to an SA establishment request, SA notification, or SA deletion.
■ Next Payload (8 bits): type of first payload in the message.
■ Mjr version (4 bits): major version of the ISAKMP protocol in use.
■ Mnr version (4 bits): the minor version of the ISAKMP protocol in use.
■ Exchange Type (8 bits): type of exchange being used. This dictates the message and payload orderings in the ISAKMP exchanges.

- Flags (8 bits): options that are set for the ISAKMP exchange for Authentication, Commit, and Encryption.
- Message ID (4 bytes): a unique value used to identify the protocol state during Phase 2 negotiations. It is randomly generated by the initiator of the Phase 2 negotiation.
- Length (4 bytes): total length of the ISAKMP header and the encapsulated payloads in bytes.

The ISAKMP payloads provide the modular building blocks for constructing ISAKMP messages. ISAKMP defines the following types of payloads, which are used to transfer information such as security association data or key-exchange data in (Domain of Interpretation) DOI-defined formats:

- NONE
- Security Association
- Proposal
- Transform
- Key Exchange
- Identification
- Certificate
- Certificate Request
- Hash
- Signature
- Nonce
- Notification
- Delete
- Vendor
- RESERVED
- Private USE

A payload consists of a Generic Payload Header and a string of octets that is opaque to ISAKMP. ISAKMP uses DOI-specific functionality to synthesize and interpret these payloads. Multiple payloads can be sent in a single ISAKMP message.

The Generic Payload Header is shown in Figure 7.8 and the fields are defined as follows:

Next Payload	RESERVED	Payload Length

Figure 7.8 Generic payload header.

- Next Payload (1 octet): identifier for the payload type of the next payload in the message. If the current payload is the last in the message, then this field will be 0. This field provides the "chaining" capability.
- RESERVED (1 octet): unused, set to 0.
- Payload Length (2 octets): length in octets of the current payload, including the generic payload header.

7.4.1.1.5 ISAKMP Protection Mechanisms

ISAKMP supports the following protection mechanisms for increased robustness:

- Anticlogging (denial-of-service).
- ISAKMP prevents connection hijacking by linking the authentication key exchange and security association exchanges.
- Man-in-the-middle attacks include interception, insertion, deletion, and modification of messages, reflecting messages back at the sender, replaying old messages, and redirecting messages.
- Support multicast key distribution.

7.4.1.1.6 Common Use

Parts of ISAKMP (and OAKLEY, see the following text) are used in the IKE protocol (described in a later section).

7.4.1.2 OAKLEY

The OAKLEY Key-Determination Protocol (OAKLEY) defined in IETF RFC 2412 is used to establish secret keying material between two communicating entities in a secure way. The name of the key can then be used later on to derive security associations for the authentication protocols AH and ESP or to achieve other network security goals.

OAKLEY is based on the Diffie–Hellman key-exchange algorithm, which allows establishment of a secret key without transmitting this key. The initiator of the key exchange offers a set of encryption, hash, and authentication mechanisms, and the responder chooses one mechanism for each group. Because OAKLEY is compatible with ISAKMP, the security association, key exchange, and authentication payloads in ISAKMP can be used to exchange the material. Through this compatibility, OAKLEY is also able to satisfy future needs for secure internet communication.

One particularly important security property provided by OAKLEY is Perfect Forward Secrecy (PFS).

7.4.1.2.1 Overview

The OAKLEY protocol allows two authenticated entities to exchange and establish secret keying material. It is designed to be a compatible component of ISAKMP. The two communicating entities negotiate methods for encryption, key derivation, and authentication. The basic mechanism of OAKLEY is the Diffie–Hellman key-exchange algorithm, which establishes a shared key without transmitting this key. For a description of the Diffie–Hellman algorithm, see Chapter 2.

7.4.1.2.2 Key Exchange

An OAKLEY key exchange is made up of a sequence of message exchanges. The goal of key-exchange processing is the secure establishment of a common keying information state in the two communicating entities. This state information consists of a key name, secret keying material, the identities of the two parties, and three algorithms for use during authentication: encryption (for privacy of the identities of the two parties), hashing (a pseudorandom function for protecting the integrity of the messages and for authenticating message fields), and authentication (the algorithm on which the mutual authentication of the two parties is based).

Each OAKLEY exchange is intended to accomplish a combination of one or more of the following five OAKLEY features:

- Stateless cookie exchange
- Perfect forward secrecy for the keying material
- Secrecy for the identities
- Perfect forward secrecy for identity secrecy
- Use of signatures (for non-repudiation)

Key exchanges are also divided into modes and the OAKLEY protocol details the services provided by each (e.g., perfect forward secrecy for keys, identity protection, and authentication).

The Initiator of the exchange begins by specifying some information in the first message. The Responder replies by supplying some information. The two sides exchange messages, supplying more information each time, until their requirements are satisfied.

The choice of how much information to include in each message depends on which options are desirable. For example, if stateless cookies are not a requirement, and identity secrecy and perfect forward secrecy for the keying material are not requirements, and if non-repudiatable signatures are acceptable, then the exchange can be completed in three messages.

Additional features may increase the number of round-trips needed for the keying material determination.

The three components of the OAKLEY key-determination protocol are the:

1. Cookie exchange
2. Diffie–Hellman half-key exchange
3. Authentication

The method of authentication can be digital signatures, public-key encryption, or an out-of-band symmetric key. The three different methods lead to slight variations in the messages, and the variations are illustrated by examples in this section.

The Initiator is responsible for retransmitting messages if the protocol does not terminate in a timely fashion. The Responder must therefore avoid discarding reply information until it is acknowledged by the Initiator in the course of continuing the protocol.

7.4.1.2.3 Common Use

OAKLEY can be used by itself or used in conjunction with ISAKMP to form a hybrid protocol. This hybrid key-exchange protocol can be used, for example, to establish VPNs and also to allow users from remote sites (who may have a dynamically allocated IP address) to access a secure network.

In particular, parts of OAKLEY and ISAKMP are used in the IKE protocol (see the following text). Also, the name of the shared key established by OAKLEY can be used to derive security associations for the authentication protocols AH and ESP or to achieve other network security goals.

7.4.1.3 IKE

IKE is the protocol that performs mutual authentication and establishes SAs between two parties for IPSec. An SA is defined as a set of information items that, when shared between two communicating parties, enables the two parties to protect the communication in some predefined way. IKE is defined in RFC 2409.

7.4.1.3.1 Overview of IKE

IKE uses parts of ISAKMP, OAKLEY, and SKEME to provide management of keys and security associations. The following summarizes the key characteristics of these three protocols from IKE's perspective:

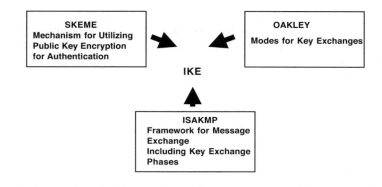

Figure 7.9   Key ISAKMP, OAKLEY, and SKEME concepts in IKE.

- ISAKMP provides a framework for authentication and key exchange but does not define them. ISAKMP is designed to be independent of the key-exchange algorithm, i.e., designed to support many different key exchanges.
- OAKLEY describes a series of key exchanges — called modes — and details the services provided by each (e.g., perfect forward secrecy for keys, identity protection, and authentication).
- SKEME describes a versatile key-exchange mechanism that provides anonymity, repudiability, and quick key refreshment.

Figure 7.9 shows some of the key concepts that have been adopted by IKE from ISAKMP, OAKLEY, and SKEME.

The following IKE definition summary highlights some of the resulting combined characteristics taken from ISAKMP and OAKLEY.

7.4.1.3.2   IKE Phases

IKE uses the ISAKMP definition of phases in the definition of IKE exchanges. IKE exchanges conform to standard ISAKMP payload syntax, attribute encoding, timeouts and retransmits of messages, and informational messages, and each exchange has an associated mode in the style of OAKLEY modes to distinguish between different types of SAs.

Thus, Phase 1 in the two ISAKMP peers use exchanges to establish a secure, authenticated channel for communicating. This authenticated channel is called the IKE SA.

In Phase 2 of each exchange, SAs are negotiated on behalf of services such as IPSec or any other service that needs the negotiation of key material and key parameters.

An ISAKMP SA is bidirectional. That is, once an ISAKMP SA is established, either party may initiate exchanges. As in ISAKMP, each SA is identified by the Initiator's cookie followed by the Responder's cookie (see the ISAKMP header), and the role of each party in the Phase 1 exchanges dictates which cookie is the Initiator's.

With this use of ISAKMP phases, an IKE implementation can accomplish very fast keying when necessary. A single Phase 1 negotiation may be used for more than one Phase 2 negotiation. Additionally, a single Phase 2 negotiation can request multiple IKE SAs.

7.4.1.3.3 IKE Exchanges

IKE exchanges performed during Phase 1 can be regarded as the initial handshake in which the two parties negotiate cryptographic algorithms, mutually authenticate, and establish a session key, creating an IKE-SA. Additionally, a first IPSec SA is established during the initial IKE SA creation.

All IKE messages that make up each exchange are request and response exchange pairs. It is the responsibility of the side sending the request to retransmit if it does not receive a timely response.

The initial exchange usually consists of two request and response pairs. (Additional request and response pairs might be needed for denial-of-service (DoS) protection if Alice attempts to use a Diffie–Hellman group that Bob does not support, or if Bob will authenticate Alice through some legacy mechanism such as a token card, OTP, or name and password.

The first pair negotiates cryptographic algorithms and does a Diffie–Hellman exchange. The second pair is encrypted and integrity protected with keys based on the Diffie–Hellman exchange. In this exchange Alice and Bob divulge their identities and prove them using an integrity check generated based on the secret associated with their identity (private key or shared secret key) and the contents of the first pair of messages in the exchange. Also, the first IPSec SA is created.

After the initial handshake, additional requests can be initiated during Phase 2 by either Alice or Bob, and consist of either informational messages or requests to establish another child-SA. Informational messages include null messages for detecting peer aliveness and deletion of SAs.

The exchange to establish an IPSec SA (also known as child-SA) consists of an optional Diffie–Hellman exchange (if perfect forward secrecy for that child-SA is desired), nonces (so that a unique key for that child-SA will be established), and negotiation of traffic selector values that indicate what addresses, ports, and protocol types are to be transmitted over that child-SA.

7.4.1.3.4 Supported Authentication Algorithms

IKE implementations *must* support the following attribute values:

- DES
- MD5 and SHA
- Authentication via preshared keys
- MODP over default group number one (see the following text)

In addition, IKE implementations *should* support 3DES for encryption; Tiger for hash (Tiger is a fast hash function, by Eli Biham and Ross Anderson); the Digital Signature Standard, RSA signatures and authentication with RSA public-key encryption; and MODP group number 2.

7.4.1.3.5 Common Use

IKE provides management of keys and security associations for protocols such as IPSec, AH, and ESP, and is commonly used in the deployment of virtual private networks (VPNs).

7.4.1.4 SKIP

Simple Key Management Protocol for IP (SKIP) is a protocol developed by Sun Microsystems to handle key management across IP networks and VPNs.

SKIP uses the Diffie–Hellman Algorithm with 1024-bit public-key-based authentication for key setup, session, and traffic key generation, along with DES-, RC2- and RC4-based traffic encryption.

SKIP is a stateless key-management scheme and eliminates the need for pseudo-session state management between two ends to acquire and change packet encrypting keys. SKIP sits on top of the IP network layer (see Figure 7.2 for the format of an IP packet with a SKIP message). As a result, SKIP provides scalable solutions that permit the dynamic rerouting of protected IP traffic through intermediate nodes for such operations as crash recovery and network route failure tolerance. Some of SKIP's key advantages include:

- No connection setup overhead
- High availability — encryption gateways that fail can reboot and resume decrypting packets instantly, without having to renegotiate (potentially thousands of) existing connections
- Unidirectional IP (for example, IP broadcast via satellite or cable)
- Scalable multicast key distribution
- SKIP gateways can be configured in parallel to perform instant failover

MAC Header	IP Header	SKIP Message

Figure 7.10 IP packet with SKIP message.

To implement SKIP, each IP-based source and destination has an authenticated Diffie–Hellman public value, which can be authenticated through the use of X.509 certificates, Secure DNS, PGP certificates, or other public methods.

Once two certificates are assigned to two IP nodes, two mutually authenticated pair-wise keys arise, simply as a result of the public value authentication process. This is because each pair of IP source and destination can acquire a mutually authenticated shared secret. The symmetric keys that are derived from these shared secrets require no set-up overhead, except for the authenticated public value distribution process itself.

All that is required for each party to compute the pair-wise symmetric key is knowledge of the other party's authenticated public value. This computable shared secret is used as the basis for a key-encrypting key to provide IP packet-based authentication and encryption.

SKIP therefore manages assignment of keys with minimal overhead, and reassignment is managed as naturally. If the source node changes the packet encryption key, the receiving IP node can discover this fact without having to perform a public-key operation. It uses the cached value to decrypt the encrypted packet key. Thus, without requiring communication between transmitting and receiving ends, and without necessitating the use of a computationally expensive public-key operation, the packet encrypting or authenticating keys can be changed by the transmitting side and discovered by the receiving side.

Figure 7.10 shows an IP packet with the SKIP message.

7.4.1.4.1 Common Use

SKIP is used as a low-overhead public-key authentication system in many IP network environments, especially in applications that rely heavily on the secure exchange of UPD traffic. For example, RFC 2356 defines the use of SKIP in Sun's SKIP Firewall Traversal for Mobile IP.

7.4.1.5 STS

The Station-to-Station (STS) protocol is the three-pass variation of the basic Diffie–Hellman protocol. It allows the establishment of a shared secret key between two parties with mutual entity authentication and mutual explicit key authentication. The protocol also facilitates anonymity — the identities of the two exchange entities may be protected from eavesdroppers.

STS employs the use of digital signatures (see the next section) and eliminates man-in-the-middle attacks.

7.4.1.5.1   Common Use

STS is often used in the deployment of VPNs.

7.5   DIGITAL SIGNATURES

As mentioned in Chapter 6, digitally signing off a message is the main technology for non-repudiation. The resulting digital signature, commonly found appended to a message sent over the network, is a key tool for ensuring both source non-repudiation and integrity of the message. The recipient of the message uses this signature to verify that the message indeed came from a person whose identity is known to the recipient and that the message has not been modified *en route*. It follows that digital signatures can be considered as both enhanced non-repudiation and message integrity technologies.

A digital signature is created by encrypting a digest of the message with a public key where the message digest is typically computed from the original message based on some mutually agreed-upon hashing algorithm, such as the checksum. The recipient side, upon reception of the message, hashes the message, decrypts the digital signature, and compares the two results. Any discrepancy indicates that the message received either did not come from the supposed sender or it has been modified *en route*.

There are three FIPS-approved algorithms for generating and verifying digital signatures: digital signature algorithm (DSA), RSA (as specified in ANSI X9.31), and Elliptic Curve DSA (ECDSA as specified in ANSI X9.62).

7.5.1   Digital Signature Standard (DSS)

On February 15, 2000, NIST announced the approval of FIPS PUB 186-2, DSS. The DSS specifies a standard set of digital signature (DS) algorithms for the generation and verification of digital signatures and some related procedures (e.g., random generator) and algorithm parameters that are appropriate for applications that require the use of digital signatures. Included in the DSS-approved DS algorithms are the three FIPS-approved digital signature generation and verifying algorithms DSA, RSA, and ECDSA.

As specified in DSS, a digital signature is computed using a set of rules and a set of parameters such that the identity of the signatory and the integrity of the data can be verified. A DS algorithm provides the capability to generate and verify digital signatures. It makes use of a private key to generate the digital signature, and the verification makes use of a public key that corresponds to, but is not the same as, the private key. Each user possesses a private and public key pair. Public keys are assumed to be known to the public in general, but private keys are never shared. Anyone can verify the signature of a user by employing that user's public key. Signature generation, on the other hand, can be performed only by the possessor of the user's private key.

7.5.1.1 Message Digest

The digital signature is typically applied not to the message itself but to a condensed representation of the message. A hash function is used to obtain such a condensed version, which is called a message digest. The message digest is then input to the DS algorithm to generate the digital signature. The digital signature is sent to the intended verifier along with the signed data (often called the message).

The hash function is specified in a separate standard, the secure hash algorithm (SHA-1), defined in the FIPS PUB 180-1 specification for the secure hash standard (SHS). The FIPS-approved DS algorithms must be implemented with SHS. Similar procedures may be used to generate and verify signatures for stored as well as transmitted data.

7.5.1.2 Key Association

Each user (i.e., the signatory) possesses a private and public key pair. Public keys are assumed to be known to the public in general but private keys are never shared. A means of associating public and private key pairs to the corresponding users is required. That is, there must be a binding of a user's identity and the user's public key. This binding may be certified by a mutually trusted party. For example, a certifying authority could sign credentials containing a user's public key and identity to form a certificate. Systems for certifying credentials and distributing certificates are beyond the scope of DSS.

7.5.1.3 DS Algorithm

A DS algorithm authenticates both the integrity of the signed data and the identity of the signatory. A DS algorithm may also be used in proving to a third party that data was actually signed by the generator of the signature. A DS algorithm is intended for use in electronic mail, electronic funds transfer, electronic data interchange, software distribution, data storage, and other applications that require data integrity assurance and data origin authentication. Whereas FIBS PUB 186 defines only DSA as

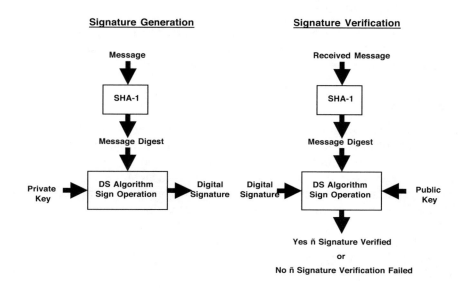

Figure 7.11   Signature generation and verification.

the only approved DS algorithm, FIBS PUB 186-2 added RSA and ECDSA as additional approved DS algorithms.

Figure 7.11 illustrates the digital signature generation and verification processes as defined in the DSS.

7.5.2   Using Digital Signature in SSL

Digital Signatures are used in SSL as a means of source non-repudiation. The following is a summary of the steps defined in SSL for the generation and verification of digital signatures:

- Step 1 — Client sends a message.
- Step 2 — Client hashes message to get a message digest.
- Step 3 — Client generates digital signature from message digest using private key.
- Step 4 — Server receives message and digital signature.
- Step 5 — Server generates message digest from message and also message digest from digital signature using public key.
- Step 6 — Server compares the two message digests for a match.

SSL is considered to be an integrated technology and will be discussed in Chapter 8.

7.5.2.1 Common Use

Digital signatures are widely used in all integrated technologies for source non-repudiation, such as higher-layer VPNs and SSL. Digital signatures have also become an integral part of digital certificates.

7.6 MAC

Besides digital signatures, another technology that can be used to achieve non-repudiation is MAC-based algorithms. A MAC is an authentication tag (also called a checksum) derived by the application of an authentication scheme, together with a secret key, to a message. MACs are computed and verified with the same key, so they can only be verified by the intended receiver, unlike digital signatures. MAC-based algorithms (often just called MACs for convenience) can be divided into different types depending on the way MACs are computed.

One widely used type of MAC is the hash-function-based MAC (HMAC). HMACs use a key or keys in conjunction with a hash function (see Chapter 2 on hash functions such as MD5 and SHA-1) to produce a checksum that is appended to the message. An example is the keyed-hash MAC (HMAC) technology. The next subsection describes HMACs in detail.

Other types of MACs use a variety of cryptographic algorithms such as stream ciphers, block ciphers, etc. For example, the DES-Cypher Block Chaining mode (DES-CBC) MAC as defined in IETF RFC 2405 is a widely used U.S. and international standard. DES-CBC is used to encrypt message blocks and output the final block in the ciphertext as the checksum.

7.6.1 HMAC

Keyed HMAC, first defined in IETF RFC 2104, is a type of MAC calculated using a cryptographic hash function in conjunction with a secret key that was first published in 1996 by Mihir Bellare, Ran Canetti, and Hugo Krawczyk. As any MAC, it may be used to verify simultaneously both the data integrity and authenticity of a message. Any iterative cryptographic hash function, e.g., SHA-1, may be used in the calculation of an HMAC and the cryptographic strength of the HMAC, will depend on the cryptographic strength of the underlying hash function and on the size and quality of the key.

FIPS PUB 198 generalizes and standardizes previous standards IETF 2104 and ANSI X9.71 on the use of HMACs.

7.6.2 Computing MACs

The following description taken from the FIPS PUB 198 document shows how a MAC is computed in HMAC.

The HMAC algorithm uses the following parameters and operations:

- B — Block size (in bytes) of the input to the Approved hash function
- H — An Approved hash function
- *ipad* — Inner pad; the byte x'36' repeated B times
- K — Secret key shared between the originator and the intended receivers
- K_0 — The key K after any necessary preprocessing to form a B byte key
- L — Block size (in bytes) of the output of the Approved hash function
- *Opad* — Outer pad; the byte x'5c' repeated B times
- t — The number of bytes of MAC
- *text* — The data on which the HMAC is calculated; *text* does not include the padded key. The length of *text* is n bits, where $0 \leq n < 2^B - 8B$
- x'N' — Hexadecimal notation, where each symbol in the string 'N' represents 4 binary bits
- $\|$ — Concatenation
- $\oplus$ – Exclusive-OR (XOR) operation

To compute a MAC over the data *text* using the HMAC function, the following operation is performed:

$$MAC(text)t = HMAC(K, text)t = H((K0 \oplus opad) \| H((K0 \oplus ipad) \| text))t$$

Table 7.1 illustrates the step-by-step process in the HMAC algorithm.

7.6.2.1 *Common Use*

Just as digital signatures, the MAC technologies are used for message integrity and source non-repudiation.

7.7 DIGITAL CERTIFICATE

A digital certificate is analogous to a driver's license and is used to verify the identity of a party that is involved in the two-way information exchange. For example, the browser has to make sure that the server to which the browser is sending sensitive information is a legitimate receiver of the information. This can be done by requiring the intended receiver to send a signed certificate to the browser. This certificate must have been issued

Table 7.1   The HMAC Algorithm

Steps	Step-by-Step Description
Step 1	If the length of $K = B$: set $K_0 = K$. Go to step 4
Step 2	If the length of $K > B$: hash K to obtain an L length string, then append $(B–L)$ zeros to create a B-byte string K_0 (i.e., $K_0 = H(K)$ ‖ 00 … 00). Go to step 4
Step 3	If the length of $K < B$: append zeros to the end of K to create a B-byte string K_0 (e.g., if K is 20 bytes in length and $B = 64$, then K will be appended with 44 zero bytes 0×00)
Step 4	XOR K_0 with ipad to produce a B-byte string: $K_0 \oplus ipad$
Step 5	Append the stream of data *text* to the string resulting from step 4: $(K_0 \oplus ipad)$ ‖ *text*
Step 6	Apply H to the stream generated in step 5: $H((K_0 \oplus ipad)$ ‖ *text*)
Step 7	XOR K_0 with opad: $K_0 \oplus ipad$
Step 8	Append the result from step 6 to step 7: $(K_0 \oplus opad)$ ‖ $H((K_0 \oplus ipad$ ‖ *text*)
Step 9	Apply H to the result from step 8: $H((K_0 \oplus opad)$ ‖ $H((K_0 \oplus ipad$ ‖ *text*))
Step 10	Select the leftmost t bytes of the result of step 9 as the MAC

by a recognized certificate authority. The browser can then validate this certificate by consulting a certificate authority.

7.7.1   X.509 Certificates

The *de facto* standard format used for digital certificates is X.509, currently at version 2. These certificates are digitally signed using the private key of the issuing CA. The following is the format of an X.509 certificate:

Certificate
    Version
    Serial Number
    Certificate Signature Algorithm
        Certificate Signature Algorithm ID
        Certificate Signature Algorithm Parameters
    Issuer
    Validity Period
        Not Before
        Not After
    Subject

> Subject Public Key Info
> > Subject Public Key Algorithm
> > Subject Public Key Parameters
> > Subject Public Key
> Issue Unique ID (optional)
> Subject Unique ID (optional)
> Extensions (optional)
> Issuer Signature
> > Certificate Signature Algorithm
> > Certificate Signature Parameters
> > Certificate Signature Value

The following is a short description of each of the fields:

- Version: version number
- Serial Number: unique identifier for each certificate generated by issuer
- Certificate Signature Algorithm
  - Algorithm Identifier ID: algorithm used to sign certificate
  - Parameters: should not be used
- Issuer Name: name of issuer (X.500 "distinguished name")
- Validity Period
  - Not Before: time
  - Not After: time
- Subject: name of subject (X.500 "distinguished name")
- Subject Public Key Info
  - Subject Public Key Algorithm: subject's signature algorithm
  - Subject Public Key Parameters: parameters applicable to subject public key
  - Subject Public Key: subject's public key
- Issuer Unique Identifier (optional): additional information about the subject
- Subject Unique Identifier (optional): additional information about the issuer
- Extensions (optional)
- Issuer Signature
  - Certificate Signature Algorithm: algorithm used for this signature
  - Certificate Signature Parameters: should not be used
  - Certificate Signature Value: encrypted signature

7.7.2 Certification Authority and Certification Path

A trusted agency that signs its certificates with its private key and then lets other parties verify the certificates by the usage of the corresponding public key is known as the Certification Authority (CA). The CA is sometimes also known as the Trusted Third Party (TTP) and should be a party that is trusted by both communicating parties.

Because two communicating parties may not always have direct access to the same CA, the verification of a certificate may need to involve a sequence of CAs. The CA sequence constitutes a CA path or chain. CAs and CA paths will be discussed further in Chapter 9 in sections 9.2 and 9.3 on PKI and FPKI technologies.

A digital certificate can be offered by a CA in the form of a software tool that a user can install in an application such as a browser. Once installed, the digital certificate identifies the user to Web sites equipped to automatically check and verify the certificate.

7.7.2.1 Common Use

Certificates are typically used by receiving parties to convey public keys to sending clients who will then use them to encrypt messages for secure transport. Public keys are used in integrated security technologies such as IPSec and SSL and in security architectures such as PKI and FPKI. See Chapter 8 (Section 8.2) and Chapter 9 (Sections 9.2 and 9.3) for descriptions of these technologies.

7.8 IEEE 802.11

Wireless networking and connectivity to a base network has been exploding in demand since portables first appeared. One technology that has become extremely popular recently is the Wireless Fidelity (Wi-Fi) wireless LAN (WLAN) defined in the IEEE 802.11 family of standards. Brief descriptions of two network security technologies that are part of the 802.11 definitions are given in the following subsections.

These WLAN security technologies as well as other WLAN topics will be described in greater detail as an overall WLAN network security architecture in Chapter 10.

7.8.1 WEP

Wired Equivalent Privacy (WEP) is IEEE 802.11's optional encryption standard implemented in the MAC Layer that most radio network interface cards (NICs) and Access Points (APs) vendors support (see Chapter 10, Section 10.1.1.2, for a description of APs). The sending station encrypts the payload (frame body and CRC) of each 802.11 frame before transmission using the RC4 stream cipher (see Chapter 2). The receiving station, also an Access Point or a radio NIC on a client station (e.g., a laptop), performs decryption upon arrival of the frame. Note that 802.11 WEP only

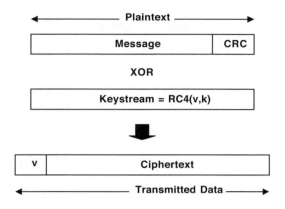

Figure 7.12 WEP encryption.

encrypts data between 802.11 stations. Once the frame enters the wired side of the network, WEP no longer applies.

7.8.1.1 WEP Encryption and Decryption Process

WEP is part of the system security of 802.11, and its goals are to provide confidentiality and data integrity and to protect access to the network infrastructure by rejecting all non-WEP packets.

WEP uses a secret key shared between the communicators. Some versions use the 40-bit key that was originally used to formulate the standard, whereas other newer versions use a 128-bit (104 in reality) key.

The encryption and decryption process is shown in Figure 7.12 and the resulting data to be transmitted is a WEP frame:

1. The data frame is checksummed (using the CRC-32 algorithm) to obtain c(M), where M is the message. M and c(M) are concatenated to get the plaintext P = (M, c(M)).
2. P is encrypted using the RC4 algorithm. This generates a keystream as a function of the initialization vector (IV) v and the secret key k, which is notated as RC4 (v, k). The cipher text results from applying the XOR function to the plaintext and the keystream. The cipher text and the IV are then transmitted via radio.

Decryption is simply the reverse of encryption.

WEP will be further discussed in Chapter 10 as part of the WLAN description.

7.8.2 802.11i

802.11i is a new security standard being developed by the IEEE Taskgroup i (TGi). It addresses the weaknesses of WEP-based wireless security. It has been known that scripting tools exist that can be used to take advantage of weaknesses in the WEP key algorithm to successfully attack a network and discover the WEP key. The Wi-Fi industry and IEEE have been actively working on solutions to tackle this problem through the TGi working group. Substantial components of the 802.11i standard have already been released or announced and products are beginning to appear in the market. Chapter 10 will provide more detailed description on 802.11i and other WLAN security topics.

7.8.2.1 Common Use

802.11 security technologies are key components in WLAN applications.

7.9 SUMMARY

CHAP is a popular enhanced authentication and authorization technology used in remote access and depends on basic technologies such as DES and MD5. Kerberos is a three-party authentication and authorization mode commonly used in SSO architectures.

Another authorization technology, the token card, uses the authentication algorithms defined in ISAKMP and OAKLEY: DSS, RSA, as well as other techniques such as time-variant passwords and challenge and response exchanges.

The enhanced authentication technology EAP is a PPP authentication extension and its framework is used in 802.11 wireless LANs. The EAP specification does not specify any particular encryption authentication protocol but supports most of the common ones such as MD5, DES, and SHA-1. MPPE is also based on PPP but is very different from EAP in that it is a tunneling VPN that utilizes RC4 to support the transfer of encrypted packets over PPP links.

ISAKMP and OAKLEY are key-management technologies, and IKE, the key-management technology used in many integrated VPN technologies such as IPSec as well as network security architectures, uses parts of ISAKMP and OAKLEY in its definitions including the use of the Diffie–Hellman algorithm for key exchange.

Another key-management technology is SKIP, which is based on the Diffie–Hellman algorithm, works over IP, and has less overhead for connectionless UDP as it saves session connection time.

STS is a three-phase Diffie–Hellman key-exchange algorithm.

Non-repudiation and message integrity technologies include the DSA, RSA, and ECDSA digital signature algorithms defined by DSS and MACs that are based on authentication algorithms used to compute MAC values. MACs, in turn, are used in authentication technologies such as AH and ESP.

Digital certificate is an enhanced authentication technology, and X.509 is the standard format used for certificates.

WEP is one of the confidentiality technologies used in earlier stages of WLAN. It uses RC4 as the cryptographic algorithm. 802.11i is an emerging security standard for WLAN.

Bibliography

1. IETF RFC 1994 (obsoletes RFC 1334) — PPP Challenge Handshake Authentication Protocol (CHAP), W. Simpson, August 1996.
2. IETF RFC 2409: The Internet Key Exchange (IKE), D. Harkins and D. Carrel, November 1998.
3. Understanding IKEv2: Tutorial, and rationale for decisions, IPSEC Working Group Internet-draft, Radia Perlman, February 2003.
4. IETF RFC 1825: Security Architecture for the Internet Protocol, R. Atkinson, August 1995.
5. IETF RFC 1510: The Kerberos Network Authentication Service (Version 5), John Kohl and B. Clifford Neuman, September 1993.
6. IETF Internet Draft: Token Card Extensions for ISAKMP/OAKLEY, J. O'Hara and M. Rosselli, November 1997.
7. FIPS PUB 186-2: Digital Signature Standard (DSS), U.S. Department of Commerce/National Institute of Standards and Technology, January 2000.
8. IETF RFC 2408: Internet Security Association and Key Management Protocol (ISAKMP), D. Maughan, M. Schertler, M. Schneider, and J. Turner, November 1998.
9. A method for obtaining digital signatures and public-key cryptosystems, R. Rivest, A. Shamir, and L. Adleman, *Communications of the ACM* 21, 1978.
10. FIPS PUB 198: The Keyed-Hash Message Authentication Code (HMAC), March 6, 2002.
11. IETF RFC 2412: The OAKLEY Key Determination Protocol, H. Orman, November 1998.
12. Security Association and Key Management — The ISAKMP and OAKLEY protocols seminar work, Robert Neumann, January 28, 2003.
13. Saadat Malik, *Network Security Principles and Practices,* Cisco Press, 2003.
14. IETF RFC 2356: Sun's SKIP Firewall Traversal for Mobile IP, G. Montenegro and V. Gupta, June 1998.
15. SKIP Security, IBM Document.
16. 802.11 WEP: Concepts and Vulnerability, J. Geier, Wi-Fi Planet Tutorial.
17. IETF RFC 2284: PPP Extensible Authentication Protocol (EAP), L. Blunk and J. Vollbrecht, March 1998.
18. Simple Key-Management for Internet Protocols (SKIP), Ashar Aziz, Tom Markson, and Hemma Prafullchandra.
19. IETF RFC 3078: Microsoft Point-To-Point Encryption (MPPE) Protocol, G. Pall and G. Zorn, March 2001.

8

INTEGRATED TECHNOLOGIES

In this chapter, we examine a number of integrated network security technologies. In the context of the network security framework formulated in Chapter 1, an integrated technology is defined in terms of one or more basic and enhanced security technologies and possibly some others that are relevant. They are relatively complex technologies that either have been designed or have evolved to support multiple network security functional elements.

The following classes of integrated technologies are discussed:

- Single-sign-on (SSO) technologies
- Higher-layer virtual private networks (VPNs)
- Firewalls

SSO technologies are defined primarily for streamlining the authentication and authorization operations required during connection establishment.

Higher-layer VPNs expand the fundamental traffic separation capabilities found in Layer 2 VPNs and the basic and enhanced tunneling protocols discussed in Chapter 5 and Chapter 6 so as to provide enhanced security capabilities. The term VPN has been widely used in the industry to refer to all the technologies that can be used to separate traffic based on connection IDs over a shared network. In this context, VPNs will include such Layer 2 VPNs as Frame Relay (FR) and ATM permanent virtual circuits (PVCs) and switched virtual circuits (SVCs), Multi-Protocol Label Switching (MPLS) VPNs, Ethernet VLANs, etc., tunneling protocols such as Generic Routing Encapsulation (GRE), L2TPv3, Extensible Authentication Protocol

Table 8.1 Typical Deployment of VPN Technologies

Typical Deployment	VPNs
Service provider defined	SVCs and PVCs
	ATM SVCs and PVCs
	MPLS connections
Client workstation-based	PPTP tunnels
	IPSec tunnels
	L2TPv3 tunnels
Client application-based	SSL
	TLS

(EAP), and Microsoft Point-to-Point Encryption (MPPE), etc., and integrated technologies such as IP Security (IPSec), Secure Sockets Layer (SSL), etc. All these technologies can be deployed to support varying secure enterprise transport of traffic over insecure, shared network infrastructures.

However, it is important to note that most VPN technologies were initially defined with somewhat different objectives and operating environments in mind. As a result, a particular VPN technology might be more suited for one situation than another. For example, MPLS has become an increasingly popular VPN technology with transport-service providers over other VPN technologies such as Point-to-Point Tunneling Protocol (PPTP). Table 8.1 shows a possible view of the typical zones of deployment for a number of the most commonly used VPNs technologies. It follows that many VPNs also need to effectively interwork together in some fashion to achieve end-to-end secure connectivity.

A firewall typically refers to a set of related hardware (e.g., a router, server, or special-purpose equipment) and software programs (e.g., Cisco's PIX firewall and Checkpoint's firewall products) that makes use of many of the basic and enhanced network security technologies described in the previous chapters.

8.1 SSO TECHNOLOGIES

To help solve the problems of juggling multiple userIDs, passwords, and log-on procedures for each user in a client/server (C/S) environment without compromising network security, many large companies maintain a single security database (which itself can be physically distributed or replicated) for distinct applications and access mechanisms, and use single-sign-on (SSO) mechanisms to streamline their access networks. SSO deals with userID and password pains by eliminating the need for users to remember the myriad of userIDs and passwords beyond their initial network log-in. SSO securely stores the userIDs and passwords that each user needs and automatically retrieves them for the user when required. This solves the problem associated with users having to remember and key in different credentials, sometimes during the same session. Figure 8.1 shows a high-level view of a typical SSO implementation.

In Figure 8.1, the user typically connects to the directory server for the initial log-in process, which performs the necessary authentication and authorization. Then the SSO takes over and, using the security capabilities implemented in it, controls the access to any application and data that the user might want to access.

There are many SSO systems defined and deployed by different vendors. Unfortunately, they are invariably based on proprietary implementations and, although efforts are being undertaken to introduce "openness" into SSO, interoperability among products from different vendors is not yet practical. The following text describes a number of these efforts.

8.1.1   The Open Group Security Forum (OGSF) SSO Model

This forum endorses consolidated user-administration systems that achieve openness by adhering to the metadirectory SSO model based on the Lightweight Directory Access Protocol (LDAP). OGSF's objective is to produce Open Group Product Standards for LDAP by developing LDAP profiles in The Open Group's Directory Interoperability Forum.

The following two diagrams, Figure 8.2 and Figure 8.3, illustrate the legacy or traditional approach to user sign-ons to multiple systems versus the OGSF's SSO approach.

In the legacy approach shown in Figure 8.2, the multiple systems act as independent domains, in the sense that an end user has to be identified and authenticated independently to each of the domains with which the user wishes to interact. The end user interacts initially with a primary domain to establish a session with it, by supplying a required set of user credentials applicable to the domain, for example, a username and password. From this primary domain session shell, the user is able to invoke the services of the other domains, such as platforms or applications.

To invoke the services of a secondary domain, an end user is required to perform a secondary domain sign-on. This requires the end user to supply a further set of user credentials applicable to that domain. Subsequently, the user has to conduct a separate sign-on dialogue with each secondary domain that he or she needs to use.

In the single-sign-on approach shown in Figure 8.3, the system collects from the user, as part of the primary domain sign-on procedure, all the identification and credential information necessary to support authentication to each of the secondary domains that he or she may potentially

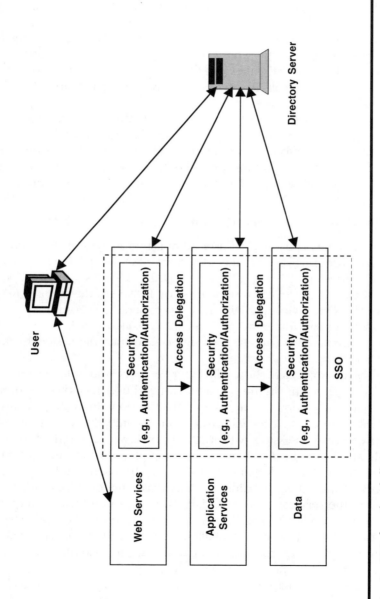

Figure 8.1 An SSO functional diagram.

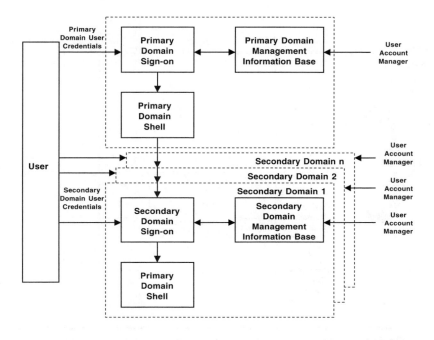

Figure 8.2   The legacy approach to user sign-on to multiple systems.

require to interact with. The information supplied by the user is then used by SSO within the primary domain to support the authentication of the end user to each of the secondary domains.

8.1.1.1   Common Use

SSOs are deployed to control and streamline log-ins to network services and applications, including remote access environments. In particular, the OGSF's SSO model is intended to achieve interoperability in LDAP implementations.

8.1.2   Service Selection Gateways (SSGs)

SSGs (such as Cisco's) typically provide a Web interface to present a service list from which the subscriber can select one or more services to connect to. Various connection features are implemented by SSG and controlled by attributes stored in the subscriber or service profiles. The following are some of the key potential features:

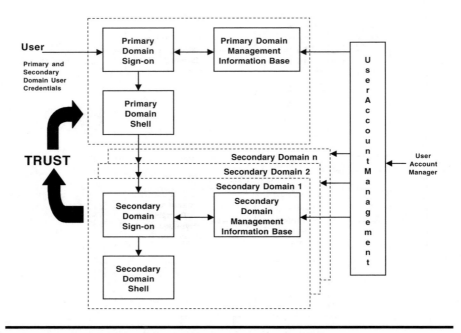

Figure 8.3   The SSO approach to user sign-on to multiple services.

- Service selection and disconnect
- Service authentication and authorization, including a choice of algorithms
- Automatic connections
- Subscriber session identifications
- Service status
- Mutually exclusive service selection

8.1.2.1   Common Use

SSGs are typically deployed to control and streamline log-ins to network and systems resources.

8.1.3   The Generic Security Service Application Program Interface (GSS-API)

This is a standard programming interface defining a set of generic functions that can be used to secure distributed applications operating in an SSO model.

The GSS-API functions enable applications in a distributed network environment to use the following security services on the network:

- Authentication — The application can verify the identity of a user or service. By using authentication, it can be guaranteed a distributed application is talking to its authentic counterpart (that is, not to an imposter).
- Integrity — The application can detect message tampering or corruption when it receives the message.
- Confidentiality — A message can be encrypted to render it unintelligible to eavesdroppers during transmission.

GSS-API has two primary design goals that are fundamental to its operation:

- Security mechanism independence
- Transport protocol independence

Because it is an open standard, GSS-API has been designed to be generic so that as security and network technologies evolve, the API does not have to change. GSS-API supports a wide range of underlying security mechanisms and technologies.

A security mechanism is a method of providing security (such as Kerberos or public-key encryption). It is not only the cryptographic technology used but also the syntax and semantics of the data that the technology employs. An application secured using the GSS-API standard may use one or more security mechanisms.

GSS-API can be used in a broad range of network environments (for example, TCP/IP, SNA, and DECnet). The standard was not designed to provide a transport mechanism. Rather, the design provides security over an arbitrary network transport. The transport must be provided by the application. The communications protocol can be an interprocess communications path or a series of networks.

GSS-API functions return information to the application, which then sends the information across the communications protocol in use. The other side of the distributed application passes the information to the GSS-API library.

For a developer securing an application using the GSS-API standard, these design goals of mechanism and transport independence provide a consistent interface that is independent of the underlying hardware and software platform — a onetime programming investment. The investment in modifications to secure an application remains constant even as the technologies evolve.

8.1.3.1 Common Use

GSS-API is typically included as a software library in Service Development Kits (SDKs) to support the programming of security features for applications operating in an SSO model.

8.2 HIGHER-LAYER VPNS

In Chapter 5, basic VPN technologies such as FR and ATM PVCs and SVCs and some basic tunneling protocols such as PPP and PPPoE were discussed. Here, newer generations of VPN technologies that allow service providers to offer a more economical way of supporting either partially or fully meshed connectivity with increased levels of network security are presented. These VPN technologies map to higher layers in the OSI Reference Model and make use of many of the basic security technologies described in previous chapters.

However, before these newer VPNs allow organizations to confidently build cost-effective private networks over insecure and shared infrastructures, the VPN service providers must be able to address diverse requirements, challenges, and issues. These challenges include scalability, flexibility, reliability, and manageability as network requirements have expanded to provide support for the necessary convergence of different traffic types that include legacy data, voice, multimedia, etc. One example of such requirements is end-to-end classes of service (COS) and the necessary underlying quality-of-service (QoS) implementations.

More important, as VPNs become an integral part of the enterprise networking landscape, different levels of network security are needed for different applications and environments, and potential security technologies such as tunneling, encryption, traffic separation, packet authentication, user authentication, and access control, in turn, become an integral part of VPNs.

In short, there is an urgent need to provide, not just basic Layer 2 VPNs but also VPNs with much more stringent security and other requirements. Some of these key VPN technologies are described in the following subsections.

Analogous to Layer 2 VPNs, it is useful to consider a distinction between a "Layer x VPN service" and a "VPN service that supports Layer x traffic." A "Layer x VPN service," or simply a "Layer x VPN," refers to a VPN that is built on top of a Layer x network. Some of these VPNs can support either Layer 2 or higher-layer traffic only, or support both Layer 2 and higher-layer traffic. For example, Any Transport over MPLS (AToM) supports the transporting of both Layer 2 and Layer 3 traffic using encapsulation.

In this chapter, for convenience, the term VPN will be taken to mean a higher-layer VPN as opposed to a Layer 2 VPN (which was described in Chapter 5).

When considering the underlying transport network, it is also helpful to consider a distinction between an IP network and an IP-based network: An IP network provides an IP layer, possibly built over some other end-to-end transport network, whereas an IP-based network is built to transport only IP traffic (e.g., IP router-based, IP over SONET, etc.) — other traffic types can be supported using encapsulation.

8.2.1 The IPSec Protocol

IP Security (IPSec) is defined as a suite of protocols used to secure traffic at the network layer through the use of cryptographic technologies.

8.2.1.1 IPSec Overview

IPSec is designed to support interoperable, high-quality, cryptographically based security communication for IPv4 and IPv6 applications. IPSec provides security services at the IP layer by enabling a system to select the required security protocols, determine the algorithms to use for the services, and put in place any cryptographic keys required to provide the requested services. IPSec can be used to protect one or more paths between a pair of hosts, between a pair of security gateways, or between a security gateway and a host. (The term security gateway is used throughout IPSec documents to refer to an intermediate system that implements the IPSec protocols. For example, a router or firewall implementing IPSec is a security gateway.)

The set of security services that IPSec can provide includes access control, connectionless integrity, data origin authentication, rejection of replayed packets (a form of partial sequence integrity), confidentiality (encryption), and limited traffic flow confidentiality. Because these services are provided at the IP layer, they can be used by any higher-layer protocol, e.g., TCP, UDP, ICMP, BGP, etc.

IPSec supports the negotiation of IP compression, motivated in part by the observation that when encryption is employed within IPSec, it prevents effective compression by lower protocol layers.

IPSec uses two protocols to provide traffic authentication — Authentication Header (AH) and Encapsulating Security Payload (ESP) (basic technologies described in Chapter 3 and Chapter 5).

- The IP AH provides connectionless integrity, data origin authentication, and an optional antireplay service.
- The ESP protocol may provide confidentiality (encryption) and limited traffic flow confidentiality. It also may provide connectionless integrity, data origin authentication, and an antireplay service. (One set of these security services must be applied whenever ESP is invoked.)
- Both AH and ESP are vehicles for access control, based on the distribution of cryptographic keys and the management of traffic flows relative to these security protocols.

These protocols may be applied alone or in combination with each other to provide a desired set of security services in IPv4 and IPv6. Each protocol supports two modes of use: transport mode and tunnel mode. In the transport mode the protocols provide protection primarily for upper-layer protocols; in the tunnel mode, the protocols are applied to tunneled IP packets.

IPSec allows the user (or system administrator) to control the granularity at which a security service is offered. For example, one can create a single encrypted tunnel to carry all the traffic between two security gateways or a separate encrypted tunnel can be created for each TCP connection between each pair of hosts communicating across these gateways. IPSec management must incorporate facilities for specifying:

- Which security services to use and in what combinations
- The granularity at which a given security protection should be applied
- The algorithms used to effect cryptographic-based security

Because these security services, in turn, use shared secret values (cryptographic keys) for authentication and integrity and encryption services, IPSec depends on a separate set of mechanisms for putting these keys in place, i.e., key distribution and management. IPSec requires support for both manual and automatic distribution of keys. IPSec specifies IKE as the public-key-based approach for automatic key management, but other automated key-distribution techniques *may* be used instead. For example, Key Distribution Center (KDC)-based systems such as Kerberos, and other public-key management systems such as SKIP could be employed.

8.2.1.2   IPSec-Based VPNs

VPNs based on IPSec have been widely deployed and typically offer very flexible, industry-standard choices as to how protections of traffic are implemented, beginning with the following:

- Tunneling can be achieved with AH or ESP.
- Encryption, if used, can be achieved with 40-bit or 128-bit RC4, 56-bit Data Encryption Standard (DES), 112- or 168-bit 3DES, 128-, 192-, or 256-bit AES.
- Authorization of users can be based on userID and password (e.g., RADIUS), userID and token and personal IDs (such as RSA SecurID cards), or some predefined shared key.
- Data integrity and non-repudiation can be achieved using X.509 Digital Certificates or hashed message authentication code (HMAC).

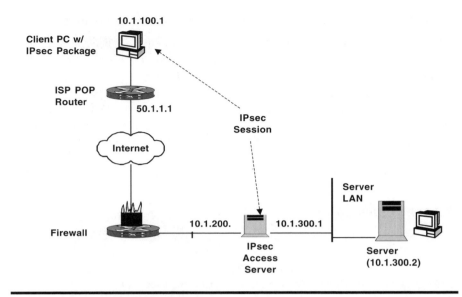

Figure 8.4   An IPSec VPN example.

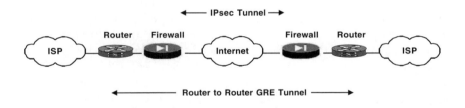

Figure 8.5   GRE over an IPSec tunnel.

Figure 8.4 shows an example of a remote access arrangement based on an IPSec VPN. An IPSec session is established between a client PC running an IPSec software package and a destination IPSec server or gateway in a secure LAN. The client PC connects through an ISP access network, passes through the destination network's firewall to the IPSec server or gateway, which in this case is behind the firewall and is located in the same LAN as the destination server or host.

In this case, the IPSec VPN is between the client PC and the IPSec server or gateway and will likely use the tunnel mode. In contrast, an end-to-end IPSec VPN between two applications or hosts will likely use the transport mode.

8.2.1.3 Interworking of IPSec and Other Tunneling Protocols

IPSec interworks with a number of other tunneling protocols; this adds to its application flexibility. For example, normal IPSec configurations cannot transfer routing protocols, such as Enhanced Interior Gateway Routing Protocol (EIGRP) and Open Shortest Path First (OSPF), or non-IP traffic such as IPX and Appletalk. Figure 8.5 shows that a GRE VPN (see Chapter 5) can be established over an IPSec tunnel so that routing OSPF-based routing traffic can be passed over IPSec VPNs between Cisco's PIX firewalls.

IPSec also works with some other tunneling protocols, including L2TP.

8.2.1.4 Common Use

IPSec works at the network layer and is supported on various operating system platforms, and IPSec VPNs are commonly used in implementations for remote access to corporate networks. IPSec is also being used in the emerging wireless LAN (WLAN) environments (see Chapter 10).

8.2.2 The SSL Standard

SSL is a mechanism for establishing a secure communication path between a client and a server. SSL was originally developed by Netscape Communications to permit secure access by a browser to a Web server over the insecure Internet. SSL has since become the *de facto* standard for establishing secure Internet connections for E-commerce, as well as other applications that depend on the transmission of information with confidentiality, integrity, and authentication. The version that is commonly deployed at the present time is SSLv3, which supports improved security algorithms compared with the previous versions.

8.2.2.1 SSL Overview

The primary goal of the SSL Protocol is, of course, to provide privacy and reliability between two communicating applications. SSL is considered to reside on top of TCP at the transport layer in the OSI Reference Model and interfaces to a user application through an SSL socket as part of an SSL connection establishment. SSL is made up of three protocols, and each SSL transaction consists of two distinct and typically sequential parts. The two main protocols are:

■ The SSL Handshake Protocol
■ The SSL Record Protocol

The third protocol is the Alert Protocol and is used to indicate questionable conditions.

At the lowest level, layered on top of a reliable transport protocol (e.g., TCP), is the SSL Record Protocol. The SSL Record Protocol is used for encapsulation of various higher-level protocols. One such encapsulated protocol is the SSL Handshake Protocol, which allows the server and client to authenticate each other and to negotiate an encryption algorithm and cryptographic keys before the application protocol transmits or receives its first byte of data. One advantage of SSL is that it is application protocol independent. A higher-level protocol can layer on top of the SSL Protocol transparently.

The SSL protocol provides connection security that has three basic properties:

- The connection is private — encryption is used after an initial handshake to define a secret key. Symmetric cryptography is used for data encryption (e.g., DES, RC4, etc.).
- The peer's identity can be authenticated using asymmetric (or public-key) cryptography (e.g., RSA, DSS, etc.).
- The connection is reliable — message transport includes a message integrity check using a keyed message authentication code (MAC). Secure hash functions (e.g., SHA, MD5, etc.) are used for MAC computations.

The Handshake Protocol demonstrates the key communicating exchanges between the client and the server.

8.2.2.1.1 The Record Protocol

The encryption for all messaging in SSL is handled in the Record Protocol. This protocol provides a common format to frame all Alert, ChangeCipherSpec, Handshake, and application protocol messages.

The SSL Record Protocol receives uninterpreted data from higher layers in nonempty blocks of arbitrary size. The Record Protocol fragments the information blocks into SSL plaintext records of 2^{14} bytes or less. Client message boundaries are not preserved in the record layer (i.e., multiple client messages may be coalesced into a single SSL plaintext record).

Once the handshake is complete, the two parties have shared secrets that are used to encrypt records and compute keyed MACs on their contents. The techniques used to perform the encryption and MAC operations are defined by the Cipher Spec. The encryption and MAC functions translate an SSL-compressed structure into an SSL ciphertext. The decryption functions reverse the process. Transmissions also include a sequence number so that missing, altered, or extra messages are detectable.

8.2.2.1.2 The Handshake Protocol

When an SSL client and server first start communicating, they agree on a protocol version, select cryptographic algorithms, optionally authenticate each other, and use public-key encryption techniques to generate shared secrets. These processes are performed in the Handshake Protocol, which is summarized in the following text.

The client sends a `client hello` message to which the server must respond with a `server hello` message, else a fatal error will occur and the connection will fail. The `client hello` and `server hello` are used to establish security enhancement capabilities between client and server. The `client hello` and `server hello` establish the following attributes: protocol version, session ID, cipher suite, and compression method. Additionally, two random values are generated and exchanged: ClientHello.random and ServerHello.random.

Following the hello messages, the server will send its certificate, if it is to be authenticated. Additionally, a `server key exchange` message may be sent, if it is required (e.g., if the server has no certificate, or if its certificate is for signing only). If the server is authenticated, it may request a certificate from the client, if that is appropriate to the cipher suite selected.

Now the server will send the `server hello done` message, indicating that the hello-message phase of the handshake is complete. The server will then wait for a client response.

If the server has sent a `certificate request` message, the client must send either the `certificate message` or a `no certificate` alert. The `client key exchange` message is now sent, and the content of that message will depend on the public-key algorithm selected between the `client hello` and the `server hello`. If the client has sent a certificate with signing ability, a digitally signed `certificate verify` message is sent to explicitly verify the certificate.

At this point, a `change cipher spec` message is sent by the client, and the client copies the pending Cipher Spec into the current Cipher Spec. The client then immediately sends the finished message under the new algorithms, keys, and secrets. In response, the server will send its own `change cipher spec` message, transfer the pending Cipher Spec to the current Cipher Spec, and send its `Finished` message under the new Cipher Spec. At this point, the handshake is complete and the client and server may begin to exchange application-layer data. See the flowchart in Figure 8.6.

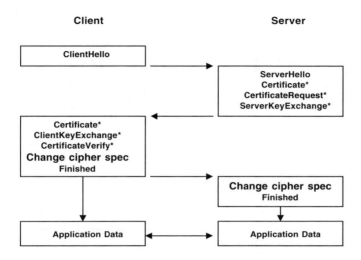

Client   **Server**

ClientHello

ServerHello
Certificate*
CertificateRequest*
ServerKeyExchange*

Certificate*
ClientKeyExchange*
CertificateVerify*
Change cipher spec
Finished

Change cipher spec
Finished

Application Data ◄───► Application Data

* Indicates optional or situation-dependent
messages that are not always sent

Figure 8.6   The Handshake Protocol.

When the client and server decide to resume a previous session or duplicate an existing session (instead of negotiating new security parameters), the message flow is as described in the following text.

The client sends a `client hello` using the session ID of the session to be resumed. The server then checks its session cache for a match. If a match is found, and the server is willing to reestablish the connection under the specified session state, it will send a `server hello` with the same session ID value. At this point, both client and server must send `change cipher spec` messages and proceed directly to finished messages. Once the reestablishment is complete, the client and server may begin to exchange application-layer data. See the flowchart in Figure 8.7. If a session ID match is not found, the server generates a new session ID, and the SSL client and server perform a full handshake.

8.2.2.1.3 The Alert Protocol

The Alert Protocol handles any questionable packets. If either the server or client detects an error, it sends an alert containing the error. There are three types of alert messages: warning, critical, and fatal. Based on the alert message received, the session can be restricted (warning, critical) or terminated (fatal).

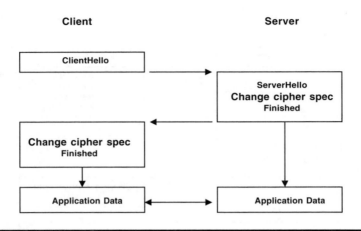

Figure 8.7   Reestablishment of handshake.

8.2.2.1.4   Key SSL Characteristics

The following are key characteristics of the SSL implementation:

- The digital signature generated by hashing a message with a public key is sent over to the other side and compared against the locally generated hashed message for a match.
- The client generally authenticates the server, and the server can optionally authenticate the client.
- The Handshake Protocol is defined as follows: the client sends ClientHello, server sends ServerHello, server sends Certificate, client sends ClientKeyExchange, client sends CertificateVerify, both send ChangeCipherSpec, and both send Finished.
- The Record Protocol is defined for bulk data transfer.
- The Alert Protocol handles questionable packets.
- Server processing bottleneck: Public-key cryptographic operation, encryption of SSL records, and MAC signature operations are all computation-intensive operations. To attain performance improvement, accelerators that are connected to switches are commonly deployed for such applications as content distribution. These are generally known as SSL accelerators. Physically external SSL accelerators are sometimes called SSL termination devices.
- SSL modes: SSL can work in transparent and nontransparent (the client address is not sent over to the server but cookies can be used to return client information) modes. Nontransparent mode is more flexible and more scalable.
- The use of SSL accelerators or other SSL optimization techniques is especially important in data centers.

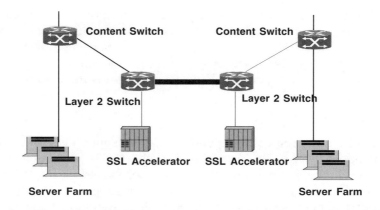

Figure 8.8 Nontransparent Mode Design Architecture.

8.2.2.2 SSL Accelerators

Server accelerators are software or hardware devices that are commonly used to off-load Web servers on such CPU-intensive operations as special query intercept and processing, TCP sessions setup and teardowns, and state maintenance. They can also be used to off-load SSL-related operations. The SSL accelerator serves as a central point for negotiating handshakes and also for encrypting and decrypting data. This allows the servers to process other Hypertext Transfer Protocol (HTTP) processes unrelated to SSL and remove the load off the Web server. In most cases the SSL accelerator is typically connected to a content switch in the path between the client and the server. This external accelerator is commonly referred to as an SSL termination device. Other SSL accelerator modules can be integrated into the content switch for the termination of SSL traffic. Figure 8.8 shows a sample network configuration where two SSL termination devices (accelerators) are being used to off-load SSL processing from server farms.

The most recommended SSL design to deploy is called *nontransparent mode*, which is also referred to as a "nontransparent proxy mode" accelerator as opposed to a "transparent proxy mode" accelerator. The reason why such an SSL accelerator is called nontransparent is that the source addresses of all the packets decrypted by the SSL accelerator have the source address of that SSL accelerator and the client source addresses do not get to the server at all. From the server perspective, the request has come from the SSL accelerator. Some customers might have a problem with this setup because they usually track the client's source address on the server. Some SSL termination devices still have the ability to send the client's source address to a syslog server for tracking purposes. In addition, with cookies, it is still possible to gather granular information about client IP address information as cookies can track where the client has come from and gone to on a Web site, as well as other personal information (e.g., passwords, shopping lists, user preferences, etc.). Nontransparent mode SSL accelerators scale better and the deployment design is more secure.

8.2.2.2.1 Common Use

SSL is application-protocol independent, and a higher-level protocol can run on top of the SSL Protocol transparently. SSL is supported in most service-development environments and is incorporated as a standard feature in most of the commonly used Web-based programs. This is convenient for users because a separate, special client program is generally not necessary as is the case with some other equivalent security technologies.

8.2.3 The Transport Layer Security (TLS) Protocol

This is a protocol that ensures privacy between communicating applications and their users on the Internet. TLS has been defined to be the successor of SSL and is often described as being better than SSL. When a server and client communicate, TLS ensures that no third party may eavesdrop or tamper with any message.

Much of the TLS protocol specification is based on the SSL 3.0 Protocol Specification as published by Netscape. The differences between TLS 1.0 and SSL 3.0 are not dramatic, but they are significant enough that TLS 1.0 and SSL 3.0 do not interoperate. The TLS protocol does contain a mechanism that allows a TLS implementation to back down to SSL 3.0. The TLS Working Group, established in 1996, continues to work on the TLS protocol and related applications.

8.2.3.1 An Overview

Just as SSL, TLS is composed of two layers: the TLS Record Protocol and the TLS Handshake Protocol. The TLS Record Protocol provides connection security with an encryption method, such as DES. The TLS Record Protocol can also be used without encryption. The TLS Handshake Protocol allows the server and client to authenticate each other and to negotiate an encryption algorithm and cryptographic keys before data is exchanged.

The TLS Record Protocol provides connection security that has two basic properties:

■ The connection is private: Symmetric cryptography is used for data encryption (e.g., DES, RC4, etc.) The keys for this symmetric encryption are generated uniquely for each connection and are based on a secret negotiated by another protocol (such as the TLS Handshake Protocol). The Record Protocol can also be used without encryption.

■ The connection is reliable: Message transport includes a message integrity check using a keyed MAC. Secure hash functions (e.g., SHA, MD5, etc.) are used for MAC computations. The Record Protocol can operate without a MAC, but is generally only used in this mode while another protocol is using the Record Protocol as a transport for negotiating security parameters.

The TLS Record Protocol is used for encapsulation of various higher-level protocols. One such encapsulated protocol, the TLS Handshake Protocol, allows the server and client to authenticate each other and to negotiate an encryption algorithm and cryptographic keys before the application protocol transmits or receives its first byte of data. The TLS Handshake Protocol provides connection security that has three basic properties:

■ The peer's identity can be authenticated using asymmetric or public-key cryptography (e.g., RSA, DSS, etc.). This authentication can be made optional, but is generally required for at least one of the peers.
■ The negotiation of a shared secret is secure. The negotiated secret is unavailable to eavesdroppers, and the secret cannot be obtained for any authenticated connection, even by an attacker who can place himself in the middle of the connection.
■ The negotiation is reliable. No attacker can modify the negotiation communication without being detected by the parties to the communication.

One advantage of TLS is that it is application-protocol independent. Higher-level protocols can layer on top of the TLS protocol transparently. The TLS standard, however, does not specify how protocols are to add security with TLS; the decisions on how to initiate TLS handshaking and how to interpret the authentication certificates exchanged are left to the judgment of the designers and implementers of the protocols that run on top of TLS.

8.2.3.2 Backward Compatibility with SSL

For historical reasons and in order to avoid a profligate consumption of reserved port numbers, application protocols that are secured by TLS 1.0,

SSL 3.0, and SSL 2.0 all frequently share the same connection port: for example, the HTTPS protocol (HTTP secured by SSL or TLS) uses port 443 regardless of which security protocol it is using. Thus, some mechanism must be determined to distinguish and negotiate among the various protocols.

TLS version 1.0 and SSL 3.0 are very similar; thus, supporting both is easy. TLS clients who wish to negotiate with SSL 3.0 servers should send `client hello` messages using the SSL 3.0 record format and `client hello` structure, sending {3, 1} for the version field to show that they support TLS 1.0. If the server supports only SSL 3.0, it will respond with an SSL 3.0 `server hello`; if it supports TLS, it will respond with a TLS `server hello`. The negotiation then proceeds as appropriate for the negotiated protocol.

Similarly, a TLS server that wishes to interoperate with SSL 3.0 clients should accept SSL 3.0 `client hello` messages and respond with an SSL 3.0 `server hello`, if an SSL 3.0 `client hello`, is received that has a version field of {3, 0}, denoting that this client does not support TLS.

Whenever a client already knows the highest protocol known to a server (for example, when resuming a session), it should initiate the connection in that native protocol.

8.2.3.3 Common Use

Just like SSL, TLS is application-protocol independent, and a higher-level protocol can run on top of the TLS protocol transparently. It can conveniently add security on many protocols that run on top of TCP. Currently, TLS is widely used with HTTP, and the most recent browser versions all support TLS.

TLS is also used in the definitions of the WLAN security protocols TTLS and PEAP within the framework of IEEE 802.11x (see the following text).

8.2.4 The TTLS and PEAP Protocols

Tunneled Transport Layer Security (TTLS) and Protected Extensible Authentication Protocol (PEAP) are proposed security protocols that are defined to work within the framework of the broadbased IEEE 802.11 wireless LAN standard for authentication known as 802.1x. PEAP and TTLS each uses TLS to set up an end-to-end tunnel to transfer the user's credentials, such as a password, without having to use a certificate on the client.

TTLS and PEAP are almost identical but are proposed by different groups of industry companies and organizations. TTLS is also known as EAP-TTLS.

8.2.4.1 The TTLS Protocol

In TTLS, the TLS handshake may be mutual; or it may be one-way, in which case only the server is authenticated to the client. The secure connection established by the handshake may then be used to allow the server to authenticate the client with existing, widely deployed authentication infrastructures such as RADIUS. The authentication of the client may use EAP, or may use another authentication protocol such as PAP or CHAP (or MS-CHAP or MS-CHAPv2).

Thus, TTLS allows legacy password-based authentication protocols to be used against existing authentication databases while protecting the security of these legacy protocols against eavesdropping, man-in-the-middle, and other cryptographic attacks.

TTLS also allows a client and server to establish keying material for use in the data connection between the client and the access point. The keying material is established implicitly between the client and server based on the TLS handshake.

8.2.4.2 The PEAP Protocol

EAP, defined in RFC 2284, provides for support of multiple authentication methods. Whereas EAP was originally created for use with PPP, it has since been adopted for use with IEEE 802.1x.

Since its deployment, a number of weaknesses in EAP have become apparent. These include:

- Lack of protection of user identity or EAP negotiation
- No standardized mechanism for key exchange
- No built-in support for fragmentation and reassembly
- Lack of support for fast reconnect

By wrapping the EAP protocol within TLS, Protected EAP (PEAP) addresses these deficiencies. Any EAP method running within PEAP is provided with built-in support for key exchange, session resumption, and fragmentation and reassembly.

8.2.4.3 Common Use

TTLS and PEAP are both used in WLAN applications.

8.2.5 Comparison of Some VPN Technologies

Table 8.2 compares the key attributes of three very commonly used VPN technologies: L2TPv3, MPLS, and IPSec.

Table 8.2 A Comparison of VPN Technologies

Attribute	L2TPv3	MPLS	IPSec
Category in network security technology hierarchy	Basic	Basic	Integrated
Base infrastructure	PPP	ATM/IP	IP
Typical use	Normally deployed in service provider network	Normally deployed in service provider network	Normally used for local (off-network) traffic
Defined for building network-based Layer 3 VPNs (e.g., IP/FR)?	No	Yes	Yes
Defined for transport of Layer 2 traffic?	Yes	Yes	No
Security	IP address, session IDs, and security IDs are spoofable	ATM-like security using Label Distribution Protocol (LDP); not spoofable	Strong authentication and confidentiality
Speed of restoration	Slower (unless the underlying IP backbone is MPLS-enabled)	Faster (MPLS fast-rerouting allows SONET-like restoration speed)	Slower
Traffic engineering	No traffic engineering capability; relies on connectionless IP	Rich traffic management capabilities (e.g, mapping of DiffServ to CRLSP; explicit routes)	Rely on underlying layers
Protocol overhead	Higher (36 bytes per packet)	Lower (8 bytes per packet)	
Scalability	No – normally used for remote access	High – normally used in carrier's backbone	No – normally used for secure remote access to headquarters
Maturity (proven implementations; advanced features such as service interoperability)	Immature	Mature	Mature

8.2.6 IPSec versus SSL

IPSec and SSL appear to be competing technologies. The difference between SSL and IPSec is that IPSec works at the network layer and secures end-to-end network connections, whereas SSL works at the application layer and secures end-to-end application sessions. IPSec and SSL are both used to provide confidentiality of data and authentication, but they achieve these goals in significantly different ways.

SSL was originally designed by Netscape to secure (HTTP) traffic passing through Web browsers and is a session-layer protocol. Unlike IPSec, SSL is based on a C/S model and is typically used for host-to-host secure transport. Because IPSec works at the network layer, it can be used to secure subnet-to-subnet, network-to-network, or network-to-host communications. This also means that IPSec traffic can be routed as each IPSec packet has IP network addresses, whereas SSL traffic cannot.

Although many people see SSL technology as competing with IPSec, this view is not entirely accurate. In most cases, IPSec and SSL are used to solve different types of problems. Also, whereas IPSec-based connections normally require a substantially larger amount of planning and implementation time, SSL implementations are relatively quicker to deploy. In particular, whereas almost all browsers support SSL, special communication software packages are likely needed for the deployment of IPSec VPNs.

8.3 FIREWALLS

A firewall is a set of related hardware and software programs, deployed strategically between a company's private network and one or more unsecured networks (particularly including the Internet). A firewall functions to protect the resources of the private network from users on the outside (external) networks.

The firewall separates the protected, private network (the inside) from the unsecured networks (the outside) and makes sure that any malicious or unintentional harm will not be done to internal resources by external forces.

A firewall is considered essential in the following areas of network applications:

- Access from one or more external unsecured networks (e.g., the Internet) to applications within the private network
- Access by users within the private network to one or more external unsecured networks (including the Internet)
- Communication with business partners through an extranet
- Remote access to the intranet

The capabilities needed in the firewall for each of the applications can be somewhat different.

The firewall examines each network packet to determine whether and how to forward the packet towards its intended destination by processing it according to a set of predefined rules. Depending on the operating environment, a firewall can simply be installed on a client PC, an access router or, for maximum security, on a dedicated router server separate from the rest of the network.

8.3.1 Classification of Firewalls

Firewalls can usefully be classified into the following four basic types:

- Packet filters — The first line of defense in firewall protection, and the most basic, is the packet filter firewall. Packet filters examine incoming and outgoing packets and apply a fixed set of rules to the packets to determine whether they will be allowed to pass. The packet filter firewall is typically very fast because it does not examine the data in the packet. It simply examines the type of the packet along with the source and destination addresses, including URLs, domain names, etc., as well as the port combinations, and then it applies the filtering rules. For example, it is easy to filter out all the packets that are destined for port 80, which might normally be the port for a Web server. The network administrator may decide that port 80 is off limits except for some specific IP subnets, and a packet filter would suffice for this purpose.
- Circuit-level gateways — This type of firewall has also been called a "stateful inspection" firewall because packets are handled on a circuit or connection basis. In a circuit-level firewall, all connections are monitored, and only those connections that are found to be valid are allowed to pass through the firewall. This generally means that a client behind the firewall can initiate any type of session, but clients outside the firewall cannot see or connect to a machine protected by the firewall.
- Application layer gateways (ALGs) — The ALG firewall forces all client applications on workstations protected by the firewall to use the firewall itself as a gateway. The firewall then handles packets for each protocol differently. There are some disadvantages to using this type of firewall. Every client program needs to be set up to use a proxy, and not all can do so. Also, the firewall must have an ALG for each type of protocol that can be used. This can mean a delay in implementing new protocols if the firewall does not support it. And, last, application proxies can be quite slow. The distinct advantage is obviously that application proxy firewalls are considered to be very secure.

A typical ALG can provide proxy services for applications and protocols such as Telnet, FTP (File Transfer Protocol), HTTP, and SMTP (Simple Mail Transfer Protocol). Note that a separate proxy must be installed for each application-level service. With proxies, security policies can be much more powerful and flexible because all the information in packets can be used by administrators to write the rules that determine how packets are handled by the gateway. It is easy to audit just about everything that happens on the gateway. You can also strip computer names to hide internal systems and evaluate the contents of packets for appropriateness and security.

■ Network address translation (NAT) — Firewalls using NAT and/or port address translation (PAT) completely hide the network protected by the firewall by translating the outgoing packets to use different addresses. In most implementations there is a single, public IP address used for the entire network. PAT needs to be added to NAT to handle port conflicts. A disadvantage of NAT is that it cannot properly pass protocols containing IP address information in the data portion of the packet. See Chapter 6 for more descriptions of NAT and PAT, which are forms of basic non-repudiation technology.

Many firewalls are implemented as a combination of the above four types. Firewalls come as either router-based software or special-purpose devices such as Cisco's PIX series of firewall devices.

Major basic and enhanced network security technologies or tools that are commonly used to implement firewalls include the following:

■ Packet filtering technologies
■ Access lists, a basic authorization technology (see Chapter 4)
■ NAT and PAT, a basic non-repudiation technology (see Chapter 6)
■ Message integrity technologies, such as tunneling protocols

8.3.2 Common Use

Firewalls are used as a major component in Internet access, extranet connectivity, and Remote Access architectures (see Chapter 9).

8.4 SUMMARY

Several integrated network security technologies have been discussed in this chapter, which make use of basic and enhanced network security technologies.

The SSO technologies aim at easing the management of user access to various network and system resources. The industry is working towards some standard, interoperable SSO architectures, and many standard tools have become available. The OGSF SSO model uses the concept of domains in defining interoperable SSOs based on LDAP. SSG defines service selection gateways employing the concept of service profiles. GSS-API is a popular API, with security services supporting a variety of security mechanisms.

IPSec is a widely used VPN technology that uses AH and ESP as authentication algorithms, RC4, DES, 3DES, and AES as encryption and decryption algorithms, and IKE for key management. HMAC and digital certificates, in particular, are used for non-repudiation. IPSec has also become an integral part of WLAN architectures.

SSL and TLS are session-layer VPNs that use the secret-key (symmetric) cryptographic algorithms of RC4 and DES and also public keys for peer authentication, as well as MACs for message integrity. Both, especially TLS, are used in WLAN applications. TTLS (also called EAP-TTLS) and PEAP are also session-layer VPNs, and they use TLS to set up tunnels and work with 802.1x. The authentication protocol used in each case can be EAP, CHAP, or PAP.

Firewalls are generally classified into four types: packet filters, circuit-level gateways (stateful), application-layer gateways (ALGs), and address translation (NAT and PAT). An actual firewall deployment can be a combination of all four types.

BIBLIOGRAPHY

1. Cisco Subscriber Edge Services Manager (SESM) document, 2003.
2. Application Security SDK, Hewlett Packard document, 2003.
3. Wedgetail Communications JCSI® SSO Product Description, 2003.
4. Introduction to Single Sign-On by the Open Group Security Forum, March 20, 1998.
5. Deploying Scalable, Secure, Dynamic Virtual Private Networks, White Paper, NetScreen Technologies, May 2003.
6. IETF RFC 2743 (obsoletes 2078): Generic Security Service Application Program Interface, Version 2, Update 1, J. Linn, January 2000.
7. IETF Internet Draft: The SSL Protocol Version 3.0, March 1996.
8. IETF RFC 2401: Security Architecture for the Internet Protocol, S. Kent and R. Atkinson, November 1998.
9. Intranet and Extranet VPN Business Scenarios, Cisco Document, January 20, 2003.
10. Configuring a GRE Tunnel over IPSec with OSPF, Cisco Document, January 14, 2003.
11. IETF RFC 2246: The TLS Protocol Version 1.0, T. Dierks, C. Allen, January 1999.
12. IETF Internet Draft: EAP Tunneled TLS Authentication Protocol (EAP-TTLS), Paul Funk and Simon Blake-Wilson, February 2002.

13. Greg Bastien and Christian Abera Degu, *CCSP Cisco Secure PIX Firewall Advanced,* Cisco Press, 2003.
14. IETF Internet Draft: Protected EAP Protocol (PEAP), Andersson, S. Josefsson, Glen Zorn, Dan Simon, and Ashwin Palekar, February 23, 2002.

9

NETWORK SECURITY ARCHITECTURES

Network security architectures are considered to define standard or *de facto* network security architectural frameworks built on basic, enhanced, and integrated technologies as well as other necessary relevant network technologies. These architectures are intended to provide guidelines for implementing large-scale security systems within the architecture's defined domain. To be considered a network security architecture, a technology must typically:

- Define a suite of network security technologies that collectively implements a number of the five network security functional elements needed to support a set of pre-defined network security services.
- Allow choices of specific basic, enhanced, or even integrated technologies to be used (e.g., encryption algorithms to be used for text confidentiality)
- Provide flexibility in implementation — features can be easily tailored to support multiple customers or organizations with diverse network security requirements

Four architectural technologies are described in this chapter:

- Random Access Architecture
- Public key infrastructure (PKI)
- Federal public key infrastructure (FPKI)
- Secure Electronic Transaction (SET) Specifications

Another emerging architectural technology, Wireless LAN (WLAN), will be described separately in Chapter 10.

9.1 REMOTE ACCESS

Remote access is the ability of a user to get access to a server or a network from a remote location. Personnel at branch offices, telecommuters, and people who are traveling may need access to the corporation's network. Home users get access to the Internet through remote access to an Internet Service Provider (ISP). Dial-up connection through a desktop, notebook, or handheld computer modem over regular telephone lines is a common method of remote access. Remote access is also possible using a dedicated line between a computer or a remote local area network and the central or main corporate local area network. A dedicated line is more expensive and less flexible but offers faster data rates. Integrated Services Digital Network (ISDN) is another method of remote access from branch offices because it combines dialup with faster data rates. Wireless, cable modem, and Digital Subscriber Line (DSL) technologies are rapidly becoming the dominant access technologies.

9.1.1 Remote Access Security Requirements

Some essential, basic security-related capabilities that are needed in all remote access systems are described in the following subsections.

9.1.1.1 Access Network Control

The first line of defense in remote access security is access network control to prevent intruders from gaining access to the remote access network. This access network control can be provided in a number of ways: the use of add-on security hardware, restricted node addresses, caller identification, and dial-back. An add-on, hardware-based security device can be a simple smart ID card that provides either a serial number or a network access code generated by the card on a one-time basis and valid for a limited period of time, which is verified by the remote access server (RAS) before network access is granted. Restricted addressing, caller ID, and dial-back ensure that a remote user can only call in from certain locations. If the access network is supplied by a service provider, only very limited security can be offered at this first line of defense because the network is normally shared and accessible to diverse users and different companies.

9.1.1.2 User Authentication and Authorization

The second line of defense is caller authentication, which ensures that no one can masquerade as an authorized user. For example, the simplest authentication method used in PPP-based remote nodes is the Password Authentication Protocol (PAP), which requires the remote node to send a nonencrypted userID and password. A more sophisticated authentication method is based on the Challenge Handshake Authentication Protocol (CHAP) whereby the RAS sends a unique 16-character code called a "challenge" to the remote user each time a log-in is attempted. The remote user's password is then encoded with a response to the challenge and sent to the server. Another CHAP-based method uses tokens along with a security device such as the RSA SecurID card.

9.1.1.3 Protection of Connection and Traffic Integrity

Once a connection or session is established, it is necessary to ensure that the integrity of the traffic exchanged between two communicating parties is preserved. Not only should messages or data reach the intended authenticated and authorized entities, but they should also not be altered en route between each remote access user's PC, or workstation or host, and the enterprise network or servers.

9.1.2 Authentication and Authorization Protocols

The initial connection established between the remote user and RAS is almost exclusively a PPP connection. To provide adequate network security, there are two basic protocols that are used for the authentication of this PPP connection: PAP and CHAP. Both protocols allow for the validation of a userID and password pair entered by RAS. PAP uses a cleartext password and is the less sophisticated authentication protocol. CHAP is the more secure protocol because it does not require the password to be transmitted over the network. Both protocols have been described earlier (PAP in Chapter 3 and CHAP in Chapter 7). The following text provides a refresher of these two protocols.

In PAP, the encrypted password is sent across the network to be compared against an encrypted password file on the access server. If the sent password matches that of the associated userID, the connection is established. Because the password can potentially be intercepted by a hacker, PAP is not considered to be secure.

CHAP addresses the PAP deficiencies by having a server send a randomly generated challenge to the client along with the hostname. The hostname is used by the client to look up the appropriate password, which is then combined with the challenge and encrypted using a one-way hashing function, and then sent to the server along with the userID. The server performs the same computation using the password and compares the result with what has been sent back by the client. If there is a match, the connection is established. Because the challenge is different in every session, a hacker cannot replay the sequence. CHAP allows

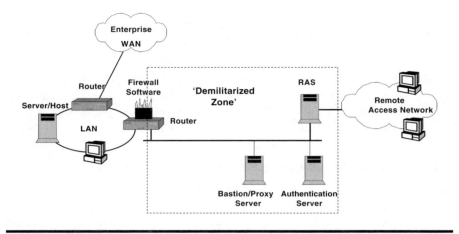

Figure 9.1 Remote Access Reference Architecture.

different types of encryption algorithms to be used. Specifically, RAS uses Data Encryption Standard (DES) and Message Digest 5 (MD5). DES, the U.S. government standard, was designed to protect against password discovery and playback. MD5, the Message Digest algorithm defined in RFC 1321, is an encryption scheme used by various PPP vendors for encrypted authentication and can be negotiated by a client when connecting to an RAS.

In most implementations, such as Windows NT, CHAP allows the RAS server to negotiate downward from the most secure to the least secure encryption mechanism used and protects whatever passwords are transmitted in the process.

Some remote access systems will find PAP adequate but most will require CHAP.

9.1.3 Remote Access Architecture

There are no formal standards defined specifically to restrict what the Remote Access Architecture should exactly be like because different corporations or organizations have different remote access requirements. However, there are functional components that have become *de facto* standards in typical remote access deployments. Figure 9.1 shows a Reference Remote Access Architecture made up of these standard functional components. Note that all remote users go through the remote access network to gain access to all network and systems resources in the enterprise network.

Again, the above architecture should be looked at as a reference architecture; there are numerous variations in actual remote access deployments. The critical components in this Reference Remote Access Architecture are considered in the following subsections.

9.1.3.1 DMZ

The DMZ (demilitarized zone) authorization technology discussed in Chapter 4 is a key element in most firewall deployments. It is used to provide a buffer between the private network and the access server that has connection to outside (external) networks.

Bastion servers are provided within the DMZ to act as go-betweens that establish two-step connections between the remote access user and the enterprise servers or hosts that the outside users want to connect to. Examples of these bastion servers are authentication servers and proxy servers (both described in the following text); these are bastion servers because they are not protected from the outside networks by a firewall.

9.1.3.2 RAS

One of the major components in the Remote Access Architecture is RAS, the computer and associated software that is set up to handle users seeking access to network remotely. Sometimes also called a communication server, RAS may include or work with a modem pool manager so that a small group of modems can be shared among a large number of intermittently present remote access users.

RAS is responsible for establishing communication with the remote user through the access network. The most common type of connection used is PPP, which can also be just the initial type of connection established between the remote user and RAS pending a more secure type of connection like one that is based on VPNs such as L2TP, PPTP, etc. Associated with the connection establishment function are a number of other IP address assignment and URL address resolution functions that need to be included in the Remote Access Architecture. These correspond to the need to have the following components: Boot Server, Dynamic Host Configuration Processor (DHCP) server, and Domain Name Server (DNS). These components can reside in separate physical servers or reside in RAS.

RAS works in tandem with the authentication server to provide the necessary authentication and authorization of remote users requesting access to the private network.

9.1.3.3 Authentication Server

The authentication server works with RAS to provide the necessary authentication and authorization functionality. For example, Windows 2000 remote access supports Extensible Authentication Protocol (EAP), CHAP, Microsoft Challenge Handshake Authentication Protocol (MS-CHAP) version 1 and version 2, Shiva Password Authentication Protocol (SPAP), and PAP.

A secure authentication scheme provides protection against replay attacks, remote access client impersonation, and remote access server impersonation. These threats are described in the following text:

- A replay attack occurs when a person captures the packets of a successful connection attempt and then replays those packets in an attempt to obtain an authenticated connection.
- Remote access client impersonation occurs when a person takes over an existing authenticated connection. The intruder waits until the connection is authenticated and then obtains the connection parameters, disconnects the user, and takes control of the authenticated connection.
- Remote server impersonation occurs when a computer appears as the remote access server to the remote access client. The impersonator appears to verify the remote access client credentials and then captures all of the traffic from the remote access client.

For mobile users, firewalls allow remote access to the private network by the use of secure log-on procedures and authentication certificates.

9.1.3.4 Proxy Server

A proxy server is a server that acts as an intermediary between a remote user and the servers that run the desired applications within the protected enterprise network so that the enterprise network can ensure its security, administrative control, and caching services. User authorization, if not done in the authentication server, might be done in the proxy server.

A proxy server receives a request for an Internet service (such as a Web page request) from a user. If the request passes filtering requirements, the proxy server, assuming it is also a cache server, looks in its local cache of previously downloaded Web pages. If it finds the page, it returns it to the user without needing to forward the request to the Internet. If the page is not in the cache, the proxy server, acting as a client on behalf of the user, uses one of its own IP addresses to request the page from the server out on the Internet. When the page is returned, the proxy server relates it to the original request and forwards it to the user.

To the user, the proxy server is invisible; all Internet requests and returned responses appear to be directly with the addressed Internet server. In reality, the proxy is not quite invisible because its IP address has to be specified as a configuration option to the browser or other protocol program.

An advantage of a proxy server is that its cache can serve all users. If one or more Internet sites are frequently requested, these are likely to be in the proxy's cache, which will improve user response time. In fact, there are special-purpose servers called cache servers. A proxy can also do logging.

Note that these components are functionally defined and therefore in actual implementation; they may or may not map into separate physical components. For example, a proxy server may be in the same machine with a firewall server or it may be on a separate server and forward requests through the firewall.

If a proxy server is located in a DMZ, then it is generally called a bastion server.

9.1.3.5   Firewall

The firewall is one of the most important components in the Remote Access Architecture. As described in Chapter 8, a firewall is a set of related hardware and software programs deployed strategically between a company's private network and one or more unsecured networks (particularly including the Internet). A firewall functions to protect the resources of the private network from users on the outside (external) networks.

The firewall separates the protected, private network (inside or internal) and the unsecured networks (outside or external) and makes sure that any malicious or unintentional harm will not be done to internal resources by external forces.

9.1.4   AAA Servers

One of the biggest headaches and sources of problems with remote access security has been the need to manage the many different components on a server-by-server basis. UserIDs, passwords, and access control lists, as well as the ever-important audit trails, have traditionally been stored on remote access servers. In addition, user accounting information and collected detailed billing records are all scattered in various devices and servers. In larger networks, the tracking and processing of all this data quickly become cumbersome and unmanageable. As a result, centralized security servers that run on many different platforms utilizing existing network operating system (NOS) directory services such as Novell's Network Directory Services (NDS) have been used to provide security management.

These centralized security servers are generally known as authentication, authorization, and auditing (AAA) servers. The two most commonly used *de facto* AAA systems are Cisco's TACACS+ and RADIUS. TACACS+ enables central control of users attempting to gain access to network resources based on separate authentication, authorization, and accounting

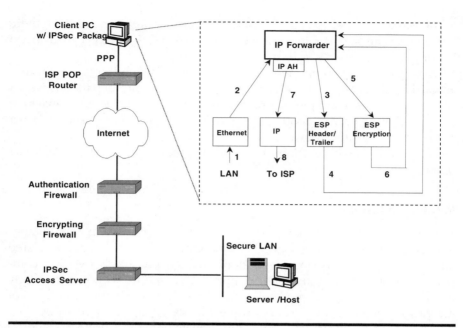

Figure 9.2 Tunneling with encryption and authentication firewall.

facilities, whereas RADIUS uses a distributed client/server (C/S) framework to combine user authentication and authorization.

9.1.5 An Illustration

There are various ways of incorporating some of the security technologies into a Remote Access Architecture. Figure 9.2 illustrates the functional steps that are needed during the formation of an IP packet to be sent over an already established IPSec VPN connection. The ability to support and execute these functional steps is implemented in the client PC software and in the access and firewall servers. (Note that the access server and firewall in the diagram are shown as logical servers and, in reality, can all reside in one physical server.)

The following briefly describes the functional steps numbered in this configuration:

1. Data packet comes in from the LAN on the Ethernet Layer 2 interface.
2. The Layer 2 packet is sent to the IP forwarder module for IP processing.
3. ESP Header and Trailer bytes are added.

4. The resulting packet gets back to the IP forwarder module to be reprocessed.
5. ESP encryption is performed on the packet.
6. The encrypted packet gets back to the IP module to be further processed.
7. An AH authentication header gets added to the encrypted packet.
8. An IP packet is generated by adding an IP header and the packet is sent out to the IP network.

The IPSec VPN could have been established using the CHAP handshaking authentication and authorization protocol.

9.2 PKI ARCHITECTURE

As business transactions become increasingly dependent on E-commerce, in which valuable information is transmitted over insecure networks such as the Internet, the question of maintaining a level of trust in all those transactions becomes critical. All of the security services presented earlier in this book must be utilized to maximize the advantages of E-commerce. PKI provides a well-conceived infrastructure to efficiently deliver these security services in a cohesive manner.

PKI is an authentication technology that defines a framework for using a combination of secret-key and public-key cryptography to enable a number of other security services including data confidentiality, data integrity, source non-repudiation, and key management. Thus, PKI allows business applications to conduct business over unsecured networks with confidence.

9.2.1 PKI Overview

PKIs are defined as the set of hardware, software, people, policies, and procedures needed for the creation, management, storage, distribution, and revocation of certificates, based on public-key cryptography. The main role of PKI is the management of keys and certificates in a trusted and efficient way for its users.

To take advantage of certificates within large distributed systems, they must be efficiently made available to all system users. One solution is the use of directory services as repositories to store information about system users and entities and allow easy access to this information by different applications. Usually, directory services follow the International Telecommunications Union-Telecommunications (ITU-T) X.500 series of recommendations. The Lightweight Directory Access Protocol (LDAP), based on X.500, is also often used to access X.500 directory services used as PKI repositories. The X.500 directory service model is based on entries that correspond to information about objects. An entry is a set of attributes and has a characteristic name known as Distinguished Name (DN) that provides unique identification.

The goal of PKI standardization is to provide interoperability, thereby allowing its use in distributed and heterogeneous environments. The Internet Engineering Task Force (IETF) has defined PKI standards for public key infrastructure X.509 (PKIX).

The Internet X.509 PKIX is an effort of the IETF PKIX Working Group to provide deterministic and automatic identification, authentication, access control, and authorization functions on the Internet. Its establishment was motivated by the fact that X.509 defines a very general framework that allows the coexistence of several incompatible X.509-compliant implementations.

9.2.2   PKI Building Blocks

PKIX uses public-key cryptographic technologies to build a security infrastructure that provides trust services. The central building blocks in PKI are digital certificates or public-key certificates that bind public keys to identifying information about their owners. The PKI infrastructure includes definitions of capabilities to create the binding and management of these certificates. Public-key certificates as defined in X.509 have been described in Chapter 7.

Although PKI derives its name from public-key cryptography, some of the services it provides have their technical roots in techniques that are outside this branch of cryptography. PKI embodies the best of these well-understood techniques. It represents the integration of public-key cryptography used for digital signatures and key management, and symmetric-key cryptography used for encryption.

9.2.3   PKI Defined

Whitfield Diffie and Martin Hellman first introduced the notion of public-key cryptography in 1976 with the publication of "New Directions in Cryptography." A great deal of progress has been made since then, including the development of public-key cryptographic algorithms such as RSA and DSA, and cryptographic algorithms based on Elliptic Curve Cryptography. In addition, technology has become available to manage the public and private key pairs, thus positioning the PKI architecture to be defined as the foundation for offering scalable key and certificate life-cycle management.

The foundation or framework for PKI is defined in the ITU-T X.509 Recommendation. The IETF PKIX Working Group has been the driving force behind setting up a formal (and generic) model based on X.509 that is suitable for deploying a certificate-based architecture on the Internet. The following subsection describes the PKIX architecture.

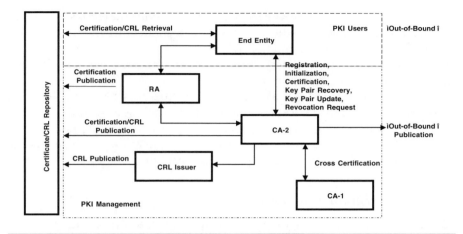

Figure 9.3 **PKIX Reference Architecture Model.**

9.2.4 The PKIX Architecture

The basic PKIX architecture has remained largely unchanged since it was first published in the original Internet Certificate and certificate revocation list (CRL) Profile defined in RFC 2459. The latest model is reflected in the most recent version of the Internet Certificate and CRL Profile defined in RFC 3280. Figure 9.3 illustrates a reference model of the PKIX architecture.

The key components in this PKIX Reference Model are considered in the following subsections.

9.2.4.1 End Entities

An End Entity can be considered as an end user, a device such as a router or a server, a process, or anything that can be identified in the subject name of a public-key certificate. End Entities can also be thought of as consumers of PKI-related services.

End Entities that will be bound to certificates, such as servers and end users, must "enroll" into the PKI before they can participate as members of the PKI. This involves an initial registration step followed by initialization and certification (see the following text).

9.2.4.2 Certification Authority

Public keys are distributed in the form of public-key certificates that are issued by certificate authorities (CAs). Public-key certificates are digitally signed by the issuing CAs. CAs are also responsible for issuing CRLs unless this has been delegated to a separate CRL Issuer.

CAs may also be involved in a number of administrative tasks such as end-user registration, but these are often delegated to the Registration Authority (RA). In implementation practice, CAs can also serve as the key backup and recovery facilities although these functions can also be delegated to a separate component.

CAs are often thought of as the source of trust in a PKI, and there are standardized frameworks for the establishment and auditing of the policies and procedures required for the operation of a PKI. Typically, End Entities are configured with one or more "trust anchors" that are then used as the starting point to validate a given certification path.

9.2.4.3 Registration Authority

An RA is an optional component that can be used to offload many of the administrative functions that a CA would have to assume in the absence of an RA. As stated earlier, the RA is normally associated with the End Entity registration process. This would include the verification of the identity of the End Entity attempting to register with the PKI. However, the RA can perform a number of other functions, including:

- Validating the attributes of the subject who is requesting the certificate
- Verifying that the subject has possession of the private key being registered (known as "proof of possession")
- Generation of shared secrets to support the initialization and certification process
- Public–private key-pair generation
- Conducting interactions with the CA (or several CAs) as an intermediary of the End Entity, including key-compromise notifications and key-recovery requests
- Parameter validation of public keys presented for registration

Note that although the RA can offload many functions from the CA, the RA can never be the issuer of a public-key certificate.

9.2.4.4 Repositories

A repository is used for storing and retrieving PKI-related information such as public-key certificates and CRLs. A repository can be an X.500-based directory with client access via LDAP, or it may be something much simpler such as retrieval of a flat file on a remote server via the File Transfer Protocol (FTP) or the Hypertext Transfer Protocol (HTTP).

9.2.4.5 Certificate Revocation List Issuers

The CRL Issuer issues CRLs. Typically, the CA that issues a given set of certificates is also responsible for issuing revocation information associated with those certificates. However, it is possible for a CA to delegate that function to another entity.

9.2.5 PKIX Management Functions

PKIX identifies a number of management functions that potentially need to be supported. The following lists some of the key management functions.

9.2.5.1 Registration

End Entities must enroll into the PKI before they can take advantage of PKI-enabled services. Registration is the first step in the End Entity enrollment process. This is usually characterized as the process whereby an End Entity first makes itself known to a CA.

9.2.5.2 Initialization

Registration is followed by initialization. At a minimum, this involves initializing the associated trust anchor with the End Entity. Additional information such as the applicable certificate policies may also be supplied. In addition, this step is usually associated with initializing the End Entity with its associated key pairs. Key-pair generation involves the creation of the public and private key pair associated with an End Entity.

It is possible that portions of this step may occur at different times. On the Internet, for example, browsers are initialized with the public keys of numerous root CAs that might be used as trust anchors. However, the end-user portion of initialization would not occur until an explicit certificate request is made.

9.2.5.3 Certification

Certification is the natural conclusion to the End Entity enrollment process. This step involves the issuance of the End Entity public-key certificate by the CA. If the key pair is generated external to the CA, the public-key component must be conveyed to the CA in a secure manner.

Once generated, the certificate is returned to the End Entity and published to a certificate repository.

9.2.5.4 Key-Pair Recovery

Key pairs can be used to support digital signature creation and verification, encryption and decryption, or both. When a key pair is used for encryption and decryption, it is important to provide a mechanism to recover the necessary decryption keys when normal access to the keying material is no longer possible; otherwise, it will not be possible to recover the encrypted data.

9.2.5.5 Key-Pair Update

Certificates are issued with fixed lifetimes (referred to as the validity period of the certificate). Although these fixed lifetimes can be rather generous (say, two to five years or so), the certificate will eventually expire. Key-pair update may also be required as a result of certificate revocation. Key-pair update involves the generation of a new key pair and the issuance of a new public-key certificate.

9.2.5.6 Revocation Request

Public-key certificates are issued with fairly generous lifetimes. However, the circumstances that existed when the certificate was issued can change before the certificate would naturally expire. Reasons for revocation include private-key compromise, change in affiliation, name change, etc.

Therefore, it is sometimes necessary to revoke a certificate before its expiration date. The Revocation Request allows an End Entity (or RA) to request revocation of a given certificate.

9.2.5.7 Cross-Certification

Cross-certification occurs between CAs. A cross-certificate is a public-key certificate that is issued by one CA to another. In other words, a cross-certificate is a public-key certificate that contains the public key of a CA that has been digitally signed by another CA.

9.2.5.8 Management Function Protocols

PKI also defines a number of message exchange protocols to support these and other PKIX management functions through the work from the PKI Forum (Section 9.2.6). For example, SCEP (Simple Certificate Enrollment Protocol) is a PKI communication protocol that leverages existing technology by using PKCS #7 and PKCS #10. SCEP is the evolution of the enrollment protocol developed by VeriSign for Cisco and now enjoys wide support in both client and CA implementations. It supports the secure issuance of certificates to network devices in a scalable manner using

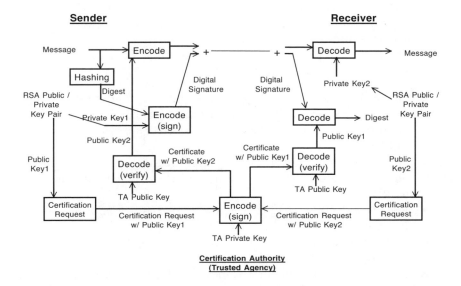

Figure 9.4   An example of PKI.

existing technology whenever possible. The protocol supports the following operations:

- CA and RA public-key distribution
- Certificate enrollment
- Certificate revocation
- Certificate query
- CRL query

9.2.6   The PKI Forum

The PKI Forum is an international, nonprofit, multivendor and end-user alliance whose purpose is to accelerate the adoption and use of PKI. It advocates industry cooperation and market awareness to enable organizations to understand and exploit the value of PKI in their e-business applications.

9.2.7   An Illustration

To illustrate the above descriptions, the diagram in Figure 9.4 shows an example application of the PKI technology. This application involves the interaction between the sender and the receiver of a message.

It is assumed that the "Sender" has an RSA public Key1 and private Key1 pair and the "Receiver" has public Key2 and private Key2 pair, both distributed in certificates by the CA.

The following steps typify the exchanges needed when the Sender wants to send a message to the Receiver:

- Sender hashes message to generate a message digest that it encodes with its own private Key1 to produce a digital signature.
- Sender retrieves public Key2 from Receiver's certificate using CA's public key.
- Sender encodes message with public Key2.
- Sender appends digital signature to encoded message and sends to Receiver.
- Receiver decodes message with private Key2 and hashes it to generate message digest.
- Receiver decodes digital message with Sender's public Key1 to get message digest.
- Receiver compares generated message digest and decoded message digest for a match.

A match of the two message digests indicates that the message has been received unaltered and that the message has been sent from "Sender."

9.3 FEDERAL PKI

Another specific application (in various stages of implementation) of the PKI architecture that is receiving a lot of attention is FPKI. FPKI will support the secure federal government use of information resources and the national information infrastructure (NII). FPKI will establish the facilities, specifications, and policies needed by federal departments and agencies to use public-key-based certificates for:

- Information system security
- E-commerce
- Secure communications, including e-mail

FPKI is defined to support secure communications and commerce among federal agencies, as well as with other branches of the federal, state, and local governments, corporate entities and the public, and to facilitate secure communications and information processing for unclassified but sensitive (UBS) applications.

FPKI does not focus inward to secure communications and information systems only within a closed government community. Rather, its purpose is to provide federal users secure information access and communications with the entire nation and the rest of the world, as well as to provide secure internal federal government information access and communications.

The great challenge of FPKI is to meld the individual agency projects that use PKI technology from a variety of commercial vendors into a broadly interoperable trust network.

Two distinct and interrelated functionalities are defined within the FPKI architecture:

- PKI — Use of public and private keys, digital signatures, and certificates (including trusted authorities) and related concepts (e.g., certification paths, etc.)
- Directory Servers — Management (including hierarchical directory architecture — federal and trusted domain-based) and access control of data (primarily certificates) in directory servers (repositories) using security features defined in border directories based on common technologies such as firewalls, etc.

The Federal PKI Technical Working Group (FPKI-TWG) is a subcommittee of the FPKI Steering Committee and is an open group focusing on resolving technical obstacles to the implementation and use of public key infrastructures by government agencies. TWG is composed of technical participants from federal agencies and industry and is chaired by NIST. Active since October 1994, TWG has developed a technical concept of operations and an X509 v3 certificate profile for a federal PKI as well as a number of other documents.

9.3.1 FPKI Security Services

The following diagram in Figure 9.5, taken from the FPKI-TWG technical concept of operations document (see reference list), gives a very informational graphical view of the major security services that are provided by these PKI and the Directory Services in the FPKI architecture. The central core of the entire structure is the PKI Certificate Management functionalities.

9.3.1.1 PKI Functionality

The PKI Functionality consists of standard PKI components that include CAs, RAs, certificate status responders, and management authorities that manage public-key certificates used by federal departments and agencies for unclassified, sensitive applications. PKI will:

- Issue public-key certificates
- Revoke public-key certificates when required

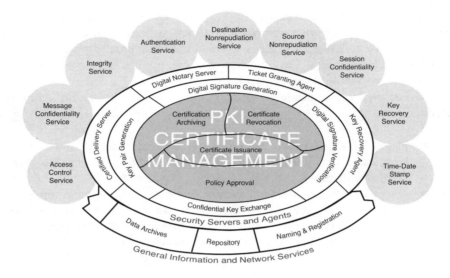

Figure 9.5   PKI-centered view of security services.

- Establish the policies that govern the issuance and revocation of certificates
- Archive the information needed to validate certificates at a later date

PKI clients will use the public-key certificates issued and managed by PKI to provide security services to federal users. PKI clients perform four primitive functions with and for certificates:

- Public–private key-pair generation
- Digital signature generation
- Digital signature verification
- Confidential key management (i.e., agreement or distribution of a session or message key to be used with a symmetric-key algorithm for confidentiality)

The first function, key-pair generation, can also be performed by CAs or RAs. However, generation of digital signature key pairs by the clients helps to maintain the integrity of the system and preserve non-repudiation because only the client then ever possesses the private key used for digital signatures. The last three functions enable a variety of public-key-based security protocols and services by direct client-to-client protocols. These services include authentication, access control based on an authenticated identity or role, non-repudiation services, and confidentiality.

A number of servers and agents support the infrastructure, and clients may obtain security services from these servers and agents. The full range of services is not fully understood and is still evolving, but they may include:

■ Digital notaries: A digital notary provides a service analogous to a notary public. A notary may provide a trusted date and time stamp for a document that proves it existed at a certain point in time, and may also verify the signatures on a signed document.

■ Key-recovery agents (KRAs): CAs may require that copies of private keys, used for confidentiality key management, be turned over to a KRA as a condition for issuing a key-management certificate. Alternatively, a client that sends an encrypted message may include the encryption session key encrypted in the public key of the KRA, with the message. The purpose of the KRA is to allow decryption of encrypted data when keys are lost, or for management supervision or law enforcement purposes.

It may be useful to separate the CA and key-recovery functions. Whereas the only secret a CA inherently needs to protect or access is its own private key, a key-recovery agent may need to store, protect, and provide carefully controlled access to a large number of client private keys.

KRAs may provide for split control of the user private keys it holds, so that the cooperation of two or more agents is required to access the keys. This applies only to key management of key pairs; private keys used for digital signatures ordinarily should never be divulged by certificate holders to any other party.

■ Certified delivery agents: These servers provide a destination non-repudiation service analogous to certified mail or process servers. The service proves that a message was received by a possibly uncooperative recipient, or that a good-faith attempt was made to deliver the message.

■ Ticket-granting agents: These agents provide cryptographic digital "tickets" that can be used for access to systems or data. They can use either public-key or symmetric-key cryptography and provide a means for centralizing and managing access control in distributed systems.

The following three general information and network services are of particular significance to PKI technology:

■ Repositories: A repository is an online, publicly accessible system for storing and retrieving certificates and other information relevant to certificates, such as revocation information. In effect, a certificate is published by putting it in a repository. Repositories also contain certification practice statements. In FPKI, the expected normal repository is a directory that uses LDAP (IETF RFC 1777). However, other forms of repositories may be used, including X.500 directories (that use the DAP directory access protocols) and HTTP or anonymous FTP servers.

■ Data archives: Archives provide long-term storage of CA files and records. The lifetime of CAs may be relatively short. But it may be important to verify the validity of signatures on very old documents. CAs must make a provision to store the information needed to verify the signatures of its users in archives that will be able to make the data available at a much later date, perhaps several decades later.

■ Naming and registration: In a distributed environment, many objects must have unique names. This is true for security objects. For example, certificate subjects and issuers must have unique names.

9.3.1.2 Federal PKI Directory Servers

FPKI will be constructed using PKI components from numerous trust domains. Some of these will be initially limited to particular applications (e.g., S/MIME signature verification), but some will be multiapplication PKIs. Because of the nature of its composition, FPKI cannot be viewed either as a monolithic structure or a single-enterprise PKI.

The approach adopted for FPKI is based on the concept of a "Bridge CA" (BCA). It provides trust (or certification) paths between PCAs for the trust domain PKIs. Industry organizations and other nations are adopting similar solutions where a designated CA cross-certifies with high-level CAs in different trust domains to create certification paths. This approach allows large-scale government, industry, national, or global PKIs to be assembled from application- or enterprise-scale PKIs. The approach is further described in the FPKI Concept of Operations.

The Federal BCA will provide cross-certification among the trust domain PKIs. Each trust domain will designate a single principal CA to cross-certify with the Federal BCA. The combination of a principal CA and its associated PKI forms a domain of trust wherein the principal CA provides a known point of trust for the domain. Trust domains currently use CA products and services from different vendors, and client products from many vendors.

To verify a digital signature, a client must build a certification path from the originator's certificate back to the certificate for an authority that the client trusts. For the BCA approach to work, directory servers must be able to retrieve the certificates and certificate revocation information from trust domains that are cross-certified via the Federal BCA.

The BCA is cross-certified with the principal CAs for the client's trust domain and the originator's trust domain. This enables the client's directory agent to build a certification path from the originator's certificate back to the client's known point of trust, allowing the client to verify the originator's signature.

The Federal BCA facilitates cross-certification among trust domains within FPKI. Access to the relevant certificates, certificate revocation information, certificate policies, and certification practice statements must be provided by publishing this information in one or more repositories to support access by users in other trust domains.

The FPKI repository includes a Federal Bridge directory server that is interconnected with a set of border directory servers.

9.3.2 Federal PKI Directory Architecture

The FPKI directory will be a distributed directory system comprising a BCA directory server and a number of other directory servers. Each trust domain will provide directory information via one or more of these directory servers. The directory servers are intended to provide a mechanism for clients within the federal government trust domains to retrieve certificates and certificate revocation information from other trust domains without requiring the client user to deal with multiple directory access protocols.

Generally, a border directory server is one that has been designated to provide the primary public directory system interface for a trust domain. By providing a separate border directory server, an organization can retain its existing directory infrastructure and still be able to communicate within FPKI.

A separate border directory server would be a new directory server specifically created to interface with FPKI. These border directory servers would implement an external interface to other FPKI directory servers and, optionally, an internal interface to the organization's internal directory infrastructure. One of the key reasons for implementing a separate border directory server is to allow the trust domain to separate the information stored in its infrastructure into information that can, and information that cannot, be provided to the public.

9.3.2.1 Directory Components

This subsection includes descriptions of the entities involved with FPKI. The definitions and terms used are consistent with those defined in the Proposed FPKI Concept of Operation.

■ Trust domains: In the federal context, a trust domain is a portion of the FPKI that operates under the management of a single Policy Management Authority. One or more CAs exist within the trust domain. Each trust domain has a single Principal CA, but may have many other CAs. Each trust domain has a domain repository. (Note: By fielding a border directory server, a trust domain can provide public access to all or only a part of its repository.) In the non-federal context, trust domains may be more loosely organized, but consist at a minimum of a group of CAs that share trust and operate under consistent policies.

■ Federal Policy Management Authority (FPMA): This management authority sets the overall policies of FPKI and determines how trust domain policies map to federal policies in providing cross-certification. It operates a Federal BCA and a repository (i.e., the Federal BCA directory server).

■ Domain Policy Management Authorities (DPMA): A policy management authority approves the certification practice statements of the CAs within a trust domain and monitors their operation. The DPMAs operate or supervise a domain repository. In the nonfederal context, a DPMA may be an association of CAs that share trust and use consistent or comparable CA policies.

■ CAs:
  – BCA: FPMA operates the Federal BCA to be a bridge of trust that provides trust paths between the various trust domains of FPKI, as well as between FPKI and nonfederal trust domains. FPMA-approved trust domains designate a principal CA that is eligible to cross-certify with the Federal BCA. Note that the BCA is not a root CA because it does not begin certification paths. When the BCA cross-certifies with CAs, it may limit the propagation of trust to other, cross-certified domains using certificate extensions such as: nameConstraints, basicConstraints, or policyConstraints.
  – Principal CA (PCA): This is a CA within a trust domain that cross-certifies with the Federal BCA. Each trust domain has one principal CA. In the case of a domain with hierarchical certification paths, the Principal CA is the root CA of the domain. In a mesh-organized domain, the principal CA may be any CA in the domain. However, it normally will be one operated by, or associated with, DPMA.

■ Directory servers: Directory servers are online repositories that provide certificates and certificate status information. In FPKI, directory servers will provide information via the LDAP protocol or X.500 DSP chained operations, but they may also provide

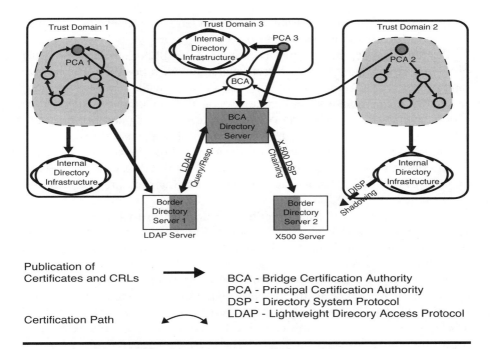

Figure 9.6   Federal Border Directory Architecture.

information in other ways. The FPMA will maintain an open BCA directory server for CA certificates and revocation information. Border directory servers contain certificates and CRLs for CAs and End Entities in their domain.

■ BCA directory server: The BCA directory server will be open to Internet access by anyone and will make the following available:
   - All certificates issued to or by the BCA
   - All cross-certificate pairs containing certificates issued to or by the BCA
   - All CA and End Entity certificates required for interoperability within the overall FPKI
   - The Federal BCA CRL
   - Other certification information, as determined by FPMA

9.3.2.2 *Architecture Overview*

Figure 9.6 illustrates the BCA with its associated directory server. The Federal BCA serves as a cross-certification entity for the principal CA associated with each trust domain. Each component PKI within FPKI will be represented by a minimum of one border directory server, which may be provided by the trust domain itself, provided by another trust domain, or outsourced to an external service provider.

Border directory servers will connect via the BCA directory server to provide a governmentwide certificate management repository. The border directory server will provide each trust domain with a publicly visible repository for certificates, certification revocation information, and certification practice statements. The border directory server need not replicate a trust domain's entire internal directory information base (DIB).

Figure 9.6 illustrates the interconnection of three trust domains, each having different internal directory structures, with the BCA directory server. (Note: External connections, such as one to the Internet, are not included in the figure.)

Trust Domain 1 publishes certificate information to border directory server 1 through any protocol it chooses. The border directory server is provided by the trust domain and supports LDAP for queries and responses from other trust domains.

Trust Domain 2 publishes information from its internal directory to its border directory server, using the X.500 Directory Information Shadowing Protocol (DISP). The border directory server supports the X.500 Directory System Protocol (DSP), using chaining to support queries and responses from other trust domains.

Trust Domain 3 does not have a separate border directory server. Instead, the PCA is responsible for posting certificate information directly to the BCA directory server.

9.3.2.3 Concept of Operation

User access to FPKI directory servers (i.e., the BCA directory server and border directory servers) should be limited to permit only interrogation services (i.e., read, compare, list, search, and abandon). We recommend that the modification and administrative services be restricted to administrative users only. In this subsection, the term "access" implies interrogation services only.

The primary use of the FPKI directory is expected to be to provide certificates for relying parties (i.e., directory users) in different trust domains to support digital signature validation. Figure 9.7 illustrates a typical scenario, wherein a relying party (the directory user) requests the signing certificate of a remote user from whom a signed message has been received.

In this scenario, the user submits a read request for the sender's directory entry (which contains the sender's public digital signature key certificate) to a local directory server.

The local server determines that the requested directory entry is not present and forwards the request to its local border directory server. (This

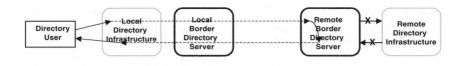

Figure 9.7   Example FPKI directory usage scenario.

is referred to as an "outgoing request.") Because the local border (in this case) includes only a subset of the information provided by the local directory infrastructure, the border directory server also determines that the requested entry is not present and forwards the request to a remote border directory server, possibly via the BCA directory server.

The remote border directory server receives this "incoming request" and retrieves the requested directory entry, sending it back to the relying party (i.e., the original directory user) as a response. Note that the remote border directory server need not retrieve information via its connection with its local directory infrastructure, as indicated by the "x" on the information flows. This model allows trust domains to limit the risk of unauthorized disclosure or modification of information within their domain infrastructures.

Incoming directory requests can be originated by trust domain users, authorized external users, or members of the public. Each trust domain must evaluate the information provided within its directory infrastructure to determine the risk associated with access by these user categories. The remainder of this subsection presents four examples of directory configurations, presented in order of increased trust domain protection, and discusses some of the protection issues relating to them.

A Certification Path is a chain of certificates between any given certificate and its trust anchor (CA). Each certificate in the chain must be verifiable in order to validate the certificate at the end of the path; this functionality is critical to the usable PKI.

9.3.3   PKI Services

PKI will provide the services and facilities needed for unclassified secure federal information processing and use of the NII, including:

- Digital signatures for
  - Authentication
  - Integrity
  - Non-repudiation
- Management of symmetric keys for UBS level confidentiality for
  - Communications sessions
  - E-mail messages

When extended by KRAs, PKI will also provide key-recovery services for encrypted data.

PKI will provide the services and facilities needed for secure information access, communication, messaging, and E-commerce with commercial and personal users employing common *de facto* and formal security standards and using mainstream commercial security products.

9.4   THE SET SPECIFICATION

SET is an open technical standard for the commerce industry developed by Visa and MasterCard as a way to facilitate secure payment card transactions over the Internet. SET uses digital certificates to create a trust chain throughout the transaction, verifying cardholder and merchant validity. Software vendors whose products pass SET Compliance Testing are eligible to display the SET Mark on their products, as are merchants, financial institutions, and promotional sites that utilize or advertise licensed software.

SET Secure Electronic Transaction LLC (SETCo) manages the SET Specification, promoting and supporting the use of SET Secure Electronic Transaction™ on the Internet.

SET uses a system of locks and keys along with certified account IDs for both consumers and merchants. Then, through a unique process of "encrypting" or scrambling the information exchanged between the shopper and the online store, SET ensures a payment process that is convenient, private and, most of all, secure. Specifically, SET:

1. Establishes industry standards to keep a customer's order and payment information confidential
2. Increases integrity of all transmitted data through encryption
3. Provides authentication that a cardholder is a legitimate user of a branded payment card account
4. Provides authentication that a merchant can accept branded payment card transactions through its relationship with an acquiring financial institution
5. Allows the use of the best security practices and system design techniques to protect all legitimate parties in an E-commerce transaction

9.4.1   Overview of SET

With SET, each user is given a digital certificate (also called electronic wallet), and a transaction is conducted and verified using a combination of digital certificates and digital signatures among the purchaser, a merchant, and the purchaser's bank in a way that ensures privacy and confidentiality.

SET makes use of Netscape's Secure Sockets Layer (SSL), Microsoft's Secure Transaction Technology (STT), and Terisa System's Secure-Hypertext Transfer Protocol (S-HTTP). SET uses some but not all aspects of a PKI.

SET defines cryptography, certificates, and signature standards to address the following seven major E-commerce business requirements:

1. Provide confidentiality of payment information and enable confidentiality of the order information that is transmitted along with the payment information.
2. Ensure the integrity of all transmitted data.
3. Provide authentication that a cardholder is a legitimate user of a branded payment card account.
4. Provide authentication that a merchant can accept branded payment card transactions through its relationship with an acquiring financial institution.
5. Ensure the use of the best security practices and system design techniques to protect all legitimate parties in an E-commerce transaction.
6. Create a protocol that neither depends on transport security mechanisms nor prevents their use.
7. Facilitate and encourage interoperability among software and network providers.

In addition to specifying concepts for using various cryptographic technologies and certification structures, SET defines a variety of transaction protocols that use the cryptographic concepts introduced to securely conduct various types of E-commerce. The following is a list of transactions defined for payment processing:

- Cardholder Registration
- Merchant Registration
- Purchase Request
- Payment Authorization
- Payment Capture
- Certificate Inquiry and Status
- Purchase Inquiry
- Authorization Reversal
- Capture Reversal
- Credit
- Credit Reversal
- Payment Gateway Certificate Request
- Batch Administration
- Error Message

9.4.2 SET E-Payment Operations

The following is a typical SET E-payment sequence of operations:

1. The customer opens a MasterCard or Visa bank account. Any issuer of a credit card is some kind of a bank.
2. The customer receives a digital certificate. This electronic file functions as a credit card for online purchases or other transactions. It includes a public key with an expiration date. It has been through a digital switch to the bank to ensure its validity.
3. Third-party merchants also receive certificates from the bank. These certificates include the merchant's public key and the bank's public key.
4. The customer places an order over a Web page, by phone, or by some other means.
5. The customer's browser receives and confirms from the merchant's certificate that the merchant is valid.
6. The browser sends the order information. This message is encrypted with the merchant's public key, the payment information, which is encrypted with the bank's public key (which cannot be read by the merchant), and information that ensures the payment can be used only with this particular order.
7. The merchant verifies the customer by checking the digital signature on the customer's certificate. This may be done by referring the certificate to the bank or to a third-party verifier.
8. The merchant sends the order message along to the bank. This includes the bank's public key, the customer's payment information (which the merchant cannot decode), and the merchant's certificate.
9. The bank verifies the merchant and the message. The bank uses the digital signature on the certificate with the message and verifies the payment part of the message.
10. The bank digitally signs and sends authorization to the merchant, who can then fill the order.

To understand more about the technical details of SET together with all the approved extensions, the reader is referred to the formal SET specifications, interface guides, and other related SET documents.

9.5 SUMMARY

Five technologies are considered to be network security architectures: Remote Access, PKI, FPKI, SET, and WLAN. The first four have been discussed in this chapter. WLAN will be described in Chapter 10.

Remote Access uses a combination of the basic, enhanced, and integrated network security technologies presented in previous chapters to support secure convenient access mechanisms for remote users and, at the same time, provide different lines of defense to protect the enterprise network and its valuable resources from malicious or unintentional attacks.

PKI defines an elaborate architecture that defines a framework for using a combination of secret-key and public-key cryptography to enable a number of other security services including data confidentiality, data integrity, source non-repudiation, and key management. Thus, PKI allows business applications to conduct business over an insecure network, such as the Internet, with confidence.

FPKI is a specific application (in various stages of implementation) of the PKI architecture. FPKI will support the secure federal government use of information resources and NII. FPKI will establish the facilities, specifications, and policies needed by federal departments and agencies to use public-key-based certificates for information system security, E-commerce, and secure communications, including e-mail. The operation of FPKI relies heavily on the FPKI Directory Servers Architecture, which is defined for use in certification and cross-certification across trust domains.

The SET Specification is an open technical standard for the commerce industry originally developed by Visa and MasterCard as a way to facilitate secure payment card transactions over the Internet. SET uses digital certificates to create a trust chain throughout the transaction, verifying cardholder and merchant validity. SET uses aspects of PKI.

BIBLIOGRAPHY

1. Symeon Xenitellis, The Open-source PKI Book: A Guide to PKIs and Open-source Implementations, 2000.
2. Working Draft: Public Key Infrastructure (PKI) Technical Specifications: Part A — Technical Concept of Operations, TWG-98-59, September 4, 1998.
3. Federal PKI Directory Concept of Operations, Cygnacom Solutions, April 20, 1999.
4. PKI Basics — A Technical Perspective, Shashi Kiran, Patricia Lareau, and Steve Lloyd, PKI Forum Document.
5. IETF RFC 2510: Internet X.509 Public Key Infrastructure Certificate Management Protocols, C. Adams and S. Farrell, March 1999.
6. Federal Agency Use of Public Key Technology for Digital Signatures and Authentication, Kathy Lyons-Burke, NIST Special Publication 800-25, September 2000.
7. W. Diffie and M.E. Hellman, New Directions in Cryptography, *IEEE Transactions on Information Theory*, IT 22:644–654, 1976.
8. ITU-T X.509 Recommendation: Information Technology — Open Systems Interconnection — The Directory Public Key and Attribute Certificate Frameworks, June 2000.

9. Pequi: A PKIX Implementation for Secure Communication, Alexandre R. Silva and Michael A. Stanton, INET 99.

10. SET Secure Electronic Transaction Specification Book 3: Formal Protocol Definition Version 1.0, May 31, 1997.

11. External Interface Guide to SET Secure Electronic Transaction, September 24, 1997.

12. SET Secure Electronic Transaction Specification Book 1: Business Description Version 1.0, May 31, 1997.

10

WLAN SECURITY
ARCHITECTURE

In this chapter, the WLAN security architecture is presented. Modern businesses require mobility and always-on connectivity to be able to compete effectively. Cell phones and Personal Digital Assistants (PDAs) have become indispensable for business to increase productivity and improve competitiveness. Laptop computers provide users with the mobility to work anytime and anywhere, and with laptops comes the demand for wireless networking and connectivity to wired base networks. One technology that has become explosively popular recently is the Wireless Fidelity (Wi-Fi) wireless LAN (WLAN). Operating at frequencies from 2.4 to 5 GHz, this is a radio-based method to link computers to networks with an acceptable connection bandwidth of 11 to 54 Mbps, as well as performance.

802.11 is the IEEE's WLAN solution of how to comprehensively network disparate computing elements over relatively short physical distances. Similar to the Infrared Data Association (IrDA) infrared link used in the Palm PDA, 802.11 aims to support communication among 802.11-equipped stations over short distances (but longer than IrDAs). The distance is increased by the use of radio waves, and the data flow has been encrypted using the Wired Equivalent Privacy protocol (WEP) to provide more security. Another wireless standard that is also gaining increased attention is IEEE 802.16, which specifies interfaces for wireless metropolitan area networks (WMANs) by focusing on the efficient use of the bandwidth between 10 and 66 GHz (802.16a, also known as WiMAX, has recently been approved by the Microwave Access Forum industry group to provide wireless, last-mile bands below 11 GHz, particularly suited for improved non-line-of-sight performance).

WLAN technologies not only offer considerable mobility but also allow for natural extensions to the wired LAN environments. As a result, WLAN interfaces have now become standard features in many PDAs and laptops, and WLANs are being deployed extensively in public places like hospitals, universities, coffee shops, restaurants, hotels, and airports, as well as in retail stores where mobility and ease of setup are premium advantages. These are also used in homes and within corporations.

As WLANs increasingly become an intrinsic part of an enterprise's IT network infrastructure, the security of information carried over WLANs receives more and more attention. Security over WLANs can be considered unique in that in a WLAN, signals are broadcast and received over the air via radio waves and so no physical barriers are presented to an unauthorized user. These signals are readily subject to interception, exposing the enterprise to the possibility of intrusions and other threats. We present in this chapter network security topics that are crucial to the success of any WLAN implementation.

10.1 OVERVIEW OF WLANS

WLAN configurations can be very simple or extremely complex. In a typical commercial WLAN configuration, a transceiver (radio transmitter cum receiver) called a Wireless Access Point (WAP) or simply Access Point (AP), also called a hotspot, connects to a customary fixed wired network. The AP is responsible for communicating with a client station through the client station's 802.11-enabled Network Interface Card (NIC). The APs, together with the communicating NICs on the client stations, form the WLAN. A WLAN is normally identified by a Network Name or a Service Set Identifier (SSID). All wireless devices on the network must use the same SSID.

The APs are responsible for the connection between the WLAN, and the wired network and server and application resources within the wired network. Each AP can support simultaneous, multiple users. Installing an additional AP effectively extends the range of the WLAN. The number of APs deployed in a WLAN is a function of the required coverage region, as well as the number and type of users to be serviced. WLANs are generally cheaper to install and maintain than wired equivalents, and offer the added advantage of easier coverage expansion.

The following are just some of the advantages of WLAN services from the users' perspective:

- WLANs allow roaming users to wirelessly connect to corporate networks.
- Most WLANs also deliver transparent bridging and roaming capabilities.

- WLANs create seamless roaming from cell to cell.
- WLAN APs also provide full mobility.

10.1.1 Secure WLAN Architecture

Figure 10.1 gives a reference WLAN architecture intended to show some of the key WLAN components.

The following subsections describe the major components defined in the WLAN architecture.

10.1.1.1 Client Stations

Each client station is typically a PDA or a laptop that is equipped with an 802.11-enabled NIC. It also normally supports higher-layer protocol stacks, as well as network and systems software to run the necessary applications.

10.1.1.2 APs

An access point in a WLAN is a service provider station that transmits and receives data (sometimes referred to as a transceiver). It forms a part of the WLAN on one side and connects to the wired network on the other. Each access point can serve multiple users within a defined network area, and as people move beyond the range of one access point, they are automatically handed over to the next. A small WLAN may require only a single access point, and the number required increases as a function of the number of network users and the physical size of the network.

10.1.1.3 Ethernet Switches

Wired Ethernet switches are deployed in secure wiring closets, which are within 100 m of every AP, and provide effective AP aggregation and VLAN-based segregation to the next layer of the architecture. These Ethernet switches and routers participate in quality-of-service (QoS) handling, deliver Power over Ethernet technology, and ensure that intermobile user communication is barred unless authorized by the WLAN Security Switch.

10.1.1.4 Security Servers

The authentication, authorization, and auditing (AAA) security servers in this reference architecture integrate all the necessary functions of networking and application-aware security, and access control for network security:

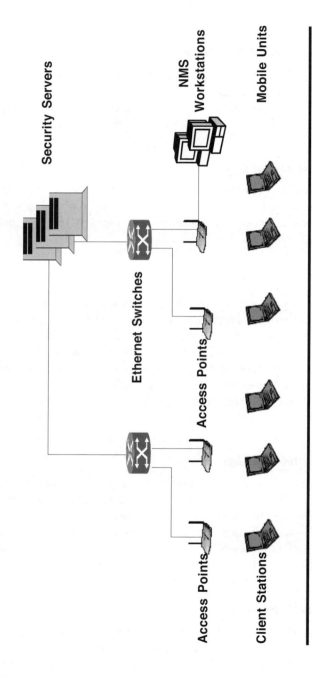

Figure 10.1 WLAN Reference Architecture.

- They support AAA and heavy-duty security in the form of traffic encryption, firewalls, and key management, and secure adaptive tunneling tailored to the application.
- They are the focal point for IP mobility, providing roaming support across subnets for enterprisewide mobility and seamless mobility.
- They interface with the fourth layer of the architecture comprised of enterprise directories, policy servers, and management systems.
- They support secure guest and contractor access using a combination of well-known network security technologies such as DMZ (demilitarized zone), firewalls, and VPNs.
- They interface with policy management, which ensures that security parameters are set consistently across multiple nodes and that multiple policies for different administrative domains all reflect enterprisewide policy, interdomain consistency, etc. Policy management addresses the full realm of security components — firewalls, authentication techniques, and more — along with a systemwide view of network environments such as found in a data center, remote office, WLAN, and campus.
- They support an interface with network management (NM) systems for various NM-related operations such as a Web Portal service for the presentation of a log-in page, password generation, update of the corporate user database, and so on.

It is important to note that the above definition of the security server is purely functional, and the actual physical implementation can be flexible.

10.1.2   WLAN Evolution

WLANs have experienced a tremendous growth over the last few years. From an architectural and technological perspective, the evolution of WLANs in the enterprise environment can be seen over time as the progression of three generations of wireless usage in LAN development.

10.1.2.1   First-Generation WLANs

Development efforts for First-Generation WLANs are principally all about basic connectivity standards and end-user benefits — much the way Ethernet LANs evolved around *ad hoc* networking, sharing network resources, and unstructured wiring during their early days. Within this early operating environment, these first-generation WLAN systems partially address security needs through proprietary designs.

Table 10.1 lists the key standards used for the development of First-Generation WLAN products.

Table 10.1   First-Generation WLAN Standards

802.11	Family of WLAN standards that originally operated at 1–2 Mbps
802.11a	A physical-layer extension standard for WLANs, supporting 54 Mbps operation in the unlicensed 5-GHz radio band. The low penetration capability of 802.11a may limit its coverage in many office environments
802.11b	A physical-layer extension for WLANs, supporting 11-Mbps operation in the unlicensed 2.4-GHz radio band

10.1.2.2   Second-Generation WLANs

Second-Generation WLANs are all about enhanced standards that put more emphasis on security, QoS, interoperability, and architectural solutions for cost–performance effectiveness. IP mobility will open the door for roaming across the entire enterprise network, not just across a few locally inter-connected wireless cells and devices. This phase is quite analogous to the widespread adoption of in-building OSI Layer 2–7 architectures based on switched Ethernet and hierarchical campus networks built around Layer 3 routing switches.

The 802.11 standards and extensions defined for the First-Generation WLANs have been significantly extended to support the additional oper-ating requirements. Table 10.2 shows the key Second-Generation WLAN standards.

10.1.2.3   Third-Generation WLANs

As Second-Generation WLANs are getting implemented and deployed, Third-Generation WLANs are being actively defined to bring down the boundaries between enterprise WLAN systems and public wireless systems for seamless roaming and to extend the application of IP mobility stan-dards, and comprehensive security and signaling mechanisms. Next-Gen-eration (so-called 2.5 and 3G) public wireless systems and a plethora of new mobility devices will have a dramatic impact on the way business works, delivering up to 11 Mbps (and beyond) throughput for data. This represents tomorrow's opportunity, which is driven first by WLAN hotspot integration with public wireless services.

10.1.3   WLAN Implementations

WLAN technologies are implemented using multiple APs to provide the required coverage and capacity. Generally, the access point is the bridge for the end clients (for example, a notebook PC) to access the enterprise

Table 10.2 Second-Generation WLAN Standards

802.11d	A supplementary 802.11 standard to allow global roaming clients; will allow access points to communicate information on the permissible radio channels with acceptable power levels
802.11e	A supplementary 802.11 standard to provide QoS support
802.11f	A "recommended practice" document that aims to achieve access point interoperability within a multivendor WLAN network by defining a common IAPP
802.11g	A physical-layer standard for WLANs in the 2.4-GHz radio band, supporting three 54-Mbps operations and a superior coding scheme (one used in IEEE 802.11a); backward compatible with 802.11b
802.11h	A supplementary 802.11 standard to comply with European regulations for 5-GHz WLANs limiting transmit power and selecting the channel for lowest interference with other systems (e.g., radar)
802.11i	A supplementary 802.11 standard to improve security; provides an alternative to Wired Equivalent Privacy (WEP) and introduces 802.1x access control, dynamic rekeying, per session key distribution mechanisms, and strong cryptographic algorithms. Centralized security management forms a key part of 802.11i
802.1x	IEEE 802.1x provides authentication/access control for the access points through the use of the Extensible Authentication Protocol (EAP), which is a set of messages for authentication negotiation and authentication transport method between client and server

network. An access point has an antenna and RF capabilities, allowing operation predominantly in the 2.4 GHz band with 11 Mbps per radio channel (IEEE 802.11b). A typical ratio of WLAN clients to access points is 10:1, although this varies between technologies and vendors. Overlapping access point cells of coverage are created when multiple access points exist around the floor or building, creating a single coverage area for mobile users.

The first three approaches to securing first-generation WLANs have major drawbacks as discussed; none of the approaches currently meet the needs for broader mobility, QoS, bandwidth management, and NM. WLANs need to be brought into the mainstream of LAN and IT infrastructures as a critical feature-rich resource that can be planned, secured, and managed. This drives the development of WLAN standards and a second-generation architecture that is functional, secure, and manageable.

Second-generation WLAN solutions that meet the needs of enterprises are founded on standards. The IEEE 802.11 committee has responded with WLAN QoS, thus allowing IP telephony and multimedia application support, and multivendor interoperability of roaming handovers across access points. All these standards present the challenge of determining which standard to use, and when and where to use it. Ideally, the 802.11 device would be able to sense what the AP is running (802.11a, b, g, d, and/or h) and dynamically connect to it. The AP may run both 802.11a and b simultaneously, or be configurable to 2.4 or 5 GHz, depending on the desired coverage area or local interference. 5 GHz has more attenuation when going through walls and windows. Ultimately, devices should be able to roam seamlessly from one standard to another (e.g., 802.11a–b).

10.2 WLAN SECURITY REQUIREMENTS

One of the key unique requirements of WLAN environments is the need to provide support for multiple options of any equivalent standard protocols or *de facto* standards in both the client station as well as the APs. This is driven by the need to have client stations communicate with APs in different domains deployed and operated by different WLAN service providers. Because different service providers support potentially different access, encryption, and other technologies based on different standards or *de facto* standards (including regional ones such as WAPI), the need to have mobility (and, therefore, roaming) dictates the need to provide support for multiple options in the stations.

Almost all large enterprises need to support WLANs as an inherent manageable and secure part of their entire enterprise network infrastructure. Thus, the WLAN network security requirements are extensions to the enterprise network security requirements. The following section provides the key aspects of these requirements that are particularly relevant to WLAN implementations.

10.2.1 Authentication and Authorization

Most large enterprise network security includes flexible user and station authentication and authorization, and single sign-on (SSO).

Authentication can be applied at the radio, networking, and application layer. As described in Chapter 7 and Chapter 9, user and station authentication capabilities are typically integrated into the enterprise Remote Access Architecture and centralized for ease of management, such as in the use of AAA servers. Before the user is allowed to access any network resources within the wired protected enterprise network, the user must first be authenticated.

In WLAN, users can be authenticated using basically the same conventional mechanisms as in wired environments: a built-in database, or existing central authentication servers such as Lightweight Directory Access

Protocol (LDAP), Remote Dial-In User Service (RADIUS), Windows NT Domain, and Active Directory. Basic authentication and authorization methods such as userID and password pairs, and more advanced authentication methods, such as token cards, certificates, and tokens all can be used.

10.2.2 Encryption

Strong encryption based on Advanced Encryption Standard (AES), for example, is applied to both physical and network layers. Because WLAN employs open airwaves for transmission of data, encryption is an essential ingredient for secure communication in WLAN. New security standards such as IEEE 802.11i (see Section 10.3.3), and VPN technologies such as IP Security (IPSec) and Secure Sockets Layer (SSL) are key to satisfying security requirements.

IPSec VPNs (see Chapter 8) operate at the network layer, are application agnostic, and require client software. For example, an IPSec-based VPN connection can be used to access e-mail, employee self-serve applications on the intranet, and the Internet.

SSL VPNs (see Chapter 8) operating at the session layer are designed primarily for Web applications, extranets, and limited application access, and do not require any special client software. The SSL VPN approach is particularly attractive for scenarios where the enterprise wants the lowest cost security solution for limited application access. It is also useful where the enterprise does not own or control the remote access devices, such as in the case of visiting customers, contractors, or suppliers.

In WLAN, to be able to simultaneously support different options of tunneling mechanisms, some vendors have implemented special adaptive tunneling mechanisms. For example, Nortel supports Mobile Adaptive Tunneling (MAT). With MAT, the security level and performance of the connection can be tailored to the application as it detects and enforces access by different types of users (e.g., general employee and restricted guest access), using devices with different security capabilities (e.g., equipped with an IPSec VPN client) and requiring different network resources.

Thus, a Nortel switch can natively support IPSec VPN clients and provide IPSec pass-through to the installed base of Secure IP Services Gateways (e.g., Nortel's Contivity). The advantages of this approach are consistency for remote, branch, and WLAN users, simplified management, and investment protection.

10.2.3 Enterprisewide Roaming

Roaming allows the users to roam from floor to floor in a building or a campus, maintaining a VPN session as they cross subnet boundaries. This permits tasks such as synchronization of e-mail and streaming sessions to be processed without interruption.

In addition, roaming has to be expanded beyond single subnet and single vendor connectivity. Several features are needed to enable solutions that meet the needs of truly mobile users:

- Dynamic Host Control Protocol (DHCP defined in IETF RFC 2132) — DHCP greatly eases the management of IP addresses by dynamically assigning IP addresses as required.
- Mobility — Mobile IP operates in a manner analogous to call forwarding in telephony networks. The WLAN cooperates to ensure that authenticated and authorized users do not need to log in again to the existing security domain and that their packet flows and sessions are uninterrupted. This implies single sign-on capabilities, and access and bandwidth controls that follow the user.
- Inter-AP Protocol (IAPP) — IAPP, defined in the IEEE 802.11f draft standard, allows APs to hand over sessions to other APs. In time, seamless enterprise IP roaming will also be extended across the public network.

10.3   WLAN NETWORK SECURITY TECHNOLOGIES

A number of very basic industry practices as well as standards-based network security solutions have been introduced since the early days of WLAN. They have since been either enhanced or replaced with more advanced standards.

The following sections describe some of the key network security technologies used in WLAN implementations.

10.3.1   Earlier Technologies

A number of industry practices as well as standards-based network security solutions have been introduced during the first-generation WLAN time period.

10.3.1.1   DMZ Isolation

This approach relies on WEP (see the following text) with all its deficiencies. It uses VLANs to segregate the WLAN traffic and to connect WLAN users to target enterprise servers placed in a DMZ area outside the corporate firewall but separate from the DMZ used for public Internet access. This prevents unauthorized users from using the corporate WLAN for Internet access, and protects the corporate LAN.

In this scenario, improvements to WEP, such as the use of rotating keys, should be implemented. The disadvantages of this approach are many, not the least of which is poor security. An unauthorized user can still easily defeat WEP using publicly available tools.

10.3.1.2   RF Isolation

This approach attempts to isolate the WLAN radio signals from the outside world. With a high-gain directional antenna, an outsider who wishes to gain unauthorized access to the WLAN can reach a WLAN from many miles away.

One method of blocking unauthorized outsiders from taking advantage of the open air availability is to provide a secure physical perimeter; another method is to surround the perimeter of the corporate grounds with APs that are not connected to the internal network.

An outsider is blocked from seeing the internal WLAN because the outside (external) APs operate at the same carrier frequency as the internal ones and offer a higher signal strength to the outsider, thereby, in effect, "jamming" the internal signal for the outsider. The disadvantage of this approach is that it is not only expensive but also not 100 percent effective.

10.3.1.3   Proprietary Methods

Some WLAN vendors have developed their own proprietary security solutions. Most are vaguely standards-based and are not interoperable with other vendors' solutions. Often these solutions are implemented in the APs themselves, thus complicating management, increasing costs, and sometimes requiring hardware upgrades.

10.3.2   802.11 Security Features

The IEEE 802.11 default authentication method defined for 802.11 is the open (system) authentication, a two-step process. The station that wants to authenticate with another station sends an authentication management frame containing the sending station's identity. The receiving station then sends back a frame, indicating whether it recognizes the identity of the authenticating station or not.

With the advent of the 802.11 standards and their extensions, more and more sophisticated security capabilities are being built into the standards. Three well-known methods to secure access to an AP are built into 802.11 networks. These basic methods are widely available and may be sufficient for some deployments such as:

- SSID
- MAC (Media Access Control) address filtering
- WEP

One or more of these methods may be implemented, but all three together provide a more robust solution.

10.3.2.1 SSID

Network access control can be implemented using an SSID associated with a single AP or a group of APs. The SSID provides a mechanism to segment a wireless network into multiple networks serviced by one or more APs. Each AP is programmed with an SSID corresponding to a specific wireless network. To access this network, client computers must be configured with the correct SSID. A building might be segmented into multiple networks by floor or department. Typically, a client computer can be configured with multiple SSIDs for users who require access to the network from a variety of different locations.

Because a client computer must present the correct SSID to access the AP, the SSID acts as a simple password and, thus, provides a measure of security. However, this minimal security is compromised if the AP is configured to "broadcast" its SSID. When this broadcast feature is enabled, any client computer that is not configured with a specific SSID is allowed to receive the SSID and access the AP. In addition, because users typically configure their own client systems with the appropriate SSIDs, they are widely known and easily shared.

10.3.2.2 MAC Address Filtering

Whereas one AP or a group of APs can be identified by an SSID, a client computer can be identified by the unique MAC address of its 802.11 NIC. To increase the security of an 802.11 network, each AP can be programmed with a list of MAC addresses associated with the client computers that are allowed to access the AP. If a client's MAC address is not included in this list, the client is not allowed to associate with the AP.

MAC address filtering (along with SSIDs) provides improved security, but it is best suited to small networks where the MAC address list can be efficiently managed. Each AP must be manually programmed with a list of MAC addresses, and the list must be kept up-to-date. In practice, the manageable number of MAC addresses filtered is likely to be less than 255. In addition, MAC addresses can be captured and "spoofed" by a client to gain unauthorized access to the network.

10.3.2.3 The WEP Protocol

Wireless transmissions are easier to intercept than transmissions over wired networks. The 802.11 standard currently specifies the WEP security protocol to provide encrypted communication between the client station and an AP. WEP employs the secret-key (symmetric) encryption algorithm Ron's Code 4 Pseudo Random Number Generator (RC4 PRNG).

Under WEP, all clients and APs on a wireless network typically use the same key to encrypt and decrypt data. The key resides in the client computer and in each AP on the network. The 802.11 standard does not specify a key-management protocol; hence all WEP keys on a network usually must be managed manually unless they are used in conjunction with a separate key-management protocol. For example, 802.1x (discussed in Section 10.3.2.4) provides WEP key management. Support for WEP is standard on most current 802.11 cards and APs.

WEP specifies the use of a 40-bit encryption key, and there are also implementations based on 104-bit keys. The encryption key is concatenated with a 24-bit Initialization Vector (IV), resulting in a 64- or 128-bit key. This key is input into a pseudorandom number generator. The resulting sequence is used to encrypt the data to be transmitted. WEP keys can be entered in alphanumeric text or hexadecimal form.

WEP relies on a secret key that is shared between a mobile station (e.g., a laptop with a wireless Ethernet card) and an access point (i.e., a base station). The secret key is used to encrypt packets before they are transmitted, and an integrity check is done to ensure that packets are not modified in transit. The standard does not discuss how the shared key is established. In practice, most installations use a single key that is shared between all mobile stations and access points. More sophisticated key-management techniques can be used to help defend against the attacks we described; however, no commercial system we are aware of has mechanisms to support such techniques.

10.3.2.3.1 WEP Encryption and Decryption

Figure 10.2 shows the formation of the WEP frame from the plaintext. The actual encryption process is as follows:

1. The data frame is checksummed (using the CRC-32 algorithm) to obtain c(M), where M is the message. M and c(M) are concatenated to get the plaintext P = (M, c(M)).
2. P is encrypted using the RC4 algorithm with a secret key k. This generates a keystream as a function of the Initialization Vector and the secret key k, and the keystream is notated as RC4 (v, k). The

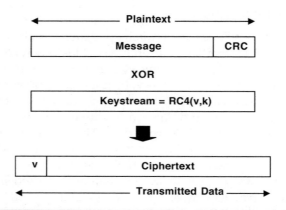

Figure 10.2 Encrypted WEP frame.

ciphertext results from applying the Exclusive-OR (XOR) function to the plaintext and the keystream. The ciphertext and the IV are then transmitted via radio.

Thus, the encrypted text, the ciphertext, and the IV v are transmitted from the sending station to the receiving station.

The decryption process is simply the reverse of the encryption process:

■ The recipient regenerates the keystream and XORs it against the ciphertext to recover the initial plaintext (P′).
■ This message (P′) is then split into the two parts of M′ and c′. Then c(M′) is computed and compared with the received checksum c′. If it does not match, the message body has changed in some manner during transmission.
■ Decryption generates the identical keystream used for encryption using the transmitted-with-the-packet IV and the shared secret key.
■ Finally, the result is XORed with the cipher text to reveal the message.

The following provides more description on the secret-key management aspect of WEP.

10.3.2.3.2 Secret-Key Management

As part of the encryption process, WEP prepares a keyschedule ("seed") by concatenating the shared secret key supplied by the user of the sending station with a random-generated 24-bit IV. The IV lengthens the life of the secret key because the station can change the IV for each frame transmission. WEP inputs the resulting seed into a pseudorandom number generator that produces a keystream equal to the length of the frame's payload plus a 32-bit Integrity Check Value (ICV).

The ICV is a checksum that the receiving station eventually recalculates and compares to the one sent by the sending station to determine whether the transmitted data underwent any form of tampering while in transit. If the receiving station calculates an ICV that does not match the one found in the frame, then it can reject the frame or flag the user.

Before transmission takes place, WEP combines the keystream with the payload or ICV through a bitwise XOR process, which produces the ciphertext (encrypted data). WEP includes the IV in the clear (unencrypted) within the first few bytes of the frame body. The receiving station uses this IV along with the shared secret key supplied by the user of the receiving station to decrypt the payload portion of the frame body.

In most cases, the sending station uses a different IV for each frame although this is not required by the 802.11 standard. When transmitting messages having a common beginning, such as the "from" address in an e-mail, the beginning of each encrypted payload will be equivalent when using the same key. After the encryption of the data, the beginnings of these frames would be the same, offering a pattern that can aid hackers in cracking the encryption algorithm. Because the IV is different for most frames, WEP guards against this type of attack. The frequent changing of IVs also improves the ability of WEP to safeguard against someone compromising the data.

10.3.2.3.3 WEP Working with Other WLAN Security Technologies

WEP encryption has been shown to be vulnerable to attack. Because of this, static WEP is only suitable for small, tightly managed networks with low-to-medium security requirements. In these cases, 128-bit WEP should be implemented in conjunction with MAC address filtering and SSID (with the broadcast feature disabled). Customers should change WEP keys on a regular schedule to further minimize risk.

For networks with high security requirements, the VPN or emerging 802.11i standards-based solutions discussed in the next subsections are preferable. These solutions are also preferable for large networks in which the administrative burden of maintaining MAC addresses on each AP makes this approach impractical. The point at which the number of wireless client systems becomes unmanageable varies, depending on the organization's ability to administer the network, the choice of security methods (SSID, WEP, and MAC address filtering), and its tolerance for risk. If MAC address filtering is used on a wireless network, the fixed upper limit is established by the maximum number of MAC addresses that can be programmed into each AP used in an installation. This upper limit varies, but the practical problem of manually entering and maintaining valid MAC addresses in every AP on a network limits the use of MAC address filtering to smaller networks.

10.3.2.4 The 802.11i Security Standard

A new security standard, 802.11i, being developed by the IEEE Taskgroup i (TGi), addresses some of the weaknesses of WEP-based wireless security. Scripting tools exist that can be used to take advantage of weaknesses in the WEP key algorithm to successfully attack a network and discover the WEP key. The industry and IEEE are working on solutions to this problem through the TGi working group. A substantial number of components in the 802.11i standard have already been released or announced with products becoming available in the market.

The 802.11i standard addresses the user authentication and encryption weaknesses of WEP-based wireless security. The components of 802.11i include:

■ IEEE 802.1x port-based authentication framework — adding 802.1x /Extensible Authentication Protocol (EAP) that can prevent the so-called man-in-the-middle attacks in which an intruder can masquerade as a host and attempt to capture passwords (see the following text)
■ Temporal Key Integrity Protocol (TKIP) — considered the next generation of WEP, providing per-packet key mixing, a message integrity check, and a rekeying mechanism, thus fixing the flaws of WEP's static keys (see the following text)
■ Advanced Encryption Standard (AES) encryption algorithm — replacing WEP's RC4 encryption
■ Key hierarchy and key management features
■ Cipher and authentication negotiation

The security requirements of AP-based (or Basic Service Set [BSS]) and *ad hoc* (or Independent BSS [IBSS]) 802.11 wireless networks are also addressed by 802.11i.

10.3.2.5 Authentication for 802.1X

The 802.1x authentication framework represents a significant improvement in security over WEP-based WLANs. This framework is included in the draft for 802.11 MAC layer security enhancements currently being developed by the IEEE 802.11 TGi. The 802.1x framework shown in Figure

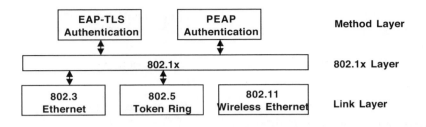

Figure 10.3 802.1x layers.

10.3 provides the link layers with extensible authentication, normally seen in higher layers.

With 802.1x, user authentication generally missing in WEP is now done through the Extensible Authentication Protocol (EAP) defined in the methods layer. Thus, whereas WEP regulates access to a wireless network based on a computer's hardware-specific MAC address, which is relatively simple to be sniffed out and stolen, EAP (see Chapter 7), on the other hand, is built on a more secure public-key encryption system to ensure that only authorized network users can access the network.

10.3.2.6 WPA

A subset of the 802.11i standard was released under the auspices of the Wi-Fi Alliance. Formerly called WECA, the Wi-Fi Alliance is a nonprofit organization that certifies interoperability of 802.11 products and promotes 802.11 as the global, wireless LAN standard.

In November 2002, the Wi-Fi Alliance announced the interim standard Wi-Fi Protected Access (WPA), which is based on those components of the 802.11i standard that are stable and may be deployed on existing 802.11 network and client equipment with a software upgrade. The fully defined 802.11i will be backward-compatible with WPA.

The initial release of WPA addresses AP-based 802.11 networks. *Ad hoc* (or peer-to-peer) networks will be addressed in the final standard. The following components of 802.11i are included in the initial WPA release:

- 802.1x authentication framework (see above).
- TKIP: Data encryption is improved through the Temporal Key Integrity Protocol (TKIP). TKIP scrambles the keys using a hashing algorithm and, by adding an integrity-checking feature, ensures that the keys have not been tampered with en route.
- Key hierarchy and management.
- Cipher and authentication negotiation.

WPA also specifies an 802.1X/RADIUS implementation and a preshared key implementation discussed that adds to its flexibility for use in large enterprise networks.

The 802.1x approach has the following advantages:

- Standards-based.
- Flexible authentication; administrators may choose the type of authentication method used.
- Scalable to large enterprise networks by simply adding APs and, as needed, additional RADIUS servers.
- Centrally managed.
- Client keys are dynamically generated and propagated.
- Because authentication is central rather than at each AP, roaming can be made as transparent as possible. At most, the user may be asked for alternate credentials if an AP requires alternate identification.

Software support for 802.1x is required on the client system and AP, as well as a RADIUS server that supports a strong EAP authentication method such as EAP-TLS and EAP-TTLS (see Chapter 8 for a description of these protocols). Currently, client operating-system support for 802.1x is still limited. Support for 802.1x is expected to expand as 802.1x matures and becomes established. Meanwhile, third-party client software exists for other PC client operating systems.

The design of 802.1x facilitates authenticating and distributing encryption keys between the wireless client and an AP. It is not an encryption protocol, nor is it designed to be a generalized VPN solution suitable for secure remote access. VPNs are still required for remote access using public APs (e.g., in airports or hotels) and from remote or home offices.

10.3.3   VPN Wireless Security

As discussed earlier in Chapter 5 and Chapter 8, VPN solutions are widely deployed to provide remote workers with secure access to the network via the Internet. In this remote user application, the VPN provides a secure, dedicated path (or "tunnel") over an "untrusted" network — in this case, the Internet. Various tunneling protocols, including the Point-to-Point Tunneling Protocol (PPTP) and Layer 2 Tunneling Protocol (L2TP) are used in conjunction with standard, centralized authentication solutions, such as Cisco's RADIUS servers.

The same VPN technologies can also be used for secure wireless access in WLANs. In this scenario, the untrusted network is the wireless network. The APs are now configured for open access with no WEP encryption, but wireless access is isolated from the enterprise network by the VPN server. The APs can be connected together via a virtual LAN (VLAN, see

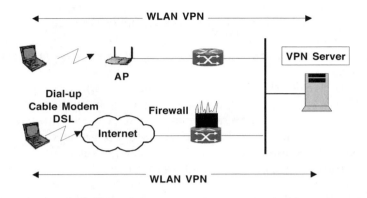

Figure 10.4   802.11 VPN wireless security.

Chapter 5) or LAN that is deployed in the Demilitarized Zone (DMZ, see Chapter 4) and connected to the VPN server. The APs should still be configured in closed mode with SSIDs for network segmentation. Authentication and full encryption over the wireless network is provided through VPN servers that also act as firewalls and gateways to the internal private network. Unlike the WEP key and MAC address filtering approaches, the VPN-based solution is scalable to a very large number of users.

Figure 10.4 shows examples that illustrate how VPN connections can provide flexible access to a private network. Remote workers can use a dial-up, cable modem, Digital Subscriber Line (DSL) or cellular data (such as General Packet Radio Service [GPRS]) connection to the Internet and then establish a VPN connection to the private network. Public wireless LAN (WLAN) networks in locations such as airports can also be used to establish a VPN connection back to the private network. Finally, on-campus 802.11 wireless access can be implemented via a secure VPN connection. The user log-in interface can be the same for each of these scenarios, so that the user has a consistent log-in interface.

The VPN approach has a number of advantages:

- Already deployed on many enterprise networks.
- Scalable to a large number of 802.11 clients.
- Low administration requirements for 802.11 APs and clients. The VPN servers can easily be administered from a central site.
- Traffic to the internal network is isolated until VPN authentication is performed.
- WEP key and MAC address list management is not needed because of security measures created by the VPN channel itself.
- Addresses general remote access with a consistent user interface in different locations such as at home, at work, and in an airport.

A drawback to current VPN solutions is the lack of support for multicasting, which is a technique used to deliver data efficiently in real time from one source to many users over a network. Multicasting is useful for streaming audio and video applications such as press conferences and training classes.

Also, as previously mentioned, mobility in wireless application is important as mobile IP is expected to operate in a manner analogous to call forwarding in telephony networks. The WLAN needs to cooperate to ensure that authenticated and authorized users do not need to log in again to the existing security domain and that their packet flows and sessions are uninterrupted. This implies single sign-on capabilities and access and bandwidth controls that follow the user. Another issue related to this is that roaming between wireless networks is not completely transparent. Users receive a log-on dialog when roaming between VPN servers on a network or when the client system resumes from standby mode. Some VPN solutions address this issue by providing the ability to auto-reconnect to the VPN.

When using a VPN solution, it is still recommended that client computers be equipped with personal firewall protection (such as Norton Internet Security, Black Ice, or the built-in firewall in Microsoft® Windows® XP) to provide increased security, including the protection against attacks by nearby wireless client systems.

VPNs are a good solution for many networks, particularly those with existing VPN infrastructure for remote access, enabling the implementers to have better control over some end-to-end connectivity features. Additional wireless security alternatives are emerging that are based on the IEEE 802.11i standard.

10.4 SUMMARY

In the first generation of 802.11 WLANs, the most widely used authentication technologies include SSID, MAC address filtering, and WEP. These authentication technologies have invariably been found to be inadequate for emerging 802.11 WLAN definitions and applications, and 802.11i with its security specifications has been formulated and is being introduced in phases to improve security in WLAN environments.

With 802.1x, the authentication protocol defined in 802.11i, user authentication generally missing in WEP is now done through EAP. Thus, whereas WEP regulates access to a wireless network based on a computer's hardware-specific MAC address (which is relatively simple to be sniffed out and stolen) EAP, on the other hand, is built on a more secure public-key encryption system to ensure that only authorized network users can access the network.

Bibliography

1. Wireless Security in 802.11 (Wi-Fi) Networks, Dell, Inc., January 2003.
2. Unified Security Architecture for Enterprise Network Security, Nortel Networks white paper: NN102060-0902, 2003.
3. The CIO's Guide to Wireless: What's Influencing Wireless in 2003, Synchrologic (Intellisync) white paper, 2003.
4. 802.11 WEP: Concepts and Vulnerability, J. Geier, Wi-Fi Planet Tutorial.
5. Wireless LAN Security, Cisco White Paper, 2002.

11

NETWORK SECURITY IMPLEMENTATION TOPICS

Basic, enhanced, integrated, and architectural technologies on network security have been presented in the previous chapters. The reader is referred to Appendix A for a summary of all the key technologies placed within the framework defined in Chapter 1. This chapter looks at a number of relevant topics that are important in the planning of the implementation and deployment of these network security technologies. They can all be considered as specialized topics, and considerable attention and research and development efforts have been given to each topic by the network security industry.

The topics can be broadly considered to fall into two categories: topics on vulnerability and topics on reducing vulnerability. Topics on vulnerability include discussions on protocol weaknesses and flaws, end-to-end connectivity, systems vulnerabilities, and other limitations. Topics on reducing vulnerability include discussions on router configurations, firewalls, adding security features to applications, etc.

Application of network security technologies (discussed in the previous chapters) is critical to the success of many business environments including the following:

- E-Commerce
- Finance and securities
- Insurance
- Business-to-business
- Private intranet
- Government-sponsored network security practices

In each of the business environments, it is essential for the network administration personnel to devise effective enterprise network security strategies. The basic guiding principles typically required to formulate these enterprise network security strategies include:

- Know your enemy
- Count your cost
- Identify your assumptions
- Control your secrets
- Remember human factors
- Know your weaknesses
- Limit the scope of access
- Understand your environment

It is useful to follow a standard SWOT (strength, weakness, opportunity, threat) approach to first identify the strengths and weaknesses of the current network environment and develop a strategy to introduce opportunities to enhance network security and reduce future potential threats. The rest of the chapter discusses a number of topics that are aimed at helping network security implementations and deployment.

11.1 STANDARDS VULNERABILITIES

Most of the network security technologies are based on defined or *de facto* standards. Algorithmic weaknesses or flaws are sometimes discovered in some of these standards as they are deployed and studied. These weaknesses and flaws potentially can be exploited to devise attacks on the implemented security systems. The typical remedy when such weaknesses and flaws are discovered in a standard is to issue a newer version or to define another more robust standard to take its place.

The following subsections show a number of such examples in:

- Cryptographic standards
- IP routing standards

Any attack on a protocol defined in a standard is considered valid if the attack results in violating some property that the protocol was intended to achieve. In other words, all attacks must be considered relative to the protocol's defined goals.

11.1.1 Cryptographic Standards

Cryptographic algorithms form the foundation of all authentication and confidentiality technologies. They need to be extremely robust for the associated network security technologies to be effective. It is therefore natural that extensive research efforts have been and will continue to be expended over the years on identifying and repairing the weaknesses and flaws of the more commonly used cryptographic standards. These efforts include the discovery and invention of ways to attack the algorithms under study. This is a very important and well-established field, and we present in the following subsections only a few such examples.

Furthermore, efforts to improve existing algorithms and standards in terms of either security or implementation efficiency are also critical to the advancement of cryptography in network security technologies. For example, RSA-PSS is a new digital signature scheme that provides increased security assurance and has been added in version 2.1 of PKCS #1.

11.1.1.1   RC4

Researchers have noted that stream ciphers (like RC4 described in Chapter 2) are vulnerable if two messages are encrypted with the same IV and secret key. If the ciphertexts are XORed together, the keystream will cancel out, and the XOR of the two plaintexts will remain. In typical messages, there is duplication of plaintext that can then lead to solving the XOR of the two. One might look for some known plaintext ("Password:" for example) which, when XORed with itself, computes to the text in the XOR of the two plaintexts. So, if the keystream is reused between messages, an attacker who has only partial knowledge of the plaintext has another chance to compromise the encryption.

11.1.1.2   IEEE 802.11

Weaknesses in some of the authentication methods used in the first generation of wireless local area network (WLAN) are described in the following subsections. The introduction of 802.11i and the associated security mechanisms are intended to plug the holes created by these weaknesses.

11.1.1.2.1   WEP

In Wired Equivalent Privacy (WEP), security is mathematically dependent on the secret key and its resistance to discovery. If RC4 is used as the stream cipher algorithm, the RC4 vulnerability mentioned earlier is carried over to the WEP implementation.

Furthermore, although the WEP standard recommends that the IV (and hence the RC4 of that IV, combined with the secret key) changes after every packet, it does not require that this has to happen. As a result, if a particular implementation of the algorithm always performs initialization to zero every time on start-up (e.g., when a 802.11 PCMIA card is inserted into a laptop), keystreams with IVs of a low value will occur frequently and would be identical for the lifetime of the secret key. An attacker would thus have multiple instantiations of the low-IV keystreams to use in cracking efforts.

There are other architectural characteristics in 802.11 that can be exploited for security attacks:

- IV dataspace is only 24 bits wide and allows IV to routinely (and somewhat predictably) repeat.
- Possibility of using only a single secret key.
- Cyclic Redundancy Code (CRC), intended to function as a message integrity guarantor, is a linear function of the message, and there are ways to control the checksum so that it is acceptable to the protocol but unlinked from the message content. CRC-32 is not immune to malicious attacks.

In more general terms, the following types of attacks are possible:

- Passive attacks to decrypt traffic, based on statistical analysis
- Active attacks to inject new traffic from unauthorized mobile stations, based on known plaintext
- Active attacks to decrypt traffic, based on tricking the access point
- Dictionary-building attacks that, after analysis of about a day's worth of traffic, allow real-time automated decryption of all traffic

As a result, WEP does not offer a high level of security, and thus other additional or alternative security measures might need to be taken. These include the use of virtual private networks (VPNs) and the newer 802.11 security definitions such as 802.11i.

Note that the attacks apply to both 40-bit and the so-called 128-bit versions of WEP equally well. They also apply to networks that use 802.11b standard (802.11b is an extension of 802.11 to support higher data rates; it leaves the WEP algorithm unchanged).

11.1.1.2.2 Use of SSID

The Service Set Identifier (SSID) is advertised in plaintext in the access point beacon messages. Although beacon messages are transparent to users, an eavesdropper can easily determine the SSID with the use of an 802.11 wireless LAN packet analyzer such as Sniffer Pro. Some access-point vendors offer the option of disabling SSID broadcasts in the beacon messages. However, the SSID can still be determined by sniffing the probe response frames from an access point.

11.1.1.2.3 MAC Address Authentication

Message authentication code (MAC) addresses are sent in the clear as required by the 802.11 specification. As a result, in WLANs that use MAC authentication, a network attacker might be able to subvert the MAC authentication process by "spoofing" a valid MAC address.

11.1.1.3 Limitations of IPSec

Though IP Security (IPSec) is the most commonly used and probably the best existing technology for the implementation of VPNs, there are certain limitations associated with the protocol. When implemented in the transport mode, IPSec is susceptible to replay attacks. Due to the limitations of Internet Security Association and Key Management Protocol (ISAKMP), IPSec is also susceptible to man-in-the-middle attacks.

Hijacking of an IPSec session can occur when an authenticating header is not used. In this type of attack, malicious data can be inserted into the payload with devastating results (e.g., an rm -r command on a Unix system can remove every file on the recipient filesystem).

Because IPSec traffic is routable, IPSec implementations may also be susceptible to source routing exploits, depending on security safeguards (or the lack thereof) that have been put in place on the routers over which IPSec traffic travels. When used in a tunnel mode, IPSec is not as vulnerable to routing exploits because the routing information is encrypted.

Though IPSec is currently not defined as part of IPv4, it is part of IPv6. Some of the weaknesses in IPSec have been corrected in IPv6. For example, in IPv4, fragmentation fields in the IP header are allowed to change. Thus, when IPSec is used in the transport mode, a hacker potentially could intercept a packet, change the fragmentation field by introducing malicious data, and then insert the packet back into the data stream. On the other hand, in IPv6, intermediate routers are not supposed to allow packet fragmentation.

11.1.1.4 Protocol-Based DoS

Protocol-based denial-of-service (DoS) attacks are one of the greatest threats to survivability of a network. Because they are implemented with the very protocols used for establishing communication, they often do not require any special privileges on the part of the attacker. Much efforts have been made to ensure that protocols are more resistant to these types of attacks but they are complicated by the fact that the very mechanisms that can be used to protect a system (e.g., cryptographic authentication) can also be used as a basis of DoS attacks themselves.

A DoS attack is a resource exhaustion attack, in which an attacker, by initiating a large number of instances of a protocol, causes a victim to waste resources until it can no longer function. Although the victim can thwart this attack by refusing to communicate with the attacker once the source of its message is known, this defense can be circumvented, or at least made more difficult, by disguising the origin of the requests. For example, the SYN attack on Transmission Control Protocol/Internet Protocol (TCP/IP) is a classic example of this type of attack. The SYN exhausts its resources, maintaining state information until timeout. Because the verification of the origin of messages in TCP/IP is based on sequence numbers that are easily forged, the victim cannot easily identify the attacker even when it is aware that it is under attack.

There are a number of defenses against this type of attack. One is to reduce the cost (i.e., risks) to a potential victim (defender of the attacks). Another is to increase the resources of the defender. A third is to introduce some sort of authentication (e.g., use of digital signatures) so that a defender could at least tell where an attack is coming from. However, the use of authentication introduces DoS risks of its own. Let us suppose, for example, that a protocol requires the defender to verify messages signed with digital signatures. Verification of such signatures is relatively resource consuming, and an attacker could introduce DoS by launching a large number of messages with bogus digital signatures, which the defender would then waste its resources verifying. Because the signatures were bogus, they would offer no assistance to the defender in tracing the origin of the attack.

A number of approaches have been used by protocol designers to reduce the DoS risks involved in participating in a protocol that uses authentication — in particular, strong authentication. These usually involve using weak authentication when the protocol is initiated but stronger authentication as it completes. Thus, the protocol provides protection against an attacker spending minimal resources in its initial stages without leaving itself vulnerable to DoS attacks that take advantage of strong authentication, but still ultimately protecting the protocol against spoofing by an attacker willing to spend greater resources. This does not leave the protocol completely invulnerable against a DoS attack by a strong opponent, but it increases the cost to an attacker. For example, cookies have become a very popular defense against DoS attacks in TCP/IP environments.

11.1.1.5 SSL and TLS

Multiple vulnerabilities have been found in different implementations of the Secure Sockets Layer (SSL) and Transport Layer Security (TLS) protocols. These vulnerabilities occur primarily in Abstract Syntax Notation One

(ASN.1) parsing code. The most serious vulnerabilities may allow a remote attacker to execute arbitrary code. The common effect is a DoS attack.

For example, an attacker can send crafted client certificate messages to a server, or attempt to cause a client to connect to a server under the attacker's control. When the client connects, the attacker can deliver a crafted server certificate message. To reduce exposure to these types of attacks, an SSL or TLS server should ignore unsolicited client certificate messages.

Again, the aforementioned are some illustrative examples of vulnerabilities and potential attacks in cryptographic standards.

11.1.2 Routing Protocols

In IP-based networks, the routing of packets plays a central role in the operations of the network as packets are forwarded hop-by-hop from their originating points to their destination-intended points by making use of information stored in routing tables. There are many routing protocols that have been defined and used. Routing Information Protocol (RIP), Interior Gateway Routing Protocol (IGRP) or Extended Interior Gateway Routing Protocol (EIGRP), Open Shortest Path First (OSPF), and Border Gateway Protocol (BGP) are the most commonly deployed. RIP, IGRP, and EIGRP are used for intra-Autonomous Systems (AS) routing, where an AS is a group of routers exchanging routing information via a common routing protocol and is normally defined to be a separate administrative domain. BGP, on the other hand, is defined to handle inter-AS routing through border routers (i.e., routers used to connect to another AS) and has two pieces that are defined similarly but used differently: Interior Border Gateway Protocol (iGBP) and Exterior Border Gateway Protocol (eGBP). Of these, iBGP is used for routing between border routers within the same AS, and eBGP is used between border routers in different ASs.

Because the separation of traffic for different connections relies on the correct operation of routing, the security capabilities in the inherent definition of routing protocols are important. All the commonly used routing protocols have security capabilities defined as part of their definitions. To illustrate such security capabilities, we look at the security-related definitions in OSPF and RIP.

11.1.2.1 OSPF Security Capabilities

All OSPF protocol exchanges are authenticated. The OSPF packet header includes an authentication-type field and 64-bits of data for use by an appropriate authentication scheme (determined by the type field).

Table 11.1 OSPF Authentication Types

AuType	Description
0	Null authentication
1	Simple password
2	Cryptographic authentication
All others	Reserved for assignment by IANA

The authentication type is configurable on a per-interface (or, equivalently, on a per-network or subnet) basis. Additional authentication data is also configurable on a per-interface basis.

Authentication types 0, 1, and 2 are defined by this specification. All other authentication types are reserved for definition by the Internet Assigned Numbers Authority (IANA). The current list of authentication types is described below in Table 11.1. A brief description of each of the authentication types is given in the following text.

11.1.2.1.1 Null Authentication

This authentication type indicates that routing exchanges over the network or subnet are not authenticated.

11.1.2.1.2 Simple Password

A 64-bit field is configured on a per-network basis. All packets sent on a particular network must have this configured value in their OSPF header 64-bit authentication field. This essentially serves as a "clear" 64-bit password. Simple password authentication guards against routers inadvertently joining the routing domain.

11.1.2.1.3 Cryptographic Authentication

A shared secret key is configured in all routers attached to a common network or subnet. For each OSPF protocol packet, the key is used to generate or verify a "message digest" or "signature" that is appended to the end of the OSPF packet. The message digest is a one-way function of the OSPF protocol packet and the secret key. Because the secret key is never sent over the network in the clear, protection is provided against passive attacks.

The algorithms used to generate and verify the message digest are specified implicitly by the secret key. This specification completely defines the use of OSPF cryptographic authentication when the Message Digest 5 (MD5) algorithm is used, as MD5 is really a hashing function.

When cryptographic authentication is used, the 64-bit Authentication field in the standard OSPF packet header is redefined with the following new field definitions:

- *Key ID* identifies the algorithm and secret key used to create the message digest appended to the OSPF packet.
- *Auth data length* indicates the length in bytes of the message digest appended to the OSPF packet.
- *Cryptographic sequence number* includes an unsigned 32-bit non-decreasing sequence number used to guard against replay attacks.

11.1.2.2   RIP Security Capabilities

The routing protocol RIP also supports authentication to prevent routing attacks. RIP's method of authentication is very similar to that of OSPF. In this case, neighboring RIP routers are provided with shared secret keys. Each sending router uses these shared secret keys to sign RIP update packet. The receiving router then uses the shared secret to check the message digest or signature and determine whether the message should be accepted.

11.2   END-TO-END CONNECTIVITY

Just as with end-to-end class of service (CoS) or quality of service (QoS), ensuring end-to-end security is not easy to do unless the network is a homogeneous one. When an end-to-end connectivity (e.g., between client workstation and a server) is made up of connection segments that use different network security technologies, these technologies should be able to work together in order to ensure the same level of security.

A common example of such connectivity is one that is made up of the following two segments:

- A remote user dials into an enterprise network gateway server, using an IPSec VPN.
- The enterprise network uses a Multi-Protocol Label Switching (MPLS) VPN to connect to the destination server.

In this case, it is important that the gateway server connecting the two VPNs (the IPSec VPN and the MPLS VPN) work correctly to ensure the secure transfer of traffic between the two ends.

Ensuring end-to-end security on one layer does not guarantee that it is ensured on another layer. For example, Simple Mail Transfer Protocol (SMTP) is not an end-to-end mechanism. Thus, if an SMTP client/server (C/S) pair decides to add TLS privacy, they are not securing the transport from the originating mail user agent to the recipient. Further, because delivery of a single piece of mail may go between more than two SMTP servers, adding TLS privacy to one pair of servers does not mean that the entire SMTP chain has been made private. Further, just because an SMTP server can authenticate an SMTP client, it does not mean that the mail from the SMTP server has been authenticated by the SMTP server when the client receives it.

Both the SMTP client and server must check the result of the TLS negotiation to see whether acceptable authentication or privacy was achieved. Ignoring this step completely invalidates the use of TLS for security. The decision about whether acceptable authentication or privacy was achieved is made locally and is implementation dependent.

11.3 SYSTEMS VULNERABILITIES

Systems software and firmware are vulnerable to attacks because of bugs, use of out-dated or incompatible versions, design flaws or incorrect configurations, and other defects.

11.3.1 OS and NOS Problems

There are many security threats, and the following are some major ones that are the results of problems in the operating systems (OSs), network operating systems (NOSs), and related systems software or firmware:

1. Viruses are computer programs written by devious programmers and designed to replicate themselves and infect computers when triggered by specific events. Viruses are countered by anti-virus software packages that keep up-to-date databases on past and new viruses, and programs to detect and clean after those viruses.
2. Trojan horse programs are delivery vehicles that are used by devious programmers to import destructive code into target computer systems. These programs appear to be harmless or useful software programs such as games.
3. Vandals are software applications or applets that cause destruction.
4. Operating system bugs or deficiencies pose security threats. Too many organizations fail to keep current on software patches.

For example, the following are a few Windows-systems vulnerabilities that have been identified and rectified:

■ Microsoft Internet Information Services (IISs) fail to handle unanticipated requests and buffer overflows, as well as breach through use of sample applications.

- Flaws in Microsoft Data Access Components (MDAC) and Remote Data Services (RDS) allow remote users to run commands with administrative privileges.
- Microsoft SQL Server vulnerabilities allow attackers to obtain sensitive information, alter database content, and compromise SQL servers or hosts.
- Improper configuration of Windows Networking Shares may expose system files or let attackers take control of the share host.
- Null sessions (anonymous log-ons) can be exploited to retrieve user and share names, or connect without authentication.
- LAN Manager Authentication password hashes are stored by default and can be easily cracked using brute force attack methods.
- Windows user accounts without passwords or with weak passwords can make it easier for attackers to gain system access.
- Multiple vulnerabilities in Internet Explorer include page spoofing, ActiveX control and scripting CVEs, MIME and content-type misinterpretation, and buffer overflows.
- Remote registry access creates a vector through which attackers can compromise a system, adjust file associations, or run malicious code.

11.3.2 Network Management Systems (NMS)

Attacks through NMS, including operation support systems (OSSs), also need to be prevented. From an NMS perspective, network security and guarding against potential malicious or unintentional attacks should be tackled on two fronts:

- Network equipment (hardware and software, e.g., routers, switches)
- User traffic carried over the network equipment

The need for this view is particularly evident for service providers who likely own the network equipment but not the end systems communicating over the network.

11.3.2.1 Protection of Network Equipment

The following are critical to the protection of network equipment (which includes NMS equipment):

- The first requirement in the protection of network equipment means secured physical installation and access control (see Chapter 4).

- The next requirement is the separation of user traffic and NMS traffic. User and NMS need to run over separate connections (e.g., PVCs, VPNs, etc.). Service providers often use separate physical networks.

11.3.2.2 Protection of User Traffic

The NMS should have capabilities that can help protect the integrity of user traffic, including the following:

- Real-time performance measurements and analysis
- Network congestion detection and release algorithms
- Management and monitoring with event alerts and automatic trouble ticketing
- Adequate levels of logs and audit trails to record user sessions and network activities
- Forward-looking client and server updates

11.4 ROUTER CONFIGURATIONS

Routers can play an important role in assuring high levels of overall network security. This section describes some general principles that need to be followed regarding the deployment and configuration of routers. The reader is referred to an extremely useful publication by the National Security Agency System and Network Attack Center (SNAC): *Router Security Configuration Guide*. A summary of this guide is included in Appendix B.

11.4.1 Protecting the Router Itself

Just as with any other network and systems equipment, before a router can protect the traffic that it carries, it must first protect itself. Some key steps to be carried out are described in the following subsections.

11.4.1.1 Physical Security

All the physical security measures (as described in Chapter 4) apply to the physical protection of a router, whether it is a backbone-network router, an access router, or a customer-premises router.

11.4.1.2 OS or NOS Vulnerabilities

The discussion earlier in this chapter on vulnerabilities in OSs or NOSs applies to routers, and steps must be taken to defend against attacks that take advantage of these vulnerabilities. For example, it is a good practice to list what features the network needs and use the resulting feature list to select the appropriate version of the OS, realizing that the very latest version of any OS tends not to be as robust in general due to its limited exposure.

11.4.1.3 Configuration Hardening

A router is similar to many computers in that it has many services enabled by default. Many of these services are unnecessary and may be used by an attacker for information gathering or for exploitation. All unnecessary services should be disabled. In addition, updates to configuration should be minimized and strictly controlled.

11.4.2 Router Configurations

Router configurations are critical not only because they tell the router how to process data correctly over the network but also to process the data correctly in the face of hostile attacks (both maliciously or unintentionally). Thus, the design and implementation life cycle of router configuration files needs to be very carefully managed.

The configuration design of routers typically proceeds after the network design is completed or in the later phases of network design. However, the management of configuration files, including the security-related aspects, can be treated as a separate entity. This life-cycle management can be looked at as the responsibility of the following:

- Design and development — Define requirements and transform them into configuration files.
- Deployment and administration — Deploy and maintain configuration files.

The maintenance of configuration is assumed to include such operations as monitoring and analysis of potential attacks. The following provides just some of the key security-related guidelines for implementing router configurations in support of network security.

11.4.2.1 Design and Development

- Base routing protocol requirements on network security requirements. Different network security requirements dictate different routing protocol needs and different routing protocol security features.

- Identify secret-key arrangements and cryptographic algorithms for use in the VPNs to be supported.
- Design ACLs based on lists of services (e.g., TFTP, SMTP, etc.) to be permitted or denied on different interfaces or connections. The lists come from user requirements.

11.4.2.2 Deployment and Administration

- Assign appropriate privilege levels to administrative personnel as part of access control. Different administrative personnel are authorized to perform different functions that incur different levels of security risks.
- Follow well-documented methods and procedures for the installation and updating of router configurations to minimize unintentional problems that can result in security risks.
- Follow secure cryptographic key-management processes to minimize disclosure of secret-key information.
- Employ constant monitoring and detailed analysis of potential attacks. Audit trails are key to the detection of attacks and planning of future defenses.
- Apply robust attack recovery procedures to minimize the cost due to successful attacks.

11.5 FIREWALLS

As described in Chapter 8, a firewall forms a crucial gateway between a network that needs to be protected and the unprotected outside world. As an integrated technology, a firewall utilizes a number of basic technologies to form a secure inside (internal) private network. The following subsections look at some implementation details for access control lists (ACLs) and network address translation (NAT) and port address translation (PAT) technologies.

11.5.1 ACLs and Packet Filtering

One of the most important router functionalities is the use of ACLs. The basic function of ACLs is to look at source and possibly destination IP addresses to make sure that only packets from and to authorized users are allowed to go through. The extended function of ACLs (see more descriptions of ACLs in Chapter 4), on the other hand, implements much more than just user authorization. One of them is packet filtering, which has been described as a basic authentication technology (see Chapter 3).

With this extended definition and usage, ACLs form an even more critical role in firewalls.

It is very important to make sure that the ACLs filter out TCP/IP packets that can do the most harm inside the firewall because of the potential usage abuse, and weaknesses and flaws in some TCP/IP services such as TFTP, ICMP, etc. Packet filtering is one of the key functions that ACLs have been asked to do.

Industrial organizations such as CERT (CERT issues regular advisories) have developed various extremely useful recommendations for system and network administrators to handle critical packet filtering issues. One of the recommendations is to have the following TCP/IP packet types filtered by a firewall:

- DNS zone transfers   Socket 53 (TCP)
- tfpd   Socket 69 (UDP)
- Link   Socket 87 (TCP) (commonly used by intruders)
- SunRPC and NFS   Socket 111 and 2049 (UDP and TCP)
- BSD UNIX "r" cmds   Sockets 512, 513, and 514 (TCP)
- lpd   Socket 515 (TCP)
- uucpd   Socket 540 (TCP)
- Openwindows   Socket 2000 (UDP and TCP)
- X windows   Socket 6000+ (UDP and TCP)

For example, packets associated with TCP socket 53 should be filtered unless they are from known secondary domain name servers. This prevents intruders from gaining additional knowledge about the systems connected to the local network.

The actual packet filtering rules to be provisioned in the firewall are very much dependent on the actual needs dictated by the applications and network environments.

Socket numbers can be used to analyze collected audit trails of known and suspected security attacks in the network to identify their patterns and to help plan future defenses.

11.5.2   NAT and PAT Limitations

As discussed in Chapter 6, NAT and PAT are address-translation technologies that are commonly used in conjunction with firewalls to allow the use of private IP addresses within enterprise networks.

NAT and PAT only examine and rewrite the IP addresses and TCP or User Datagram Protocol (UDP) port numbers in the network-layer headers in the IP packets as they pass in and out of the network. The following is a list of NAT limitations:

- NATs work at Layer 3 (IP layer).
- NATs modify the source and destination of IP addresses.
- NATs do not modify Layer 4, Layer 5, Layer 6, and Layer 7 addresses embedded within the IP payload.
- Many applications embed IP addresses at OSI Reference Model Layer 4 through Layer 7.
- NAT breaks the end-to-end model of IP for routability, encryption, etc., due to the embedded Layer 4 through Layer 7 IP addresses.

There are many applications that place the IP address and port information within the IP-layer payload (e.g., in one of the higher-layer headers), in which case it will not be sufficient to just have NAT and PAT rewrite IP addresses and port numbers in the IP-layer headers for the applications to work correctly.

This limitation of the NAT feature can be overcome with added intelligence to the relevant NAT software. For example, Cisco IOS NAT and PIX firewall support a feature called Native Support or Fixup Protocol for various applications such as File Transfer Protocol (FTP), Hypertext Transfer Protocol (HTTP), H.323, Session Initiation Protocol (SIP), and SMTP. The following subsections look at a number of these applications.

11.5.2.1 VoIP

Voice-over-IP (VoIP) presents a problem for NAT. In VoIP, IP phones, terminals, and gateways typically use one of a number of protocol suites for call signaling, call control and media capability exchanges, and the actual VoIP packet transmission. The most commonly used protocol suites are H.323, SIP, Media Gateway Control Protocol (MGCP) and Media Gateway Control (Megaco), all sitting on top of TCP or UDP or both. The protocol stack for SIP is shown in Figure 11.1 as an example.

VoIP packets containing voice samples are carried as Real-Time Transport Protocol (RTP) or Real-Time Transport Control Protocol (RTCP) payloads. Other messages use the SIP and Session Delivery Protocol (SDP) layers.

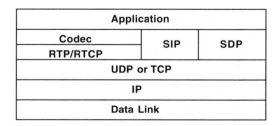

Figure 11.1 SIP protocol stack.

In each of these protocol suites, call signaling, call control, and media capability exchanges are all done through the exchanges of messages defined within the respective protocol suites, typically through a Call Control Element (CCE) (also called the gatekeeper in H.323). In all these messages, the IP addresses and port numbers are embedded within the data payload of the IP packets. This causes end-to-end routing problems between the endpoints if the embedded IP addresses are private IP addresses, and address and port number translations are required. If address translation is done only on the network-layer header IP addresses, then the most likely result is that the call will be directed to the wrong destination, be unsuccessful, or remain in some hung state.

One solution is to employ a special application layer gateway (ALG) that examines and rewrites IP addresses and ports not only on the IP headers but also within the SIP or SDP layers.

11.5.2.2 IPSec VPN

Some VPN technologies do not support NAT and PAT without enhancements. IPSec currently is one of these technologies, and therefore an IPSec connection cannot traverse "NATed" environments.

11.5.3 Special Application Layer Gateways

Special tools continue to be introduced as different types of attacks are injected, and protection of networks becomes a perpetual catch-up game. For example, many specialized devices (hardware and software packages) have become commercially available to tackle the e-mail attack phenomenon of spam that has been causing widespread DoS problems to not only enterprise networks but also Internet Service Providers (ISPs). These devices invariably employ the use of blacklists, and sometimes whitelists, and known spam recognition techniques to filter out SMTP messages before they arrive at the enterprise mail servers.

As another example, the deployment of separate intrusion detection systems (IDSs) to continually, passively or actively, monitor incoming packets to discover if a hacker is attempting to break into a system (or cause a DoS attack) is now being done in some form in most major enterprise networks.

From a high-level perspective, these special tools can all be classified as ALGs (Chapter 8).

11.6 ADDING SECURITY TO APPLICATIONS AND SERVICES

Security capabilities have been added to many applications and services to ensure an acceptable level of security, regardless of what kinds of transport network are being used. The following subsections provide just a few examples.

11.6.1 Network Services

11.6.1.1 S-HTTP

S-HTTP (Secure HTTP) is an extension to the HTTP that allows the secure exchange of files on the World Wide Web. Each S-HTTP file is either encrypted or contains a digital certificate, or both. For a given document, S-HTTP is an alternative to another well-known security protocol, SSL. A major difference is that S-HTTP allows the client to send a certificate to authenticate the user, whereas using SSL, only the server can be authenticated. S-HTTP is more likely to be used in situations where the server represents a bank and requires authentication from the user that is more secure than a userID and password.

S-HTTP does not use any single encryption system, but it does support the Rivest–Shamir–Adleman public-key infrastructure encryption system. SSL works at a program layer slightly higher than the TCP level. S-HTTP works at an even higher level of the HTTP application. Both security protocols can be used by a browser user, but only one can be used with a given document.

A number of popular Web servers support both S-HTTP and SSL. Newer browsers support both of them. S-HTTP (not to be confused with HTTP over SSL [HTTPS]) is defined in IETF RFC 2660.

11.6.1.2 S/MIME

Secure/Multipurpose Internet Mail Extensions (S/MIME), defined in IETF RFC 2311, provide a consistent way to send and receive secure MIME data. Based on the popular Internet MIME standard, S/MIME provides the following cryptographic security services for electronic messaging applications: authentication, message integrity and non-repudiation of origin (using digital signatures), and privacy and data security (using encryption).

S/MIME can be used by traditional mail user agents (MUAs) to add cryptographic security services to mail that is sent and also interpret them in mail that is received. However, S/MIME is not restricted to mail; it can be used with any transport mechanism that transports MIME data, such as HTTP. In this way, S/MIME takes advantage of the object-based features of MIME and allows secure messages to be exchanged in mixed-transport systems.

Further, S/MIME can be used in automated message transfer agents that use cryptographic security services that do not require any human intervention, such as the signing of software-generated documents and the encryption of FAX messages sent over the Internet.

11.6.1.3 SMTP

SMTP allows servers and clients to normally communicate in the clear over the Internet. In many cases, this communication goes through one or more routers that are not controlled or trusted by either entity. Such untrusted routers might allow a third party to monitor or alter the communications between the server and client.

Further, there is often a desire for two SMTP agents to be able to authenticate each other's identities. For example, a secure SMTP server might only allow communications from other SMTP agents it knows, or it might act differently regarding messages received from an agent it knows rather than one it does not know.

RFC 2487 defines an extension to the SMTP service that allows an SMTP server and client to use TLS to provide private, authenticated communication over the Internet. This gives SMTP agents the ability to protect some or all of their communications from eavesdroppers and attackers.

11.6.2 Web Applications

Web applications typically refer to applications that use TCP port 80 (HTTP) for traffic pass-through. Many application-layer attacks that target Web applications cannot easily be detected and handled by traditional firewalls. Attacks of these kinds include, for example, the following:

- Command (e.g., SQL commands) injection
- Buffer overflow caused by injection and execution of shell code
- Access to unauthorized directories through forceful browsing

In these cases, special Web-application firewalls can be deployed to stop hackers from exploiting Web-application vulnerabilities. They can be deployed either separately or as part of the ALGs.

11.7 SUMMARY

The topics discussed in this chapter fall broadly into two categories: network vulnerability and reducing network vulnerability. Because of various weaknesses, flaws, and limitations in various network protocols, work on improving network security is actively pursued in many arenas, including protocol design or improvement, stringent equipment-configuration guidelines (e.g., in router configurations), and network topology (e.g., firewalls, demilitarized zones [DMZs], etc.) requirements, as well as adequate network management sophistication.

Bibliography

1. *Router Security Configuration Guide by System and Network Attack Center (SNAC)*, National Security Agency, Updated: March 25, 2002, Version: 1.0k, Report Number: C4-054R-00.
2. IETF RFC 2487: Service Extension for Secure SMTP over TLS, P. Hoffman, January 1999.
3. A Framework for Denial of Service Analysis, C. Meadows, Third Information Survivability Workshop — ISW-2000, October 24–26, 2000.
4. The CERT® Guide To System and Network Security Practices, Julia Allen, May 30, 2001.
5. VoIP traversal of NAT and Firewall, Cisco Document, March 26, 2003.
6. IETF RFC 2328 (obsoletes 2178): OSPF Version 2, J. Moy, April 1998.
7. Wireless LAN Security, Cisco White Paper, 2003.
8. IETF RFC 2311: S/MIME Version 2 Message Specification, S. Dusse, P. Hoffman, B. Ramsdell, L. Lundblade, L. Repka, March 1998.
9. Burt Kaliski, "Raising the Standard for RSA Signatures: RSA-PSS," RSA Laboratories, February 26, 2003.

Appendix A

SECURITY TECHNOLOGIES: A HIERARCHICAL GUIDE

	Authentication	Authorization	Confidentiality	Message Integrity	Non-Repudiation
Architecture			RAS PKI FPKI SET WLAN/802.11		
Integrated			Firewalls: Packet filter, Circuit-level gateway, ALG Higher-layer VPNs: IPsec, SSL, TLS, TTLS, PEAP SSOs: OGSF SSO, SSG, GSS-API		
Enhanced	UserID and password: CHAP, Kerberos EAP Digital certificate	UserID and password: CHAP, Kerberos Token card	Encrypted VPN: MPPE Key management: ISAKMP, OAKLEY, IKE, SKIP, STS Wi-Fi: WEP, 802.11i	Digital signature: RSA, DSA, ECDSA MAC	Digital signature: RSA, DSA, ECDSA MAC
Basic	Authentication headers: AH, ESP Packet filtering: Static, dynamic UserID and password	Physical access control UserID and password: PAP, SPAP ACLs DMZ	Hashing algorithms: MD5, SHS (SHA-1, SHA-256, SHA-384, and SHA-512) Secret-key cryptography: DES, 3DES, AES, RC4 Public-key cryptography: RSA, DSA, ECDSA, Key exchange: Diffie-Hellman	L2 VPNs: FR, ATM, MPLS, Ethernet VLAN Tunneling protocols: PPP, PPPoE, PPP over SONET/SDH, GRE, PPTP, L2TP Authentication headers: AH, ESP	Digital signature MAC NAT and PAT

Appendix B

NSA AND SNAC ROUTER SECURITY CONFIGURATION GUIDE SUMMARY (FROM NATIONAL SECURITY AGENCY/SYSTEM AND NETWORK ATTACK CENTER)

EXECUTIVE SUMMARY

This card is a supplement to the NSA and SNAC Router Security Configuration Guide version 1.1. It describes quick but effective ways to tighten the security of a Cisco router, along with some important general principles for maintaining good router security. For more information, consult the sections of the main guide listed with each recommendation.

GENERAL RECOMMENDATIONS

1. Create and maintain a written router security policy. The policy should identify who is allowed to log in to the router, who is allowed to configure and update it, and should outline the logging and management practices for it [Section 3.4].
2. Comment on and organize offline master editions of your router configuration files! This sounds superficial despite being a big

security win. Also, keep the offline copies of all router configurations in sync with the actual configurations running on the routers. This is invaluable for diagnosing suspected attacks and recovering from them [Section 4.1].

3. Implement access lists that allow only those protocols, ports, and IP addresses that are required by network users and services, and that deny everything else [Section 3.2 and Section 4.3].

4. Run the latest available General Deployment (GD) IOS version [Section 4.5.5 and Section 8.3].

5. Test the security of your routers regularly, especially after any major configuration changes [Section 6].

SPECIFIC RECOMMENDATIONS: ROUTER ACCESS

1. Shut down unneeded services on the router. Servers that are not running cannot break. Also, more memory and processor slots become available. Start by running the show proc command on the router, then turn off clearly unneeded facilities and services. Some servers that should almost always be turned off and the corresponding commands to disable them are listed below [Section 4.2 and Section 4.5.3].
    - Small services (echo, discard, chargen, etc.)
        - no service tcp-small-servers
        - no service udp-small-servers
    - BOOTP — no ip bootp server
    - Finger — no service finger
    - HTTP — no ip http server
    - SNMP — no snmp-server

2. Shut down unneeded services on the routers. These services allow certain packets to pass through the router or send special packets, or are used for remote router configuration. Some services that should almost always be turned off and the corresponding commands to disable them are listed below [Section 4.1 and Section 4.2].
    - CDP — no cdp run
    - Remote config — no service config
    - Source routing — no ip source-route

3. The interfaces on the router can be made more secure by using certain commands in the Configure Interface mode. These commands should be applied to every interface [Section 4.1 and Section 4.2].
    - Unused interfaces — shutdown
    - No Smurf attacks — no ip directed-broadcast

- Mask replies — no ip mask-reply
- *Ad hoc* routing — no ip proxy-arp

4. The console line, the auxiliary line, and the virtual terminal lines on the router can be made more secure in the Configure Line mode. The console line and the virtual terminal lines should be secured as shown below. The auxiliary line should be disabled, as shown below, if it is not being used [Section 4.1].
   - Console line
     - line con 0
     - exec-timeout 5 0
     - login
   - Auxiliary line
     - line aux 0
     - no exec
     - exec-timeout 0 10
     - transport input none
   - VTY lines
     - line vty 0 4
     - exec-timeout 5 0
     - login
     - transport input telnet ssh

5. Passwords can be configured more securely as well. Configure the Enable Secret password, which is protected with an MD5-based algorithm. Also, configure passwords for the console line, the auxiliary line, and the virtual terminal lines. Provide basic protection for the user and line passwords using the service passwordencryption command. See examples in the following text [Section 4.1].
   - Enable secret — enable secret 0 2manyRt3s
   - Console line
     - line con 0
     - password Soda-4-jimmY
   - Auxiliary line
     - line aux 0
     - password Popcorn-4-sara
   - VTY lines
     - line vty 0 4
     - password Dots-4-georg3
   - Basic protection — service password-encryption

6. Consider adopting SSH, if your router supports it, for all remote administration [Section 5.3].

7. Protect your router configuration file from unauthorized disclosure.

SPECIFIC RECOMMENDATIONS: ACCESS LISTS

1. Always start an access-list definition with the privileged command
   no access-list *nnn* to clear out any previous versions of
   access list number *nnn* [Section 4.3].

   ```
   East(config)# no access-list 51
   East(config)# access-list 51 permit host 14.2.9.6
   East(config)# access-list 51 deny any log
   ```

2. Log access list port messages properly. To ensure that logs contain
   correct port number information, use the port range arguments
   shown below at the end of an access list.

   ```
   access-list 106 deny udp any range 1 65535
       any range 1 65535 log
   access-list 106 deny tcp any range 1 65535
       any range 1 65535 log
   access-list 106 deny ip any any log
   ```

   The last line is necessary to ensure that rejected packets of protocols other than TCP and UDP are properly logged [Section 4.3].

3. Enforce traffic address restrictions using access lists. On a border
   router, allow only internal addresses to enter the router from the
   internal interfaces, and allow only traffic destined for internal
   addresses to enter the router from the outside (external interfaces).
   Block illegal addresses at the outgoing interfaces. Besides prevent-
   ing an attacker from using the router to attack other sites, it helps
   identify poorly configured internal hosts or networks. This
   approach may not be feasible for complicated networks [Section
   4.3, also RFC 2827].

   ```
   East(config)# no access-list 101
   East(config)# access-list 101 permit ip
       14.2.6.0 0.0.0.255 any
   East(config)# access-list 101 deny ip any any log
   East(config)# no access-list 102
   East(config)# access-list 102 permit ip
       any 14.2.6.0 0.0.0.255
   East(config)# access-list 102 deny ip any any log
   East(config)# interface eth 1
   East(config-if)# ip access-group 101 in
   East(config-if)# exit
   East(config)# interface eth 0
   ```

```
East(config-if)# ip access-group 101 out
East(config-if)# ip access-group 102 in
```

4. Block packets coming from the outside (untrusted network) that are obviously fake or have source or destination addresses that are reserved, for example networks 0.0.0.0/8, 10.0.0.0/8, 169.254.0.0/16, 172.16.0.0/20, and 192.168.0.0/16. This protection should be part of the overall traffic filtering at the interface attached to the external, untrusted network [Section 4.3; see also RFC 1918].

5. Block incoming packets that claim to have a source address of any internal (trusted) networks. This impedes TCP sequence number guessing and other attacks. Incorporate this protection into the access lists applied to interfaces facing any untrusted networks [Section 4.3].

6. Drop incoming packets with loopback addresses, network 127.0.0.0/8. These packets cannot be real [Section 4.3].

7. If the network does not need IP multicast, then block multicast packets.

8. Block broadcast packets. (Note that this may block DHCP and BOOTP services, but these services should not be used on external interfaces and certainly should not cross border routers.)

9. A number of remote probes and attacks use ICMP echo, redirect, and mask request messages; block them. (A superior but more difficult approach is to permit only necessary ICMP packet types.)

The example below shows one way to implement these recommendations.

```
North(config)# no access-list 107
North(config)# ! block our internal addresses
North(config)# access-list 107 deny ip
        14.2.0.0 0.0.255.255 any log
North(config)# access-list 107 deny ip
        14.1.0.0 0.0.255.255 any log
North(config)# ! block special/reserved addresses
North(config)# access-list 107 deny ip
        127.0.0.0 0.255.255.255 any log
North(config)# access-list 107 deny ip
        0.0.0.0 0.255.255.255 any log
North(config)# access-list 107 deny ip
        10.0.0.0 0.255.255.255 any log
North(config)# access-list 107 deny ip
        169.254.0.0 0.0.255.255 any log
```

```
North(config)# access-list 107 deny ip
      172.16.0.0 0.15.255.255 any log
North(config)# access-list 107 deny ip
      192.168.0.0 0.0.255.255 any log
North(config)# ! block multicast (if not used)
North(config)# access-list 107 deny ip
      224.0.0.0 15.255.255.255 any
North(config)# ! block some ICMP message types
North(config)# access-list 107 deny icmp
      any any redirect log
North(config)# access-list 107 deny icmp
      any any echo log
North(config)# access-list 107 deny icmp
      any any mask-request log
North(config)# access-list 107 permit ip
      any 14.2.0.0 0.0.255.255
North(config)# access-list 107 permit ip
      any 14.1.0.0 0.0.255.255
North(config)# interface Eth 0/0
North(config-if)# description External interface
North(config-if)# ip access-group 107 in
```

10. Block incoming packets that claim to have the same destination and source address (i.e., a 'Land' attack on the router itself). Incorporate this protection into the access list used to restrict incoming traffic into each interface, using a rule like the one shown below [Section 4.3].

```
access-list 102 deny ip host 14.1.1.250
      host 14.1.1.250 log
interface Eth 0/1
ip address 14.1.1.250 255.255.0.0
ip access-group 102 in
```

11. Configure an access list for the virtual terminal lines to control Telnet access. See example commands below [Section 4.1 and Section 4.6].

```
South(config)# no access-list 92
South(config)# access-list 92 permit 14.2.10.1
South(config)# access-list 92 permit 14.2.9.1
South(config)# line vty 0 4
South(config-line)# access-class 92 in
```

SPECIFIC RECOMMENDATIONS: LOGGING AND DEBUGGING

1. Turn on the router's logging capability and use it to log errors and blocked packets to an internal (trusted) syslog host. Make sure that the router blocks syslog traffic from untrusted networks. See example commands below [Section 4.5].

   ```
   Central(config)# logging on
   Central(config)# logging 14.2.9.1
   Central(config)# logging buffered
   Central(config)# logging console critical
   Central(config)# logging trap informational
   Central(config)# logging facility local1
   ```

2. Configure the router to include time information in the logging. Configure at least two different NTP servers to ensure availability of good time information. This will allow an administrator to trace network attacks more accurately. See example commands below [Section 4.2 and Section 4.5].

   ```
   East(config)# service timestamps log datetime
   localtime show-timezone msec
   East(config)# clock timezone GMT 0
   East(config)# ntp server 14.1.1.250
   East(config)# ntp server 14.2.9.1
   ```

3. If your network requires SNMP, then configure an SNMP ACL and hard-to-guess SNMP community strings. The example commands below show how to remove the default community strings and set a better read-only community string, with an ACL [Section 4.5].

   ```
   East(config)# no snmp community public ro
   East(config)# no snmp community private rw
   East(config)# no access-list 51
   East(config)# access-list 51 permit 14.2.9.1
   East(config)# snmp community BTR18+never ro 51
   ```

ROUTER SECURITY CHECKLIST

The following security checklist is designed to help you review your router security configuration and remind you of any security area you might have missed:

- Router security policy written, approved, distributed
- Router IOS version checked and up to date

- Router configuration kept offline, backed up, access to it limited
- Router configuration well documented and commented
- Router users and passwords configured and maintained
- Password encryption in use, enable secret in use
- Enable secret difficult to guess, knowledge of it strictly limited (if not, change the enable secret immediately)
- Access restrictions imposed on Console, Aux, VTYs
- Unneeded network servers and facilities disabled
- Necessary network services configured correctly (e.g., DNS)
- Unused interfaces and VTYs shut down or disabled
- Risky interface services disabled
- Port and protocol needs of the network identified and checked
- Access lists limit traffic to identified ports and protocols
- Access lists block reserved and inappropriate addresses
- Static routes configured where necessary
- Routing protocols configured to use integrity mechanisms
- Logging enabled and log-recipient hosts identified and configured
- Router's time of day set accurately, maintained with NTP
- Logging set to include consistent time information
- Logs checked, reviewed, archived in accordance with local policy
- SNMP disabled or enabled with good community strings and ACLs

Appendix C

KEY NETWORK SECURITY TERMS AND DEFINITIONS

The following are some useful terms and definitions used in the area of network security:

Basic Service Set (BSS): A set of 802.11-compliant stations that operate as a fully connected wireless network.

Block Cipher: An algorithm that encrypts (and decrypts) data organized in fixed-size blocks (for example, 64 contiguous-bits blocks) as opposed to one byte at a time.

Certification Path: A chain of certificates between any given certificate and its trust anchor (CA). Each certificate in the chain must be verifiable in order to validate the certificate at the end of the path; this functionality is critical to the usable PKI.

Checksum: The checksum of an input data is a value computed by adding together all the numbers in the data. If the sum of all the numbers exceeds the highest value that a checksum can hold, the checksum equals the modulus of the total — i.e., the remainder that is left over when the total is divided by the checksum's maximum possible value plus 1. The checksum method is the simplest method of verifying the integrity of digitally transmitted data.

Ciphertext: The text that is the output from an encryption algorithm and is unreadable until it is decrypted with the correct key.

Cookie: A piece of text that a Web server can store on a user's hard disk. Cookies allow a Web site to store information on a user's machine and later retrieve it. The pieces of information are stored as name–value pairs.

Domain of Interpretation (DOI): The DOI defines payload formats, the situation, exchange types, and naming conventions for certain information such as security policies or cryptographic algorithms. It is also used to interpret ISAKMP payloads.

End Entity: An End Entity can be considered an end user, a device such as a router or a server, a process, or anything that can be identified in the subject name of a public-key certificate. End Entities can also be thought of as consumers of PKI-related services.

Exchange Type: Exchange type defines the number of messages in an ISAKMP exchange and the ordering of the used payload types for each of these messages. Through this arrangement of messages and payloads, security services are provided by the exchange type.

Feistal Network: A Feistal Network generates blocks of keystream from blocks of the message itself, through multiple rounds of groups of permutations and substitutions, each dependent on transformations of a key.

Independent Basic Service Set Network (IBSS Network): Independent Basic Service Set Network is an IEEE 802.11-based wireless network that has no backbone infrastructure and consists of at least two wireless stations. This type of network is often referred to as an *ad hoc* network because it can be constructed quickly without much planning.

IP Spoofing: IP (Address) Spoofing is a technique used to gain unauthorized access to computers or network devices, whereby the intruder sends messages with an IP source address to pretend that the message is coming from a trusted source.

Message Authentication Code (MAC): Message authentication code is a one-way hash computed from a message and some secret data. It is difficult to forge without knowing the secret data. Its purpose is to detect if the message has been altered.

Nontransparent Proxy Mode Accelerator: In a Nontransparent Proxy Mode Accelerator, the source addresses of all the packets decrypted by the SSL accelerator have the source address of that SSL accelerator and the client source addresses do not get to the server at all. From the server perspective, the request has come from the SSL accelerator.

Perfect Forward Secrecy: Perfect forward secrecy means that even if a private key is known to an attacker, the attacker cannot decrypt previously sent messages.

Public Key Cryptography Standards: Public Key Cryptography Standards (PKCS) are specifications produced by RSA Laboratories in cooperation with secure systems developers worldwide for the purpose of accelerating the deployment of public-key cryptography.

Proxy Server: Proxy server is a server that acts as an intermediary between a remote user and the servers that run the desired applications.

Salt: A string of random (or pseudorandom) bits concatenated with a key or password to reduce the probability of precomputation attacks.

Security Association: A set of parameters that defines all the security services and mechanisms used for protecting the communication. A security association is bound to a specific security protocol.

Security Parameter Index (SPI): An identifier for a security association within a specific security protocol. This means that a pair of security protocol and SPI may uniquely identify a security association, but this is implementation dependent.

Session Key: A randomly generated key that is used one time and then discarded. Session keys are symmetric (used for both encryption and decryption). They are sent with the message, and protected by encryption with a public key from the intended recipient. A session key consists of a random number of approximately 40 to 2000 bits. Session keys can be derived from hash values.

Situation: A set of all security-relevant information. The decision of an entity on which security services it requires is based on the situation.

Stream Cipher: An algorithm that encrypts (and decrypts) data one byte at a time.

Strong Authentication: Refers to systems that require multiple factors for authentication and use advanced technology, such as dynamic passwords or digital certificates, to verify a user's identity.

Substitution–Linear Transformation Network: A practical architecture based on Shannon's concepts for secure, practical ciphers with a network structure consisting of a sequence of rounds of small substitutions, easily implemented by table lookup and connected by bit-position permutations or linear transpositions.

Appendix D

LIST OF COMMON TCP AND UDP WELL-KNOWN PORTS

WELL-KNOWN PORT NUMBERS

The port numbers are divided into three ranges: Well-Known Ports, Registered Ports, and Dynamic and Private Ports.

- Well-Known Ports are those from 0 through 1023.
- Registered Ports are those from 1024 through 49151.
- Dynamic and Private Ports are those from 49152 through 65535.

Well-Known Ports are assigned by the Internet Assigned Numbers Authority (IANA) and on most systems can only be used by system (or root) processes or by programs executed by privileged users.

Ports are used in TCP (RFC793) to name the ends of logical connections that carry long-term conversations. For the purpose of providing services to unknown callers, a service contact port is defined. This list specifies the port used by the server process as its contact port. The contact port is sometimes called the "Well-Known Port."

To the extent possible, these same port assignments are used with UDP (RFC768).

The range for assigned ports managed by the IANA is 0–1023.

COMMON WELL-KNOWN PORT NUMBERS

The following are some commonly used TCP and UDP Well-Known Ports:

Port	UDP	TCP	Definition
7	x	x	echo
9	x	x	discard
11	x	x	systat
13	x	x	daytime
17	x	x	quote of the day
19		x	character generator
20		x	ftp — data
21		x	ftp — control
23		x	telnet
25		x	smtp mail transfer
37	x	x	timeserver
39	x		rlp resource location
42	x	x	nameserver
43		x	nicname whois
53	x	x	dommainlein name server
67	x		bootpc bootstrap protocol
68	x		bootpc bootstrap protocol
69	x		tftp trivial file transfer
70		x	gopher
79		x	finger
80		x	http
88	x	x	kerberos
101		x	hostname nic
102		x	iso-tsap class 0
107		x	rtelnet
109		x	pop2
110		x	pop3
111	x	x	sunrpc
113		x	identification protocol
117		x	uucp
119		x	nntp
123	x		ntp
135	x	x	epmap
137	x	x	netbios — name service
138	x		netbios — dgm
139		x	netbios — ssn
143		x	imap
158		x	pcmail — srv
161	x		snmp
162	x		snmptrap

Port	UDP	TCP	Definition
170		x	print — srv
179		x	border gateway protocol
194		x	irc internet relay chat
213	x		ipx
389		x	ldap
443	x	x	https (ssl)
445	x	x	microsoft — ds
464	x	x	kpasswd
500	x		isakmp key exchange
512	x	x	remote execute
513	x	x	login/who
514	x	x	shell cmd/syslog
515		x	printer spooler
517	x		talk
518	x		ntalk
520	x	x	router/efs
525	x		timeserver
526		x	tempo
530		x	rpc
531		x	conference chat
532		x	netnews newsreader
533	x		netwall
540		x	uucp
543		x	klogin
544		x	kshell
550	x		new — rwho
556		x	remotefs
560	x		rmonitor
561	x		monitor
636		x	ldaps over tls/ssl
666	x	x	doom id software
749	x	x	kerberos administration
750	x		kerberos version iv
1109		x	kpop
1167	x		phone
1433	x	x	ms-sql-server
1434	x	x	ms-sql-monitor
1512	x	x	wins
1524		x	ingreslock
1701	x		l2tp

Port	UDP	TCP	Definition
1723		x	pptp point to point
1812	x		radius authentication
1813	x		radius accounting
2049	x		nfs server
2053		x	kerberos demultiplexor
9535		x	man remote server

Appendix E

RSA PUBLIC-KEY CRYPTOGRAPHY EXAMPLE

The following example is taken from "An RSA Laboratories Technical Note" by Burton S. Kaliski Jr., Revised November 1, 1993, in support of RSA Data Security, Inc., Public Key Cryptography Standards (PKCS).

GENERATING A KEY PAIR AND PROTECTING THE PRIVATE KEY

An example user, called Test User 1, generates an RSA key pair according to PKCS #1 and protects the private key with a password according to PKCS #5 and #8. The process of generating a key pair and protecting the private key can be broken down into five steps:

1. Generating an RSA key pair according to PKCS #1
2. Encoding values of type RSAPublicKey and RSAPrivateKey according to PKCS #1 to represent the key pair in an algorithm-specific way
3. Encoding values of type PrivateKeyInfo according to PKCS #8 to represent the private key in an algorithm-independent way
4. Encrypting the PrivateKeyInfo encoding with a password according to PKCS #5
5. Encoding a value of type EncryptedPrivateKeyInfo according to PKCS #8 to represent the encrypted PrivateKeyInfo value in an algorithm-independent way

Step 1: Generating an RSA Key Pair

Test User 1 generates an RSA key pair according to PKCS #1.

In the example, the modulus n is the following 508-bit integer:

```
n = 0a 66 79 1d c6 98 81 68 de 7a b7 74 19 bb 7f b0 c0
    01 c6 27 10 27 00 75 14 29 42 e1 9a 8d 8c 51 d0 53 b3
    e3 78 2a 1d e5 dc 5a f4 eb e9 94 68 17 01 14 a1 df e6
    7c dc 9a 9a f5 5d 65 56 20 bb ab
```

The prime factors p and q of the modulus are:

```
p = 33 d4 84 45 c8 59 e5 23 40 de 70 4b cd da 06 5f bb
    40 58 d7 40 bd 1d 67 d2 9e 9c 14 6c 11 cf 61
```

```
q = 33 5e 84 08 86 6b 0f d3 8d c7 00 2d 3f 97 2c 67 38
    9a 65 d5 d8 30 65 66 d5 c4 f2 a5 aa 52 62 8b
```

The public exponent e is $F4$ (65537):

```
e = 01 00 01
```

The private exponent d and other private-key parameters are as follows:

```
d = 01 23 c5 b6 1b a3 6e db 1d 36 79 90 41 99 a8 9e a8
    0c 09 b9 12 2e 14 00 c0 9a dc f7 78 46 76 d0 1d 23 35
    6a 7d 44 d6 bd 8b d5 0e 94 bf c7 23 fa 87 d8 86 2b 75
    17 76 91 c1 1d 75 76 92 df 88 81
```

```
d mod p-1 = 04 5e c9 00 71 52 53 25 d3 d4 6d b7 96 95 e9
            af ac c4 52 39 64 36 0e 02 b1 19 ba a3 66 31 62 41
```

```
d mod q-1 = 15 eb 32 73 60 c7 b6 0d 12 e5 e2 d1 6b dc d9
            79 81 d1 7f ba 6b 70 db 13 b2 0b 43 6e 24 ea da 59
```

```
q-1 mod p = 2c a6 36 6d 72 78 1d fa 24 d3 4a 9a 24 cb
            c2 ae 92 7a 99 58 af 42 65 63 ff 63 fb 11 65 8a 46 1d
```

Step 2: Encoding RSAPublicKey and RSAPrivateKey Values

Test User 1 encodes values of type RSAPublicKey and RSAPrivateKey according to PKCS #1 to represent the key pair in an algorithm-specific way.

The BER-encoded RSAPublicKey value is:

```
30 47
   02 40                                                    modulus = n
      0a 66 79 1d c6 98 81 68 de 7a b7 74 19 bb 7f b0
```

```
      c0 01 c6 27 10 27 00 75 14 29 42 e1 9a 8d 8c 51
      d0 53 b3 e3 78 2a 1d e5 dc 5a f4 eb e9 94 68 17
      01 14 a1 df e6 7c dc 9a 9a f5 5d 65 56 20 bb ab
   02 03 01 00 01                            publicExponent = e
```

The RSAPublicKey value is later used in a certificate.
The BER-encoded RSAPrivateKey value is:

```
30 82 01 36
   02 01 00                                        version = 0
   02 40                                        modulus = n
      0a 66 79 1d c6 98 81 68 de 7a b7 74 19 bb 7f b0
      c0 01 c6 27 10 27 00 75 14 29 42 e1 9a 8d 8c 51
      d0 53 b3 e3 78 2a 1d e5 dc 5a f4 eb e9 94 68 17
      01 14 a1 df e6 7c dc 9a 9a f5 5d 65 56 20 bb ab
   02 03 01 00 01                            publicExponent = e
   02 40                                  privateExponent = d
      01 23 c5 b6 1b a3 6e db 1d 36 79 90 41 99 a8 9e
      a8 0c 09 b9 12 2e 14 00 c0 9a dc f7 78 46 76 d0
      1d 23 35 6a 7d 44 d6 bd 8b d5 0e 94 bf c7 23 fa
      87 d8 86 2b 75 17 76 91 c1 1d 75 76 92 df 88 81
   02 20                                          prime1 = p
      33 d4 84 45 c8 59 e5 23 40 de 70 4b cd da 06 5f
      bb 40 58 d7 40 bd 1d 67 d2 9e 9c 14 6c 11 cf 61
   02 20                                          prime2 = q
      33 5e 84 08 86 6b 0f d3 8d c7 00 2d 3f 97 2c 67
      38 9a 65 d5 d8 30 65 66 d5 c4 f2 a5 aa 52 62 8b
   02 20                               exponent1 = d mod p–1
      04 5e c9 00 71 52 53 25 d3 d4 6d b7 96 95 e9 af
      ac c4 52 39 64 36 0e 02 b1 19 ba a3 66 31 62 41
   02 20                               exponent2 = d mod q–1
      15 eb 32 73 60 c7 b6 0d 12 e5 e2 d1 6b dc d9 79
      81 d1 7f ba 6b 70 db 13 b2 0b 43 6e 24 ea da 59
   02 20                             coefficient = q–1 mod p
      2c a6 36 6d 72 78 1d fa 24 d3 4a 9a 24 cb c2 ae
      92 7a 99 58 af 42 65 63 ff 63 fb 11 65 8a 46 1d
```

Step 3: Encoding a PrivateKeyInfo Value

Test User 1 encodes a value of type `PrivateKeyInfo` according to PKCS #8 to represent the private key in an algorithm-independent way.

In this example, the private key is identified by PKCS #1's `rsaEncryption`, which has the object identifier value {1 2 840 113549 1 1 1}. There are no attributes in the private-key information.

The BER-encoded `PrivateKeyInfo` value is the following 340-octet string:

```
30 82 01 50
  02 01 00                                          version = 0
30 0d                          privateKeyAlgorithmIdentifier
  06 09                           algorithm = rsaEncryption
    2a 86 48 86 f7 0d 01 01 01
  05 00                                      parameters = NULL
04 82 01 3a               privateKey = RSAPrivateKey encoding
  30 82 01 36 … 65 8a 46 1d
```

Step 4: Encrypting the PrivateKeyInfo Encoding

Test User 1 encrypts the `PrivateKeyInfo` encoding with a password according to PKCS #5.

In this example, the selected password-based encryption algorithm is "MD2 with DES-CBC." There are three steps to this algorithm: a DES key and initializing vector are derived from the password with MD2, given a salt value and an iteration count; the `PrivateKeyInfo` encoding is padded to a multiple of eight bytes; and the padded `PrivateKeyInfo` encoding is encrypted under DES.

The message M is the `PrivateKeyInfo` encoding.

The password P is the ASCII string "password":

```
P = 70 61 73 73 77 6f 72 64
```

The salt value S (which happens to be derived deterministically from the MD2 message digest of the octet string $P \parallel M$) is:

```
S = 53 7c 94 2e 8a 96 04 4b
```

The iteration count c is 1.

The result of one iteration of MD2 on the octet string $P \parallel S$ is the following 16-octet string:

```
13 1a 55 51 fe 1f d2 a4 3a d9 95 74 66 6b 67 ce
```

The DES key K (with odd parity) and the initializing vector IV derived from the message digest are:

```
K = 13 1a 54 51 fe 1f d3 a4
IV = 3a d9 95 74 66 6b 67 ce
```

The padding string PS for the message M is:

```
PS = 04 04 04 04
```

because the length of the message M is 340 octets, which is four less than a multiple of eight.

The ciphertext C resulting from encrypting the octet string $M \parallel PS$ under DES with key K and initializing vector IV is the following 344-octet string:

```
20 d4 dd 6a 50 5f 0d ea e3 da a6 98 22 a0 10 0e 70 ef e2
8f 4b 07 ff ee 77 b2 34 3f c7 ee 61 25 84 b3 7e 13 c3 d8
fd ad 83 94 0c a3 5b 70 67 2d 48 9c 10 23 57 31 77 b1 48
2a c2 65 40 ce 10 33 40 87 cf f8 7b 2a 05 0e 3f 3a 9e c7
4e a1 08 7f 02 9e a9 06 7a a5 9a 7e 64 cd 03 1a 49 6b 47
b0 64 6d 04 65 8b 31 d7 3a 12 58 24 80 da 44 73 0a c4 0f
af 4a 00 8e 8f d3 5b 22 1e 84 1c 54 20 37 50 b3 c2 94 74
60 64 51 65 a1 41 ca a7 34 68 a1 c1 e3 59 be 9b 42 54 14
06 ae 17 b4 f4 f3 75 9f 6d 29 96 ef 3e 5c aa 6d 61 4d d8
5d d3 b5 7d fd c4 54 c8 63 0e a1 22 90 28 a9 11 a6 e6 dd
41 93 75 76 f1 b3 e5 6a 0f 85 7b 19 95 a2 94 9b 25 3c e2
fe 27 aa d6 1e f2 d7 bb 00 cb 62 fa b7 87 c9 bd 6a fa 5c
ce 22 b7 2b 6c 8c 29 4b e3 f2 2b be fa 44 42 dc 31 11 0a
f2 6d ad 82 9c c3 2a 15 ca 1f 00 c3 93 e8 1a fc 4b 5d 99
75 77 f4 f7 fd 17 65 9e 6e 7f a0 66 05 b0 28 b3 ef c0 65
4e bb ea 34 78 36 cf d3 ae 38 dd 79 45 f7 f0 b8 99 cb 71
27 64 c5 c7 d3 61 9d fb 6e ba 4c e6 a4 22 dd 11 8d e8 88
63 77 4a 4a 8f 88 40 b5 1d 01 12 e5 ea fe 71 b6 b3 7e 71
c8 cf
```

Step 5: Encoding the EncryptedPrivateKeyInfo Value

Test User 1 encodes a value of type `EncryptedPrivateKeyInfo` according to PKCS #8 to represent the encrypted `PrivateKeyInfo` value in an algorithm-independent way.

In this example, the encryption algorithm is identified by PKCS #5's md2WithDES-CBC, which has the object identifier value {1 2 840 113549 1 5 1}.

The BER-encoded `EncryptedPrivateKeyInfo` value is:

```
30 82 01 78
  30 1a                                      encryptionAlgorithm
    06 09                      algorithm = pbeWithMD2AndDES-CBC
      2a 86 48 86 f7 0d 01 05 01
    30 0d                                              parameter
      04 08 53 7c 94 2e 8a 96 04 4b    salt value
      02 01 01                          iteration count = 1
  04 82 01 58                                      encryptedData
    20 d4 dd 6a ... 7e 71 c8 cf
```

Test User 1 can now store this encoding and transfer it from one computer system to another. The private key is obtained by reversing steps 3, 4, and 5.

Appendix F

ACRONYMS

3DES — Triple Data Encryption Standard
AAA — Authentication, Authorization, Auditing (or Accounting)
AAL5 — ATM Adaptation Layer Type-5
ABR — Available Bit Rate
ACL — Access Control List
AES — Advanced Encryption Standard
AH — Authentication Header
ALG — Application Layer Gateway
ANSI — American National Standards Institute
AP — Access Point
API — Application Program(ing) Interface
AS — Autonomous System, or Authentication Server
ASA — Adaptive Security Algorithm
ASN.1 — Abstract Syntax Notation One
ATM — Asynchronous Transfer Mode
AToM — Any Transport over MPLS
BCA — Bridge CA
BECN — Backward-Explicit Congestion Notification
BER — Bit Error Rate, or Basic Encoding Rule
BGP — Border Gateway Protocol
C/S — Client/Server
CA — Certification Authority
CBAC — Context-Based Access Control
CBC — Cypher Block Chaining
CBR — Constant Bit Rate
CCE — Call Control Element
CDV — Cell Delay Variation
CDVT — CDV Tolerance
CERT — Computer Emergency Response Team

CHAP — Challenge Handshake Authentication Protocol
CLP — Cell Loss Priority
CLR — Cell Loss Ratio
CO — Central Office
COS — Class of Service
CRC — Cyclic Redundancy Code
CRL — Certificate Revocation List
CTD — Cell Transfer Delay
DCE — Data Communication Equipment
DE — Discard Eligibility
DER — Distinguished Encoding Rule
DES — Data Encryption Standard
DHCP — Dynamic Host Configuration Processor
DIB — Directory Information Base
DiffServ — Differentiated Services
DISP — Directory Information Shadowing Protocol
DLCI — Data-Link Connection Identifier
DMZ — Demilitarized Zone
DN — Distinguished Name
DNS — Domain Name Server
DOI — Domain of Interpretation
DoS — Denial of Service
DS — Digital Signature
DPMA — Domain Policy Management Authorities
DSA — Digital Signature Algorithm
DSL — Digital Subscriber Line
DSP — Directory System Protocol
DSS — Digital Signature Standard
DTE — Data Terminal Equipment
EA — Extended Address
EAP — Extensible Authentication Protocol
eBGP — Exterior Border Gateway Protocol
ECDSA — Elliptic Curve Digital Signature Algorithm
EIGRP — Enhanced Interior Gateway Routing Protocol
ESP — Encapsulating Security Payload
F4 — Fermat Prime F4 (65537)
FCS — Frame Check Sequence
FEC — Forward Equivalent Class
FECN — Forward-Explicit Congestion Notification
FIPS — Federal Information Processing Standards
FPKI — Federal Public Key Infrastructure
FPMA — Federal Policy Management Authority
FR — Frame Relay

FTP — File Transfer Protocol
GFC — Generic Flow Control
GPRS — General Packet Radio Service
GRE — Generic Routing Encapsulation
GSS-API — Generic Security Service Application Program Interface
HDLC — High-Level Data Link Control
HEC — Header Error Control
HMAC — Keyed-hash Message Authentication Code
HTTP — Hypertext Transfer Protocol
IANA — Internet Assigned Numbers Authority
IAPP — International Association of Privacy Professionals
iBGP — Interior Border Gateway Protocol
ICMP — Internet Control Message Protocol
ICV — Integrity Check Value
IDS — Intrusion Detection System
IETF — Internet Engineering Task Force
IGMP — Internet Group Management Protocol
IGRP — Interior Gateway Routing Protocol
IKE — Internet Key Exchange
IP — Internet Protocol
IPsec — IP Security
IrDA — Infrared Data Association
ISAKMP — Internet Security Association and Key Management Protocol
ISDN — Integrated Services Digital Network
ISP — Internet Service Provider
IT — Information Technology
ITU–T — International Telecommunications Union–Telecommunications
IV — Initialization Value
KDC — Key Distribution Center
KRA — Key Recovery Agent
L2F — Layer 2 Forwarding
L2TP — Layer 2 Tunneling Protocol
LDAP — Lightweight Directory Access Protocol
LDP — Label Distribution Protocol
LEAP — Lightweight EAP
LER — Label Edge Router
LSP — Label Switched Path
LSR — Label Switch Router
MAC — Media Access Control, or Message Authentication Code
MAN — Metropolitan Area Network
MAT — Mobile Adaptive Tunneling
MBS — Maximum Burst Size
MCR — Minimum Cell Rate

MD5 — Message Digest 5
MIT — Massachusetts Institute of Technology
MODP — Modular Exponential
MPLS — Multi-Protocol Label Switching
MPPE — Microsoft Point-to-Point Encryption
MSP — MAN Service Provider
NAS — Network Access Server
NAT — Network Address Translation
NDS — Network Directory Services
NIC — Network Interface Card
NII — National Information Infrastructure
NIST — National Institute of Standards and Technology
NM — Network Management
NNI — Network-to-Network Interface
NOS — Network Operating System
nrt-VBR — non-real-time Variable Bit Rate
NSA — National Security Agency
OS — Operating System
OGSF SSO — Open Group Security Forum SSO
OSI — Open Systems Interconnection
OSPF — Open Shortest Path First
OSS — Operations Support System
PAC — PPTP Access Concentrator
PAP — Password Authentication Protocol
PAT — Port Address Translation
PCA — Principal CA
PCR — Peak Cell Rate
PDA — Personal Digital Assistant
PDU — Packet Data Unit
PEAP — Protected Extensible Authentication Protocol
PFS — Perfect Forward Secrecy
PGP — Pretty Good Privacy
PKCS — Public Key Cryptography Standard
PKI — Public Key Infrastructure
PNS — PPTP Network Server
PPP — Point-to-Point Protocol
PPPoE — PPP over Ethernet
PPTP — Point-to-Point Tunneling Protocol
PRNG — Pseudo Random Number Generator
PT — Payload Type
PVC — Permanent Virtual Circuit
QoS — Quality of Service
RA — Registration Authority

RADIUS — Remote Authentication Dial-In User Service
RAS — Remote Access Server
RC4 — Ron's (or Rivest's) Code
RF — Radio Frequency
RIP — Routing Information Protocol
RSA — Rivest–Shamir–Adelman
RSA-PSS — RSA-Probabilistic Signature Scheme
RSVP — Resource Reservation Protocol
RTCP — Real-Time Control Protocol
RTP — Real-Time Protocol
rt-VBR — real-time Variable Bit Rate
SA — Security Association
SCEP — Simple Certificate Enrollment Protocol
SCR — Sustainable Cell Rate
SDK — Service Development Kit
SDP — Session Delivery Protocol
SET — Secure Electronic Transaction
SHA — Secure Hash Algorithm
SHS — Secure Hash Standard
S-HTTP — Secure Hypertext Transfer Protocol
SIP — Session Initiation Protocol
SKEME — Secure Key Exchange Mechanism for Internet
SKIP — Simple Key Management for Internet Protocol
S/MIME — Secure/Multipurpose Internet Mail Extensions
SMTP — Simple Mail Transfer Protocol
SNAC — System and Network Attack Center
SNMP — Simple Network Management Protocol
SPAP — Shiva Password Authentication Protocol
SPI — Security Parameter Index
SSG — Service Selection Gateway
SSID — Service Set Identifier
SSL — Secure Socket Layer
SSO — Single Sign-On
STS — Station-to-Station
STT — Secure Transaction Technology
SVC — Switched Virtual Circuit
SWOT — Strength, Weakness, Opportunity, Threat
TACACS+ — Terminal Access Controller Access Systems+
TCP — Transmission Control Protocol
TGS — Ticket Granting Service
TGi — Taskgroup i
TKIP — Temporal Key Integrity Protocol
TLS — Transport Layer Security

TTLS — Tunneled Transport Layer Security
UBR — Unspecified Bit Rate
UBS — Unclassified But Sensitive
UDP — User Datagram Protocol
UNI — User-to-Network Interface
VC — Virtual Circuit, or Virtual Container (SONET/SDH)
VCI — Virtual Channel Identifier
VLAN — Virtual LAN
VPI — Virtual Path Identifier
VPN — Virtual Private Network
WAP — Wireless Access Point
WAPI — Wired Authentication and Privacy Infrastructure
WEP — Wire Equivalent Privacy
WLAN — Wireless LAN
WMAN — Wireless MAN
WPA — Wi-Fi Protected Access
XOR — Exclusive OR

INDEX